DEEPER HEAVEN

A Reader's Guide to C. S. Lewis's Ransom Trilogy

Christiana Hale

ROMAN ROADS PRESS

MOSCOW, IDAHO

Deeper Heaven: A Reader's Guide to C. S. Lewis's Ransom Trilogy

Published by Roman Roads Press
Moscow, Idaho

RomanRoadsPress.com

DeeperHeaven.com

Interior Layout: Carissa Hale
Cover and interior illustrations: Joey Nance Design

Deeper Heaven: A Reader's Guide to C. S. Lewis's Ransom Trilogy / Christiana Hale
ISBN 13: 978-1-944482-56-5
ISBN 10: 1-944482-56-3

Version 1.0.2 May 2021

To my parents, Jim & Anita, who gave me story,

To my siblings, Cassandra, Carissa & Isaac, who give me laughter,

And to Pastor Douglas Wilson who inspired this project.

l'amor che move il sole e l'altre stelle

CONTENTS

PART I:

Out of the Silent Planet

PART II:

Perelandra

PART III:
That Hideous Strength

Conclusion

Appendices

A Map of the Ransom Trilogy Cosmology

according to C. S. Lewis

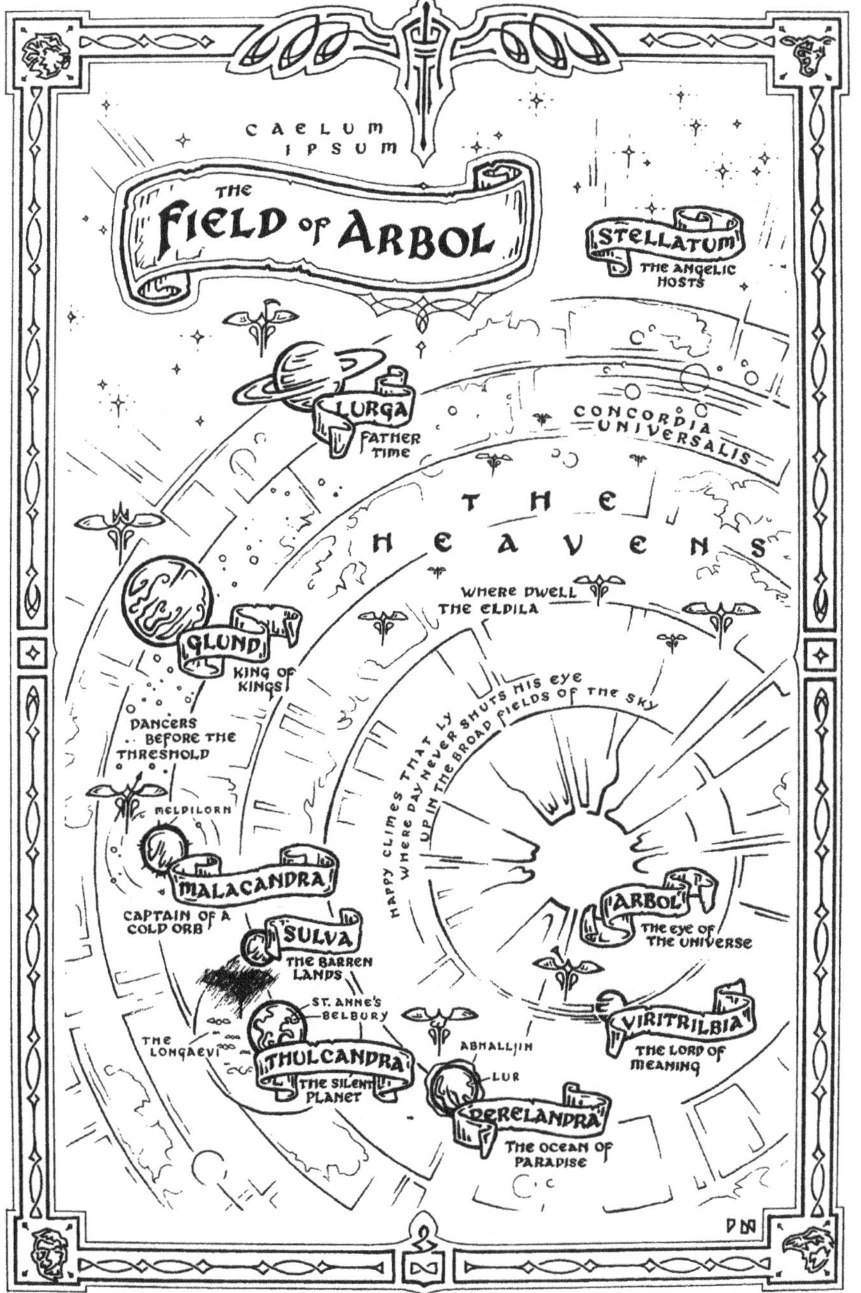
CAELUM IPSUM
THE FIELD OF ARBOL
STELLATUM
THE ANGELIC HOSTS
LURGA
FATHER TIME
CONCORDIA UNIVERSALIS
THE HEAVENS
WHERE DWELL THE ELDILA
GLUND
KING OF KINGS
DANCERS BEFORE THE THRESHOLD
HAPPY CLIMES THAT LY
WHERE DAY NEVER SHUTS HIS EYE
UP IN THE BROAD FIELDS OF THE SKY
MELDILORN
MALACANDRA
CAPTAIN OF A COLD ORB
ARBOL
THE EYE OF THE UNIVERSE
SULVA
THE BARREN LANDS
ST. ANNE'S
BELBURY
THE LONGAEVI
THULCANDRA
THE SILENT PLANET
ABHALLJIN
LUR
VIRITRILBIA
THE LORD OF MEANING
PERELANDRA
THE OCEAN OF PARADISE
DM

FOREWORD

The Ransom Trilogy

One of the great ironies surrounding the publication and continued popularity of C. S. Lewis's space trilogy is the fact that everybody still calls it the space trilogy. If there was one thing that Lewis wanted people to quit calling the heavens, it would be *space*. Space makes us think of vast expanses, full of nothing but dead blackness, punctuated here and there by shapeless asteroids and inchoate oceans of flaming gas.

In fact, the popular concept of "space" has actually resulted in many moderns imagining it to be something pretty close to the biblical description of damnation—the outer darkness. This should perhaps indicate to us that one of Screwtape's relatives was likely involved in all of this, with the result that things heavenly have come to have hellish connotations for us. Something has gone seriously wrong somewhere.

This was in fact one of the dragons that Lewis came to slay, and yet for some reason his publishers continue to put "space trilogy" on these books. Contrast this with the experience that Ransom had when he was first becoming acclimatized to the "heavens":

> But Ransom, as time wore on, became aware of another and more spiritual cause for his progressive lightening and exultation of heart. A nightmare, long engendered in the modern mind by the mythology that follows in the wake of science, was falling off him. He had read of 'Space': at the back of his thinking for years had lurked the dismal fancy of the black, cold vacuity, the utter deadness, which was supposed to separate the worlds. He had not known how much it affected him till now—now that the very name 'Space' seemed a blasphemous libel for this empyrean ocean of radiance in which they swam. (*Out of the Silent Planet*)

Apart from the collision that results with Lewis's vision, there is also the fact that the phrase is actually not descriptive enough. How many science fiction writers have there been to date? And how many of them have produced trilogies? Many of them cannot be *kept* from producing trilogies. So the chances are pretty good that the number of space trilogies can be reckoned by the score, and yet, such is Lewis's continued authorial dominance that his remains *the* space trilogy. If we are fortunate, we may be able to create some room for the others.

So words do matter, but they do not matter as much as the vision behind the words matters. Despite the fact that "space trilogy" is emblazoned right there on my set of the three books, the fact remains that Lewis has nevertheless opened up the heavens for countless readers. I am not speaking here of Heaven—although Lewis is responsible for large numbers of people coming to understand *that* better as well. Not only so, but he is also responsible for a large number of people *going* there. His vision of Heaven, as seen for example in *The Last Battle* and *The Great Divorce*, is a subject worth considering in its own right, but I am concerned here with Lewis and the heavens.

The final Heaven and the heavens we can see at night are not two separated subjects. They are closely related to one another. To the ancient and medieval eye what we could see in the night sky was not the ultimate Heaven, obviously not. But what we could see was thought of as the anterooms of Heaven, the outskirts. We were like sailors centuries ago approaching the coasts of an undiscovered and unexplored Chinese empire, knowing that the great rumors were still only fables to us. The capital city with its "stately pleasure dome" was still out of sight. What we had heard about was still far inland, if it existed at all. When we first made landfall, we could see none of that. But we could see the coastland. We could see *that* with our own eyes.

Has any mortal seen Heaven? Well, actually, all of us have seen the outskirts.

If you ask a typical modern if he has ever seen an angel, you will likely get laughed at. You are likely to get this treatment even if the modern you ask happens to be a professing Christian. "Seeing angels" is something our more excitable brethren on the charismatic fringes do, and *we* by contrast are sober, responsible, upright, not drunk, and pretty duddy. And so when one of these buttoned-up-tight Christians tells you that he has never seen an angel, has it ever occurred to you to point at the night sky and ask, "So what are those?"

After you have worked through the initial consternation, and the "are you serious?" follow up questions, you will have yourself a serious cosmological discussion. And Lewis was deadly serious about provoking such discussions. It was an essential part of his project.

> "In our world," said Eustace, "a star is a huge ball of flaming gas."
>
> "Even in your world, my son, that is not what a star is but only what it is made of." (*The Voyage of the* Dawn Treader)

I own an older version of *The New Bible Dictionary*, and in the entry for "Host of Heaven", the writer is talking about the identification of celestial beings and celestial bodies, and he says this:

> No doubt to the Heb. mind the distinction was superficial, and the celestial bodies were thought to be closely associated with heavenly beings. In fact, the implied angelology of C. S. Lewis's novels (*Out of the Silent Planet*, etc.) would probably have commended itself with some force to the biblical writers. (*The New Bible Dictionary*, J. D. Douglas, ed., Eerdmans, Grand Rapids, 1962, 543)

The heavenly host refers to God's armies, and it also refers to the stars in all their vast array. What we are looking at through our telescopes is not the debris field and leftover gasses from a large and rather unfortunate explosion. "Lord Sabaoth is his name/from age to age the same/and He must win the battle." Lord Sabaoth means Lord of hosts, Lord of the armies, Lord of all the stars.

We have trained ourselves in a deliberate form of intellectual schizophrenia. We believe in the modern cosmology, just as it was handed to us in our science classes and *Star Wars* movies, and if we are conservative evangelicals, we *also* believe in the account of the Star of Bethlehem, and the message delivered by the host of heaven to the shepherds keeping watch over their flocks by night. It never once occurs to us to try to put all those things together in one coherent whole. And if some aspiring liberal presses us on the Star of Bethlehem we defend ourselves by retreating to something called "the spiritual realm," which is something like the 17th dimension. The main virtue of this place is that nothing can be falsified there.

> Your man has been accustomed, ever since he was a boy, to having a dozen incompatible philosophies dancing about together inside his head. (*The Screwtape Letters*)

The distance from Jerusalem to Bethlehem is about six miles. Herod's scholars sent the wise men to Bethlehem on the basis of Micah 5:2, but it was a *star* that led the wise men to a particular house in that same town. Now if the Bible is the Word of God, without error in all that it affirms, then stars are not what we have all been quietly assuming them to be. Either the wise men were doing some serious astrological math on the backs of camels in the dark, or a star stopped over the right house, say fifty feet up. If the former, then astrology is valid, and if the latter then a star is not millions of miles in diameter, for that would have burned all of Bethlehem, and our entire planet, to a cinder. The solution, for those who are prepared to read Lewis sympathetically, from Narnia to *The Discarded Image*, from *The Discarded Image* to the descent of the gods on Ransom's bedroom, is straightforward, obvious, and manifestly biblical.

And that goes double for the angels who announced peace on earth, good will toward men. Angels, stars, Oyarsa, all the same kind of thing. When Luke tells us that the angels went away from them back into heaven (Luke 2:15), it would perhaps be best to visualize them as *thwapping* back into their spots, kind of like what the stars do in *Star Trek* whenever the ship goes into hyperdrive. Not that we put any exegetical weight on that.

Christiana Hale is particularly suited to the task of writing a reader's guide to the Ransom Trilogy. She is an intelligent lover of all things Lewis, and is a dedicated student of this material. She reads carefully, widely, and wisely, and is not hampered by having to read her material with modernist blinkers that help us all to deny what the texts are obviously saying. I have been privileged to have known Christiana as a student in a number of settings, and this book is one that I can happily commend and recommend. You will come away from it the wiser.

Douglas Wilson
Christ Church, Moscow
November 2020

WHAT IS THIS BOOK?

In 1936, two of the greatest authors of the twentieth century agreed to take on a challenge. This challenge remained incomplete, but it nevertheless led to the creation of one of the most complex and enchanting stories ever written. C. S. Lewis and J. R. R. Tolkien, both scholars of the highest caliber and each a genius in his own right, were dissatisfied with the lack of the kinds of stories they loved.[1] Lewis suggested that he take on the task of writing a space-travel story while Tolkien created a time-travel story. Tolkien never completed his end of the bargain and abandoned "The Lost Road," a time-travel story intended to link his Middle-earth with our world.[2] Lewis, on the other hand, went beyond the call of duty. Between 1938 and 1945 he completed not just one but three space-travel stories. And the Ransom Trilogy—commonly and erroneously called the Space Trilogy (more on this later)—has captivated and bewildered readers and critics alike ever since.

C. S. Lewis remains one of the most popular authors of the twentieth century. Read and beloved by both Christians

1 J. R. R. Tolkien to Dora Marshal, March 3, 1955, in *The Letters of J. R. R. Tolkien*, ed. Humphrey Carpenter (Boston: Houghton Mifflin, 1981), 209.

2 Tolkien to Stanley Unwin, February 18, 1938, in *The Letters of J. R. R. Tolkien*, 29.

and non-Christians, his writings span an impressive range of subjects and genres and even those who do not share his faith recognize his genius. His Narnia books remain on the list of best-selling children's novels to date and will, no doubt, stay there for generations to come. Hundreds of books have been written about Lewis, his life, and his writings, but surprisingly very few concern the Ransom Trilogy, a series of books that is arguably one of Lewis's most complex works.

The trilogy itself lies somewhat hidden among Lewis's greater-known works, and many readers who love Lewis are yet unaware the trilogy exists, like a treasure mine buried in a familiar backyard. And those who have read the trilogy tend to number it among the unapproachables—just some of those books that are simply too strange and fantastical and, well, *weird* to really like. I love this series deeply, but I still relate to those people. On the surface, the Ransom Trilogy bears the marks of a sci-fi adventure. But then there are all those philosophical passages, and there's an awful lot of time spent just *talking* on Perelandra, and then Merlin (of all people!) shows up and don't even get started on Mr. Bultitude… It is for these people—indeed, for my former self—that I have written this book.

Lewis's Ransom Trilogy is a much-neglected and yet critically important part of his works. It is a distillation in novel form of one of Lewis's favorite subjects, a subject whose melody is woven into almost every other thing that Lewis ever wrote: the medieval conception of the cosmos.

Lewis's love for medieval literature and culture is no great secret. It was part of his job description. He held the position of Chair of Medieval and Renaissance Literature at Magdalene College in Cambridge University from 1954 until 1963, just a few months before his death. Strangely, this manifest passion for medieval literature throughout Lewis's fiction goes virtually unnoticed. But unless we understand his love for the medieval world and his self-proclaimed efforts to re-awaken respect and admiration for the Medieval Model of the cosmos in the modern mind, we will misinterpret or even neglect many of Lewis's writings as strange and unintelligible. No work of Lewis's suffers more from this than his Ransom Trilogy. Where many readers stumble through the trilogy in a fog of disconnected themes and seemingly meaningless characters, there is, in fact, a deep underlying unity in the trilogy—one that can be fully understood only through the lens of medieval thought and literature.

The Ransom Trilogy's importance in the canon of Lewis's writings is, I believe, difficult to overstate. It is a synthesis of Lewis's ongoing project of exploring the imaginative and emotional effects of the medieval cosmology and the different ways these effects can be utilized in literature. We need to read and study this trilogy because it is Lewis's first foray into demonstrating how the Medieval Model retains value, even in the modern world. In the wake of the Copernican revolution, we have been far more affected by the Enlightenment than we may realize. Science is idolized and empiricism is still the reigning epistemology (despite its slow mummification in our postmodern age where truth is whatever we want it to be). So when we are confronted with medieval cosmology, our question is: *why* should we care? And until we answer that question, we cannot understand the importance of the Ransom Trilogy.

In Lewis's non-fiction treatment of the Medieval Model of the cosmos, *The Discarded Image*, Lewis says that the purpose of literature is "to teach what is useful, to honour what deserves honour, to appreciate what is delightful."[3]

3 C. S. Lewis, *The Discarded Image* (Cambridge: University Press, 1964), 214.

The medieval cosmology, while not "true" in the sense of being *scientifically accurate*, is nevertheless true in a deeper sense. Lewis shows this truth throughout his writings. His project is to demonstrate the potent usefulness, honor, and delight that the Medieval Model wields, particularly in the literary realm. The Ransom Trilogy is this project incarnated.

We need to read and study the Ransom Trilogy because it gives us a deeper understanding of the world we live in, the world God created. These books may seem daunting—the waves are high and the ocean is dark and deep. But if we dive into these books, the jeweled realm of the coral reef awaits, teeming with shimmering fish and twisting shapes and colors, dazzling in its diversity and yet harmonious and interwoven. It is waiting to be explored and each time we take the plunge even more magic awaits.

NOTE ON HOW TO USE THIS BOOK

This book acts as a guide: a Beatrice to your Dante. There are several ways you can use this book. All of them are helpful and informative and will enhance your appreciation for Lewis's Ransom Trilogy and the deep riches that are to be found there. If you have already read the trilogy, first of all, well done, and now jump into this guide! The water is warm and the reef awaits. If you are a first-time reader of the trilogy, I would recommend reading *Out of the Silent Planet* before reading the corresponding section of this book, then reading *Perelandra*, and so forth.

However you implement the resources included in this project, my hope is that you will walk away with a deeper understanding of and admiration for the Ransom Trilogy as a whole. This trilogy is woven together with threads from many different works of the medieval and renaissance era. It is shot through with Lewis's love for the cosmology of that period, as well as his belief that this cosmology is necessary to a renewal of man's imaginative and emotional faculties.

So where do we start? We start as Lewis would have us start—by walking outside on a clear night and casting our eyes up towards the heavens.

INTRODUCTION

1

MAPPING THE UNIVERSE

The Medieval Cosmos

> I hope to persuade the reader not only that this Model of the Universe is a supreme medieval work of art but that it is in a sense the central work, that in which most particular works were embedded, to which they constantly referred, from which they drew a great deal of their strength. (Lewis, *The Discarded Image*)

Before we turn to the trilogy itself, there are some essential landmarks that we must introduce. Being familiar with these landmarks will not only enhance our enjoyment of the journey through Lewis's work but will also give much needed coherence and clarity to what otherwise appears murky and disconnected.

Lewis was a medieval scholar. That was his day job, so to speak, and he was not only good at it—he loved it. And as with everything else that Lewis loved, elements of the medieval world are integrated into every part of his writings, both scholarly and otherwise. As Owen Barfield once said, what Lewis thought about everything was contained in what he said about anything.[1] So we should not be surprised when we find traces of Lewis's love for medievalism and the medieval cosmos in particular throughout his other works.

Understanding the layout of the medieval cosmos is like having an insider's road-map to the Ransom Trilogy and many of Lewis's other books—a road-map drawn by someone who knows the ins and outs of the city, the little back roads and alleys where all of the interesting shops and charming nooks and crannies are hiding. With this map in hand, we have already taken a large step towards a deeper appreciation of the world of treasures yet to be discovered.

What is a cosmology? The word *cosmos* comes from the Greek word κόσμος meaning *order*. We also get our word *cosmetology* from this word (but don't confuse the two!). Cosmology is not just a study of the heavens or, as a modern man might call it, outer space. A cosmology is a system into which every aspect of reality is placed. Everything is *ordered*. And how you order things matters.

Not all cosmologies are created equal. Different ways of arranging things lead to different characteristics and personality quirks. Most of the people that we meet have eyes and ears and noses; they have the same basic features. And yet the *arrangement* of these features on the face—different nose shapes and eye colors, and so on—means that no one (with a few exceptions) looks exactly the same. People's faces express their personalities and give them individuality and character. The same can be said of cosmologies. Every cosmology puts together a model of the entire created order, arranging the

---

1 Owen Barfield, *Owen Barfield on C. S. Lewis* (Middletown: Wesleyan University Press, 1989), 22.

elements in a particular order. But *how* those elements are arranged leads to a multitude of different characteristics.

The Copernican Revolution did more than just swap out the earth for the sun on the map of the universe. It marked a definitive worldview shift (or *cosmos*-view shift) in the minds and imaginations of men and women. The old Ptolemaic map of the cosmos looked very different from the one we know today (as we will see more fully later on) but it also presented a completely different idea about what the world and the universe were *like*. The Enlightenment, that age of science and reason, led to a materialism that largely stripped the cosmos (particularly that part that used to be called the "heavens") of its wonder and enchantment. And with the age of space exploration, that enchantment has been almost entirely removed.

We are all familiar with the modern view of the universe. Space is dark and empty and cold, punctuated by occasional dead rock or the harsh, uninhabitable planets we have so far observed and discovered. Stars are blazing balls of burning gas. Earth, thus far, is the only haven of life and light in our known universe. If there are any other forms of life out there, they will be (by necessity) barbaric and cruel, even if more technologically advanced and sophisticated.

As we turn to consider the medieval cosmology, we must recognize that understanding the *physical architecture* of the cosmos is essential to understanding the imaginative and emotional effects of that model on a culture and a people. In other words, physical design has an emotional impact. And so we must understand the *physical* makeup of the medieval cosmos before we can grasp why it had such a unique emotional impact on the people who embraced it. Lewis frequently emphasized the emotional and imaginative differences between the medieval cosmos and the modern cosmos

Architecture of the Medieval Cosmos

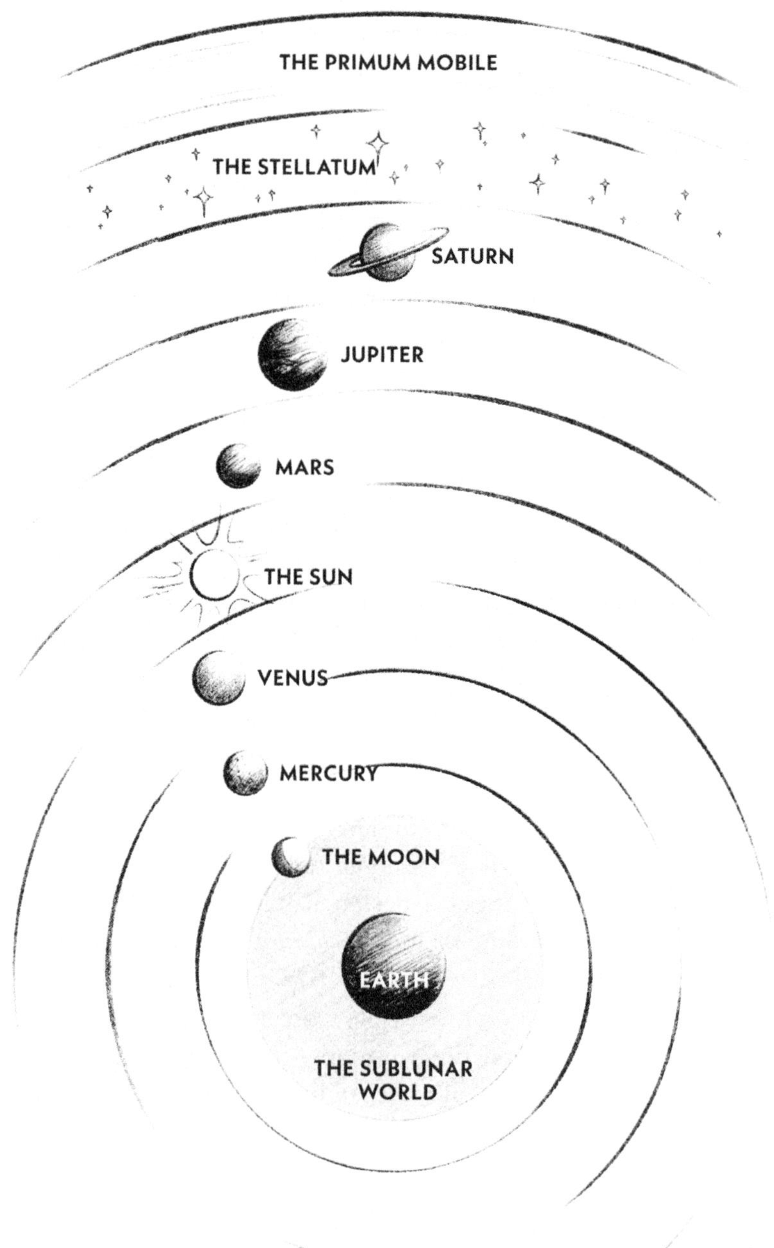

described above. These differences stem primarily from the *physical* arrangement of the cosmos, as well as from other unique features of the Medieval Model. The movement away from the Medieval Model that occurred in the wake of the Copernican revolution had a ripple effect, especially concerning the imagination:

> And on our thoughts and emotions (which concern a literary historian more) it [the Copernican model] was destined to have profound effects. By reducing Nature to her mathematical elements it substituted a mechanical for a genial or animistic conception of the universe.[2]

In the medieval period, the concept of "space"—a wild, black expanse of darkness and silence—never entered man's thought or imagination, let alone his literature. Rather, the medieval man was "like a man being conducted through an immense cathedral, not like one lost in a shoreless sea."[3] Let us explore this cathedral.

Architecturally, the Medieval Model[4] of the cosmos consists of a series of hollow and transparent globes called the spheres. Earth sits at the center surrounded by these spheres, one atop the other, like Russian nesting dolls. There are seven of these spheres (also called the seven heavens) and each sphere is governed by a planet (or "luminous body") which is fixed within each sphere. The order of the planets, starting from Earth and working outward, is the Moon, Mercury, Venus, the Sun, Mars, Jupiter, and Saturn.

---

2 C. S. Lewis, *English Literature in the Sixteenth Century* (Oxford: Clarendon Press, 1976), 3.

3 Lewis, *Discarded Image*, 100.

4 For a fuller treatment of the Medieval Model and its literary history and significance see the entirety of Lewis's *The Discarded Image.*

Beyond the spheres is the Stellatum, the realm of the "fixed stars" (meaning that the stars do not appear to move across the sky in relation to each other, unlike the planets, whose name comes from the Greek word πλανῆται, "wanderers"). Beyond the Stellatum is the Primum Mobile, which means the "first moveable." This is the outermost sphere whose spinning in turn sets all of the other spheres in motion. And beyond this is the Empyrean, the *caelum ipsum* or "very heaven," the abode of God.

Earth exists in the sublunar world, the world beneath the Moon. (The word *sublunar* is an important one to keep in mind and we will use it often in this book.) The Moon is the boundary line between the mutable (changeable) earthly realm and the transcendent realm of the Heavens. Beneath the Moon, disease and decay hold sway.[5] The Moon marks the divide between the cold, deathly realm and the realm of light and life. The medievals believed that only the created order beneath the Moon has been affected by the Fall. Everything above the Moon's sphere is perfect and unfallen, still singing the praises of the Lord as it has since its creation. But while the heavens are full of dancing and the music of the spheres, beneath the Moon, all is silent.

So, how does this architectural structure of the medieval cosmos affect our emotional and imaginative faculties? While the medieval cosmos was "unimaginably large," it was still bounded by specific dimensions.[6] It was *finitely* large. And, as Lewis himself notes, this actually served to make our smallness, the smallness of Earth, felt more keenly, because we have something specific to compare it to. While the modern man looks out into space as into an infinite sea of nothingness, the medieval man looked up into

5 *Discarded Image*, 94.

6 Ibid., 99.

the Heavens as one who looks up the side of a skyscraper: massive and towering, but also crafted and shaped.

> [...] To look out on the night sky with modern eyes is like looking out over a sea that fades away into mist, or looking about one in a trackless forest—trees forever and no horizon. To look up at the towering medieval universe is much more like looking at a great building. The "space" of modern astronomy may arouse terror, or bewilderment or vague reverie; the spheres of old present us with an object in which the mind can rest, overwhelming in its greatness but satisfying in its harmony.[7]

If we can look at the night sky with medieval eyes, adopting a more Ptolemaic understanding of the cosmos, our emotional state will shift. A medieval looking up into the vast expanse of the shimmering heavens would feel small, just like we do, but it would be the smallness and awe that you feel looking up the side of a castle or cathedral, not the shiver of terror we feel when looking into dead, empty "space."

We begin to see how the shape of the cosmos affects how we look at the world around us, especially as we start to see the Heavens rather than mere "space." But to truly understand the feelings that were evoked in the medieval men by looking at this sort of cosmos, we must move beyond the architecture and layout. We must bring the whole thing to life. The Medieval Model was more than just a map, more than a two-dimensional pen and ink drawing on paper. The medieval cosmos was whirling, sparkling, dazzling, and teeming with life, music, and dance. We have assembled our instrument—now let's make it sing.

7 Ibid.

2

KINDLY ENCLYNING

The Influence and Personality of the Planets

> Darkness, our own darkness, draws the veil and we catch a glimpse of the high pomps within; the vast, lighted concavity filled with music and life [...] the revelry of insatiable love. (Lewis, *The Discarded Image*)

One of the most unique and dynamic features of the Medieval Model is the personalities of the planets themselves. This is arguably Lewis's favorite feature of the Model. Unlike our modern materialistic view of the universe, in which all is reduced to matter and atoms, the medieval cosmos was teeming with personality, with a spiritual dimension which makes the universe not just enchanting but *alive.*

In the Medieval Model, the planets are not just physical balls of matter floating out in space. They are worlds with rulers, and those rulers, those celestial beings, are full of exuberant individuality. While the planets exist in the translunar realm, their influences are strong enough to pierce the boundary marked by the Moon and affect Earth and mankind. Now remember, the planets exist in an unfallen realm; the medievals believed that only the creation *under* the Moon was subject to the consequences of the Fall. Hence, the planets and their personalities are not tainted by sin. Yet the influences which are powerful enough to penetrate the lunar barrier could be corrupted on Earth, since Earth is located in the sublunar realm of disease and decay. We will see more on the planetary personalities later on.

Each of the planets is named after an ancient Greek or Roman god or goddess, names with which we are still familiar: Mars, Venus, Jupiter, Mercury, etc. But if we are going to discuss the vibrant personalities of these planets, questions will inevitably arise. What did medieval man think about the planetary beings themselves? Were they the same as the Greek and Roman gods and goddesses? What about the actual physical planet in the sky?

Lewis explains this quandary in his book *The Discarded Image*. He says that the Christian medieval poets wouldn't have thought in terms of those distinctions. The physical luminous body in the night sky, the god or goddess of ancient Greece or Rome (with all of its attendant mythologies and quirks), and the planetary being itself (with its influential personality) were all one and the same.

> They are planets as well as gods. Not that the Christian poet believed in the god because he believed in the planet; but all three things—the visible planet in the sky, the source of influence, and the god—generally acted as a unity upon his mind. I have not

> found evidence that theologians were at all disquieted by this state of affairs.[1]

In a world less concerned with defined lines, where Heaven has infiltrated Earth and where God has become flesh, it becomes less a question of "which is it?" and more a matter of "how does each one intersect and relate?"

It was Lewis's opinion that we don't just need to know *of* the planetary characters, but that we need to know the planetary characters *themselves*—to know them like we know our friends and family, to know them down to our bones. But why? What is so important about the characters of the planets? Doesn't this seem like an archaic, uninformed, and well, *medieval* superstition?

To the contrary, Lewis said that the planetary characters have "*permanent* value as spiritual symbols."[2] He believed the Model yet has value, that it offers truths we ought to learn from. For one thing, the imaginative and emotional potential of planetary personalities for literature alone is vast, as Lewis's works themselves display and as we will explore in more depth in this book. But beyond this, these planetary characters teach us about the one true God. Under the lordship of Christ, the planetary personalities place various attributes of God under a microscope, magnifying them and embodying them in separate planetary characters so that we can understand each one better. The personalities of the planets give us examples in microcosm of the way that God Himself works in the world. We will come back to this theme again and again throughout the book.

1 *Discarded Image*, 105.

2 C. S. Lewis, "The Alliterative Metre," in *Selected Literary Essays*, ed. Walter Hooper (Cambridge: University Press, 1969), 24, emphasis mine.

Michael Ward, author of the ground-breaking book *Planet Narnia*, was the first scholar to recognize the sheer depth of the influence of the planetary figures on Lewis's writings. Ward's thesis—that the seven Narnia stories correspond to the seven planets of medieval cosmology—has been revolutionary in the world of Lewis scholarship. Like the Copernican revolution itself, Ward's discoveries regarding the "secret" behind the Narnia books has reordered the entire universe of the study of Lewis's works. The value of *Planet Narnia* and the debt we owe to Ward cannot be overstated. *Planet Narnia*, as well as Lewis's *The Discarded Image*, are essential to understanding how deeply and intricately Lewis weaves medieval cosmology throughout his writings. These two books cannot be ignored, and this reader's guide itself exists largely because of them.

Let's look at the descriptions of each planet and its influence on the Earth. We will see these personalities in action as we dive into discussing the Ransom Trilogy itself. Though the planets are typically called by their Roman names, I will also supply their Greek counterparts.

The Moon: The Moon (also Luna; Selene to the Greeks) marks the barrier between the sublunar/terrestrial realm and the heavenly realm. She is the boundary line. Her pock-marked visage still bears evidence of the great war for the cosmos that occurred when Satan fell "like lightning" (Luke 10:18). Lady Luna is associated with all things watery and damp. Her metal is silver and the influence of her rays can cause the wandering of both mind and body. In some people, this is simply the desire to travel; in others, the wandering of wits. This is where we get our word *lunacy*.

Mercury: The Mercurial spirit is a difficult one to pin down—as it should be. Lewis describes the various attributes and symbols that are associated with Mercury, but he ends by simply saying: "It is better just to take some real mercury in a saucer and play with it for a few minutes. *That* is what 'Mercurial' means."[3] Mercury is associated with men of action. He is the lord of language—of words and their meanings, of learning and the study of literature. Mercury is multi-faceted ("Merry multitude of meeting selves, same but sundered"[4]) and is associated with thieves and deceptions. Mercury was the messenger god of the Romans (to the Greeks, he was Hermes). Speed and nimbleness, both physical and intellectual, are possessed under his sway. Lewis's best attempt at describing the unity of all these characteristics is "skilled eagerness" or "bright alacrity."[5]

Venus: Venus is *Fortuna Minor*, meaning she is the most benevolent planet second only to Jupiter. Known as Aphrodite to the Greeks, Venus is the goddess of love, beauty, and fortuitous events in history. She produces fertility and abundance. She is the archetypical mother, bountiful and fruitful, and therefore sensual. When twisted, her influence can become lewd or tasteless in the translunar world. On Earth, Venus's influence can produce "beauty and amorousness" in mortals.[6] She produces copper in

---

3 *Discarded Image*, 108.

4 C. S. Lewis, "The Planets," in *Poems*, ed. by Walter Hooper (London: Harcourt, 1964), 13.

5 *Discarded Image*, 108.

6 Ibid., 107.

the earth[7] and hence burnished, ruddy gold is a color frequently connected with her personality. We will examine her character even more deeply in our study of *Perelandra.*

Sol (the Sun): The sun god Apollo (both in Greek and Roman mythology) is the god of archery, music, dance, prophecy, healing, and more. His is the sphere of the philosophers and theologians, wise men and sages. Apollo was also known as Apollo Sauroktonos (the "dragon-slayer") because of his famous slaying of the python, and so dragons are frequently associated with the Sun as well. The Sun brings fortunate events, but in the sublunar realm he can also produce greed and avarice. He produces gold and is associated with wisdom, benevolence, and generosity.

Mars: Mars (or Ares to the Greeks) is the god of war and soldiers. He gives men a temperament towards war and military excellence. He also produces a "sturdy hardiness,"[8] strength and courage, justice and heroism. The Martial metal is iron: a war-like metal used for the forging of weaponry. Yet Mars is also the god of farmers. He was known as *Mars Silvanus*, the god of trees and the woods. Below the Moon where all is muddled and imperfect, the Martial influence can lead to cruelty, tyranny, despotism, and hardness of heart.

Jupiter: Jupiter (or Jove) is the King of the planets. He is *Fortuna Major*: the best planet, bringing the most

7 Venus is the "Lady of Cyprus," being especially worshiped in that island, and Cyprus was once famed for its copper mines (copper = "cyprium"), *Discarded Image*, 107.

8 Ibid., 106.

good fortune. Jove (Zeus to the Greeks) was the king of all the gods, king of the sky and lightning. His sign was the eagle, which is why the eagle became the standard of Roman legions. Jove produces a "jovial" spirit in men. This word has been stripped of much of its depth and is commonly understood to simply mean "cheerful". But the true jovial spirit is not an easy one to grasp. It is cheerful and festive, yet tranquil and temperate, like a king "at peace, enthroned taking his leisure, serene."[9] Lewis himself claimed to have been born under Jove's influence and appointed himself Jove's "standard-bearer,"[10] always trying to make the jovial character more widely understood. Jove's metal is actually tin which, as Lewis notes, is somewhat disappointing to our modern sensibilities. But the shining metal worked differently upon the medieval imagination. Post-canning industry, the metal appears to us worthless and common, but in the Middle Ages tin was bright, beautiful, and rare. We will explore the Jovial spirit in more depth in our study of *That Hideous Strength.*

Saturn: Saturn is *Infortuna Major*, the "most unfortunate" planet. The Roman god Saturn was the god of agriculture, death and rebirth, and time. His Greek equivalent was Kronos, also the god of time. Saturn's influence produces a melancholy complexion in men. In the sublunar realm, he is connected with sickness and old age. Saturn is the most terrible of the seven planets, his sublunar influence promoting "fatal accidents, pestilence, treacheries, and ill luck in

9 Ibid.

10 Michael Ward, *Planet Narnia* (New York: Oxford University Press, 2008), 44.

general."[11] In earth, he fittingly produces lead: dull, gray, and heavy.

These brief explanations of the planetary personalities feel a bit like writing a speaker introduction to be read at a conference before each panelist takes the stage. They highlight just a few of the most obvious characteristics. But in order to truly know the planets, we must get to know them like friends, not just memorize facts about them. We must spend time with them. We must go to their homes, meet their friends, get to know their family. We must soak in the atmosphere that they create and learn about their personalities from firsthand experience. We all know what it is like to walk into various homes and feel the different atmospheres. The planetary personalities work in the same way, but because they exist in the unfallen, translunar realm, their personalities have an influence so strong that they can pierce the boundary of the Moon and make their presence known even on the sealed-off, silent planet of Earth.

Through the rest of this book, we will be slowly getting to know these planets and their unique atmospheres by spending time with them in the Ransom Trilogy.

11 *Discarded Image*, 105.

3

WHATNESS & WHICHNESS

Donegality and Atmosphere

If a man loves wine and yet hates one of the strongest wines, then surely the sole source of pleasure in wine cannot be the alcohol? (Lewis, "On Stories")

We've talked about the architecture of the medieval cosmos and we've set it spinning by discussing the dynamic personalities of the planetary figures themselves. But how does Lewis actually *use* the Model? Which literary method does he use to implement his knowledge of the planetary characters in his writing and pass that knowledge on to his readers? As we saw at the end of the last chapter, the personalities of the planets create their own unique *atmosphere*. Each one is a friend who we must come to know better by spending time with them. Lewis helps us do this by using their personalities to shape and craft the atmosphere of his stories.

In Lewis's essay "On Stories," he makes an important distinction between two different types of pleasure in reading a story. There is the pleasure in the *plot* itself—the adventures and exploits of the characters and the dangers they find themselves facing and conquering. But then there is a different sort of pleasure, not unrelated to or unaffected by the first, and that is the pleasure to be found in a story due to its *atmosphere*, the world that gives the story its own unique flavor and feel. This elusive, yet essential, element of good storytelling is what makes a story truly unforgettable. It is this element that shapes childhoods and draws readers back again and again to the same story.

The atmosphere of a book can go unnoticed if done well, but we would all notice if it were gone. Narnia and Middle Earth, Sherlock Holmes's London and Tom Sawyer's Mississippi River, Robin's Sherwood Forest and King Arthur's Camelot—we all go back to these books, whether we realize it or not, in order to live in the world of that book again. We visit them like we visit old friends and we would not trade one for the other. Each story is different because they have different personalities that go beyond the action of the plot. They have different atmospheres.

A story that lacks atmosphere can still keep you glued to the book, just as action and adventure movies do. Those stories can still be exciting and enjoyable in their own right, but they cannot really hold us beyond the first reading. They don't invite us to re-read them. Lewis's problem with books that only offer "excitement" is precisely this lack of atmosphere:

> If to love Story is to love excitement then I ought to be the greatest lover of excitement alive. But the fact is that what is said to be the most 'exciting'

> novel in the world, *The Three Musketeers*, makes no appeal to me at all. The total lack of atmosphere repels me. There is no country in the book—save as a storehouse of inns and ambushes. There is no weather. When they cross to London there is no feeling that London differs from Paris [...] It all means nothing to me.[1]

Lewis describes this idea of atmosphere in terms of a unique sense of place. Books like *The Three Musketeers* lack this sense of *place*, the place that has a peculiar *placeness* that is all its own and that we want to experience again and again. Once we've had our excitement, there is nothing left to go back to. The story has done its job. In contrast, Lewis sees *place* as the primary reason that we re-read the books we love: we want to return there.

> [...] when such stories are loved at all, they are re-read perhaps more than any others. Re-reading them is like going back to a fruit for its taste; to an air for...what? for *itself*; to a region for its whole atmosphere—to Donegal for its Donegality and London for its Londonness. It is notoriously difficult to put these tastes into words; and in a similar way the taste for a narrative 'world' is difficult to talk about.[2]

Michael Ward adopts this word *donegality* from the above quote and uses it as a technical term to refer to this phenomenon—atmosphere, the qualitative sense of place within certain books. And this is what Ward argues the

1 C. S. Lewis, "On Stories," in *Of This and Other Worlds*, (New York: Harcourt, 1982), 29.

2 C. S. Lewis, *Spenser's Images of Life* (Cambridge: University Press, 1967), 115.

planetary characters give to the Narnia stories. Each of the seven Narnia stories possesses a donegality, an intoxicating and pervasive atmosphere, that is determined by a specific planetary character.

This is how Lewis implements the medieval cosmology at a pervasive yet nearly invisible level in many of his writings. In the Ransom Trilogy in particular, Lewis mines the vast caves of the planetary personalities and uses them to shape both the plot and the donegality of the books. The goal of the whole trilogy is, in essence, to rediscover and recover the Medieval Model, a "discarded image." From viewing Earth as the "Silent Planet" mentioned in the title of the first book, to the presence of Merlin in the third, every twist and turn of the plot is influenced by the mythology attached to the medieval cosmology.

Pinning down the way the planets influence the donegality or atmosphere of the books can be as difficult as explaining why Grandpa's study feels different than any other study, or why Aunt Jane's house feels different from Uncle Bob's. We can list the ways that Lewis uses words and imagery associated with the different planets. We can try to dissect his use of adjectives and metaphors, action and plot twists. But as another great writer once said, "He that breaks a thing to find out what it is has left the path of wisdom."[3] In the end, Lewis has taken his own advice. He knows these planetary characters from the inside out, and so he writes from *inside* this atmosphere. To ask how he does it would be to ask someone how they breath the air around them. We can explain it scientifically, down to the atoms of air and the exchange of gases. But at root there is still something

---

3 J. R. R. Tolkien, *The Fellowship of the Ring*, (New York: Houghton Mifflin, 1994), 252.

magical and mysterious that we cannot define, we can only experience. There is a spiritual dimension and we cannot escape it. It is woven into the world. If we step into that world, we will feel it.

That said, there are certain characteristics and methods that Lewis uses that we can point to when we are trying to describe the donegality of any particular book. In *Out of the Silent Planet*, we will see the characteristics and personality of Mars shape the setting and atmosphere of Malacandra. Nearly all of *Perelandra* takes place on the planet Venus, and so we will explore the way in which the spirit and influence of that fruitful, maternal character shapes the whole story. And finally, in *That Hideous Strength*, we see the great lord, Jupiter the Priest-King, shape not only the atmosphere of the book but the character of Ransom himself.

Ultimately, this is what the Ransom Trilogy is all about: recovering the image of a cosmos that is potent enough to create worlds that breathe on the page, characters real enough to teach us about God's sovereignty and man's freedom, a cosmos leaping with the life of the Triune God and singing His praises. This world is a living world, which means that it is both matter and spirit, and is therefore far more complex than we can begin to imagine. These planetary figures, vivacious and powerful, are not merely characters, though they are that. They pervade and influence every word on every page of Lewis's remarkable work. Lewis does not just tell us that the planets exert an influence on the Earth—he *shows* us. From the sphere of Mars to the influence of the kingly planet himself, Lewis stands *inside* and beckons us to join him in seeing firsthand how the spirit of the medieval cosmos is still alive.

PART I:

Out of the Silent Planet

SUMMARY

Ransom, a middle-aged Cambridge don and philologist, is on a walking tour through the English countryside. He offers to assist a country woman who is worried when her somewhat dimwitted son does not return from his job at a large house nearby. In his attempt to send the boy home, Ransom meets the masters of the house, Weston and Devine. Ransom is drugged by the men and kidnapped, waking up to find himself aboard a space-ship bound for the planet Malacandra (Mars). He finds out that Weston and Devine intend to offer him as a human sacrifice to the natives of Malacandra, but manages to escape their clutches once they reach the planet's surface.

The book focuses on Ransom's ensuing adventures on Malacandra, in which he meets the inhabitants and learns more truths about the universe. In the end, Ransom is brought before the Oyarsa of Malacandra (the angelic being given charge over the planet). Weston and Devine are captured by the Malacandrians and stripped of their weapons, and then all three men are sent back to Earth in the space-ship, having been warned that this breach of the barrier between the Silent Planet and Deep Heaven has become a turning point in a cosmic conflict—the Earth is no longer as sealed off as it had been before.

4

THE PEDESTRIAN & THE PILGRIM

Dante's Influence and Importance

> The last drops of the thundershower had hardly ceased falling when the Pedestrian stuffed his map into his pocket, settled his pack more comfortably onto his tired shoulders, and stepped out from the shelter of a large chestnut-tree into the middle of the road. (Lewis, *Out of the Silent Planet*)

Lewis was a medieval and renaissance scholar. Although he was called to many things and ended up wearing many different hats throughout his life, his scholarly work was a large part of who he was and, as we have already seen, it deeply influenced his fictional work as well. Lewis's love for his subject matter was unparalleled and it was that love that enabled not only his excellence in his field, but also the influence of medieval thought and imagination to permeate his life and writings.

Among the many authors that inspired and influenced his life and writings, Dante, the great Florentine poet of the Middle Ages, stands tall. No discussion of the Medieval Model (or Lewis's love for it) would be complete without Dante. He will pop up again and again throughout this book, so we need to take a moment to get to know him and see why Lewis loved him so much.

Born around 1265 in Florence, Italy, Dante Alighieri is best known for his epic poetic masterpiece *La commedia*, later called *La divina commedia* (*The Divine Comedy*), one of the greatest works of medieval literature. Dante's use of the Italian vernacular in this beautiful work was groundbreaking at the time and changed the course of literature. The *Comedy*'s poetry is sophisticated and full of imagery and imagination despite being told in the "common" language.

The poem is an allegory that takes the reader on a journey through the three realms of the afterlife. The work is divided into three volumes: *Inferno*, *Purgatorio*, and *Paradiso*. Each volume is divided into thirty-three cantos (or chapters). Dante himself is the main character and he is guided through these realms of Hell, Purgatory, and finally Paradise itself. His guide for the first two stages of the journey is the great Roman poet Vergil. However, Vergil disappears at the entrance to the earthly paradise of Eden in the seventh level of Purgatory to be replaced by a new guide: Beatrice, Dante's muse, and, historically, the woman that the poet Dante loved.

The entirety of Dante's masterpiece is written from *inside* the medieval cosmology. Hell is lowest and central: the cesspit of the universe, containing the dregs of all humanity. While we moderns think that centrality equates *importance*, the medievals saw centrality as an indication of *unimportance*. The center is the lowest point. Therefore, Earth's centrality did not place it in the position of highest significance, but rather of greatest insignificance. Earth possesses the most central, the very lowest position in the cosmos, and Hell is the most central and lowest part of the Earth. Hell is the lowest of the low. From Hell, Dante is led up the mountain of Purgatory and then through the seven heavens of Paradise. Each of these seven heavens corresponds to the seven planets that we have already discussed. The saints that Dante's Pilgrim encounters within each of these spheres possess virtues that correspond to the planet ruling that sphere.

Dante's poetry encapsulates everything that Lewis loved about the medieval cosmos: the light and life, the bursting vivacity and creativity, and the rich tapestry of ideas and images, emotions and languages that the Medieval Model presents.

Lewis first read the *Inferno* in Italian when he was a teenager. He later read *Purgatorio* when he was in hospital recovering from wounds that he received in World War I. He finally read *Paradiso* for the first time years later in 1930. This was before he became a Christian, but after he had reluctantly decided that there was *a* God. He was still very much conflicted as to the nature of God and whether or not there was such a thing as an afterlife. This was his state of mind when he read Dante's *Paradiso.*

After finishing the work, Lewis told his dear friend Arthur Greeves:

> I think it reaches heights of poetry which you get nowhere else; an ether almost too fine to breathe. It is a pity I can give you no notion what it is like. Can you imagine Shelley at his most ecstatic combined with Milton at his most solemn & rigid? It

> sounds impossible I know, but that is what Dante has done.[1]

The year after reading *Paradiso*, Lewis became a believing Christian. While we may never know how significant a role Dante played in his actual conversion, the role that Dante played in the rest of the areas of Lewis's life shows us that it could not have been insignificant.

Lewis echoes Dante several times in the opening pages of his trilogy. Dante's *Inferno* begins with a Pilgrim (Dante) in a dark wood:

> Midway along the journey of our life
> I woke to find myself in a dark wood,
> For I had wandered off from the straight path.[2]

In the opening chapter of *Out of the Silent Planet*, Lewis likewise introduces us to a pilgrim ("the Pedestrian") in a dark wood. For scholars of Dante, reading this opening scene is like running into an old friend. Both Dante's Pilgrim and Lewis's Pedestrian are in a dark wood, and they are of similar age: the Pilgrim is "midway along the journey of life"[3] and the Pedestrian is "thirty-five to forty years of age."[4] The Pedestrian is Ransom, but this first page of the trilogy is the only place where Lewis gives him this title. In referring to Ransom as "the Pedestrian," Lewis immediately sets him up as a kind of Everyman, a figure that Dante also implements in his Pilgrim. For those first few pages, Ransom, just like

1 C. S. Lewis to Arthur Greeves, Hillsboro, July 8, 1930, in *The Collected Letters of C. S. Lewis*, ed. Walter Hooper (London: HarperCollins, 2000), 1:915.

2 Dante Alighieri, *Inferno*, 1.1-3.

3 Ibid., 1.1.

4 C. S. Lewis, *Out of the Silent Planet* (New York: Scribner, 1938), 10.

Dante's Pilgrim, is a nameless, middle-aged walker: he could be anyone or no one. And then, a light appears over the hill:

> I raised my head and saw the hilltop shawled
> In morning rays of light sent from the planet
> That leads men straight ahead on every road.[5]

Ransom also encounters this light over the hill, a sign of a change, the appearance of a guide that was unasked for, but nonetheless needed.

Another connection with Dante's great work is seen in the *characters* of Ransom and Dante themselves. Ransom is a philologist, a studier of language and words. Dante's Pilgrim (a characterization of Dante himself) is also a poet, a lover of language, the author who wrote a work entitled *De vulgari eloquentia* ("On Eloquence in the Vernacular"). Ransom and Dante are both turned back from their planned journeys: Dante is turned back from climbing the mountain and Ransom is turned back from the inn. Using these small details and allusions, Lewis subtly and deftly recreates the opening scene of Dante's *Inferno*, using similar language and images without in any way being heavy-handed. This is one of those passages that echoes and reverberates with the sounds of a vast literary lineage, and yet it is so naturally done that many readers don't notice until it is pointed out. Once you see it, however, you can't ignore it.

The similarity between these two passages—the opening of the Ransom Trilogy and the first lines of *The Divine Comedy*—invites us to begin a comparison between Elwin Ransom and Dante's Pilgrim. If we know that Dante's Pilgrim is led from the dungeons to the heights of the

5 *Inferno*, 1.1.

cosmos, we might expect that Ransom, too, is going to set out on a journey that is very different from the one he originally planned. He is about to enter realms that he could scarcely imagine. Lewis hints at this impending surprise when he says that Ransom "set out at once with the determined stride of a good walker who has lately realized that he will have to walk *farther than he intended*."[6] If Ransom only knew…

Dante's Pilgrim is already on the road in the beginning of *The Divine Comedy*, but he also takes an unexpected path through the hidden places of the universe, descending into the depths of Hell before rising through Purgatory and on to the blissful realm of Paradise and the Empyrean itself. Likewise, Ransom is on holiday, backpacking through the English countryside. He is already on a journey. But just like Dante's Pilgrim, Ransom has no idea of the *kind* of journey it really is and what the consequences will be when he steps out from the shadow of the wood and pursues the light that shines out through the darkness over the hill. He, too, will travel through the different realms of the cosmos. In imitation of Dante's Pilgrim, Ransom goes through Hell, Purgatory, and the deepest Heaven. But, as we will explore more deeply in later chapters, Lewis puts these realms in places we might not expect. Ransom goes through Hell on Mars, Purgatory on Venus, and, at the last, rather than travel to the deepest parts of heaven himself, he himself is the bridge whereby Deep Heaven descends to Earth, the Silent Planet.

Yet Dante's influence on the Ransom Trilogy runs deeper than narrative structure or overarching themes or small echoes like the ones I've just described. Even as Dante's brilliance struck the young, unconverted Lewis with its glory and sublime artistry, flooding his imagination and shaping

---

6 *Silent Planet*, 9, emphasis mine.

his thought, so too does that same influence shape these books. Just as the influence of the planets themselves weave metals through the earth, Dante's influence worked veins of gold through Lewis's thought and imagination. It planted seeds that germinated deep under the earth, spreading their roots wide like nets, and once we discover a connection, the whole plant comes up, rich dirt clinging to the life-giving tendrils. As we continue our exploration of the trilogy, more examples of Dante's influence will come to light.

5

"BY JOVE!"

Lewis's Use of Language

"Do you find it easy to get drunk on words?" "So easy that, to tell you the truth, I am seldom perfectly sober." (Dorothy Sayers, *Gaudy Night*)

Before we explore how Lewis uses language, we need to consider language itself. Language is made up of sound. Air and vocal chords and sound waves work together to produce something that somehow mysteriously makes sense to those who hear it. The very nature of language is an argument against materialism, one of Lewis's foremost philosophical adversaries. Let's take a minute to discuss this materialism.

Materialism views spiritual realities (including morality, religion, faith, etc.) as results of chemical processes. Everything has a material explanation; everything is "simply" matter. This view can also be referred to as *materialistic reduc-*

tionism in the sense that the entire cosmos is *reduced* to merely the material. Nothing exists apart from physical matter. Created things are *just* matter: no more.

Materialistic reductionism leads also to a rejection of any moral code or ethic or even epistemology (the theory of knowledge or how we know things). Knowledge and information are themselves spiritual realities—they are more than the sum of their material parts.

This worldview is ultimately untenable as it leads logically to a rejection of the rational arguments that are used to support it. In order to exist in this world, we are forced to *behave* as if materialism is false. If our thought processes are mere chemical reactions, then why should we build our entire view of reality from thoughts that we concocted *using* those chemical reactions?

To bring this back to the subject of language, we see that language itself is a refutation of materialistic reductionism. In order for us to communicate with each other, there must be something *beyond* the physical elements of air and cartilage and sound waves, because the meaning that we communicate by these physical means is not itself able to be touched or seen.

Human beings are word-oriented people by nature. We have been created by the Word of the eternal Creator. Christians in particular are people of the *Word.* "And the Word became flesh and dwelt among us, and we beheld His glory, the glory as of the only begotten of the Father, full of grace and truth" (John 1:14). It is undeniable that words matter and no words matter more than the ones that God has given to us in the Bible. He gave us His Word, He gave us words (in language), and He gave us the blessing of multiple languages. Babel, a curse upon a prideful people, has been redeemed by Christ's coming. In Pentecost we see this reversal, as all nations and peoples and tribes and languages and nations see the glory of the Gospel. In Christ, all things are made new, and so now we see the glory of a multiplicity of languages. Every language has its own splendor, each their own sounds and characteristics that give them personality. The flowing dance of French. The earthy percussion of German. The rumble bumble of Anglo-Saxon or the lilting cadence of Irish Gaelic. Harsh or harmonious, rigid or fluid, languages all teach us something about the way the world works.

Lewis was a lover of words and languages. He could read and speak Greek, Latin, Italian, French, German, Anglo-Saxon, Old Norse, and a smattering of others. He delighted in the sounds and the meanings of words. Anyone can tell from his writings that he was not above the humor found in puns or double meanings. He was an expert deep-sea diver of language, plumbing the depths of etymology and history to recover rare jewels of meaning from the shipwrecks of ancient and classical knowledge. Lewis also never chose a word at random; if his word choice ever strikes us as odd, we are simply not as well-versed in its usage and history as Lewis! He sets words in order purposefully, like polished stones in a kingly crown, and so we should seek to understand his reasons for choosing those words.

In the Ransom Trilogy in particular, language holds a central thematic place. For Ransom the philologist, words and language comprise his entire occupation. As a character, Ransom is thinking about language all the time, and as the author, Lewis consistently plays with words and their etymological significance and connotations. Studying Lewis's use of language in his prose is like studying a portrait in an art gallery. We don't need to know anything about the artist, the painting style, or the backstory of the subject of the portrait in order to appreciate the painting on a superficial level. But understanding the subject, context, and history behind the painting nevertheless gives us a *deeper* appreciation for the portrait. The connotations enrich our experience and enjoyment. In the same way, if we join Lewis on his deep dive into the roots and origins of some of his most distinctive words, we will discover an additional layer to the world and atmosphere that he is crafting in these books.

One example is his use of exclamations. Ward speaks about this in *Planet Narnia* while illustrating the planetary influences on each of the seven Narnia books. For example, the exclamation "by gum!" occurs most frequently in *The Magician's Nephew*, the book influenced by the spirit of Venus. The Mediterranean island of Cyprus was known for trees that produced a particular resin, or gum. These trees were connected to the worship of Venus which flourished on the island and is the reason for another one of Venus's many names: *Cypris* (the lady of Cyprus). Lewis clearly uses the expression "by gum!" to emphasize the influence of Venus on *The Magician's Nephew*.[1] Likewise, the exclamation "by Jove!", while found in many of the Chronicles, occurs most frequently in the book under the strongest Jovial influence: *The Lion, the Witch, and the Wardrobe*. All of these exclamations are not mere colloquialisms or catchphrases that Lewis throws into his characters' dialogue at random. They are loaded with cosmological meaning. When Lewis uses them, he uses them purposefully.

In *Out of the Silent Planet*, "by Jove!" is uttered twice: first by Devine and the second time by Weston, the two men who kidnap Ransom and take him to Malacandra. Let us examine one of these instances.

1 *Planet Narnia*, 183.

Devine's use of "by Jove" is perhaps the more surprising of the two. Devine is not a serious or superstitious character in the slightest. He is glib and flippant on the outside, while inside he is just greedy. Where Weston has some sense of a higher purpose or philosophy (more on that later), Devine simply wants money. We might easily overlook his use of "by Jove" because it seems like something that Devine would say without thinking anything of it, and so we don't think anything of it either. It is hidden in plain sight. But once we understand the influence of the Medieval Model on these books, *any* mention of Jove in *any* form should draw our attention.

Devine uses the word in response to Ransom telling him his name. Devine responds, "By Jove…not Ransom who used to be at Wedenshaw?"[2] By seeming "coincidence," Ransom has run into an old acquaintance (a schoolfellow whom he disliked) and Devine's response is to exclaim in wonder. But knowing, as we do, that Jove is the greatest of the planets, the King over the others, *the one who orders all things*, we know that Ransom running into Devine is no coincidence at all. Jove is *Fortuna Major*, the benevolent monarch. By invoking Jove in the mouth of a flippant character, Lewis is telling us, very plainly, that this apparent total coincidence has literally occurred *by Jove.* The truth is that countless events over the years have worked together in order to bring Ransom to this precise spot and moment in time. Jove himself has orchestrated the event, this unexpected shift. In other words, Lewis is telling us that Ransom's imminent arrival on Malacandra is just the beginning of a bigger story, the tipping point of a great movement.

2 *Silent Planet*, 14.

Besides exclamations, there are a couple of key words that have cosmological significance for Lewis but that can be easily overlooked if we are not familiar with their etymology. One of these words is *tingle*. Our English word *tingle* comes from the Anglo-Saxon word for star, *tingul*. In the Ransom Trilogy, *tingle* is often used to describe Ransom's sensations when he either sees the heavens for what they really are or encounters various angelic beings: the *eldila* or the Oyerésu. The word *tingling* is not merely descriptive. It is appropriate that Ransom feels the effects of his cosmological shift in a particularly cosmological way. His view of the stars has been rewritten and this is felt in his body as a tingling—we could say *starriness*. He has seen the stars for what they are and he feels it down to his bones.

Another word with a similar cosmological background is *consider*, which comes from the Latin *considerare* which means "to examine/reflect upon." But this word is comprised of another Latin word, *sidus*, and the prefix *con*. *Sidus* means "star" or "constellation/group of stars." So, *to consider* literally means "to gaze at the stars." Back when astrology did not carry the negative connotations that it does today, generations of wise men, sages, magi, and prophets looked to the stars for guidance and wisdom. Far from being purely fictitious and superstitious, astrology was the *study of the stars*. But the way the medievals viewed the cosmos was far less dualistic and materialistic than the way we view it. Because of this, in their thought, the line between what we would call superstition and science was less defined. The stars are not just "balls of burning gas" and they have something to say to those who have ears to hear. Like the Magi led to a single stable in Bethlehem, the medievals looked to the sky with more than just observational interest. There was something spiritual to be understood from looking at the heavens.

Lewis was not unaware of this ancient meaning. Early in the book, when Ransom is first taken among the stars, Ransom's sanity forbids him to "consider" the possibility that he is really dead when he awakens in the space-ship.[3] And later Ransom tells the madman Weston: "I consider *your* philosophy of life raving lunacy."[4] Here Lewis uses two cosmologically relevant words in the same sentence. Lunacy is a result of the influence of Luna, the Moon, whose rays cause a wandering of the wits. But Ransom specifically considers Weston's ideas to be lunacy. And Lewis never uses a word like this lightly. As we shall see as we learn more about Weston and the medieval cosmology, Ransom hits the nail on the head. Weston's ideas are not just insanity, they are directly *under the sublunar influence*. The Moon was the battleground of Satan's great rebellion, and half of the Moon fell to the enemy. That half, the fallen half, is under the sway of the ideology of death and sterility. Later, in *That Hideous Strength*, it is Weston's philosophies that lead the men and women of Belbury to attempt to turn the Earth into a second Luna: cold and barren. Ransom has *considered* these philosophies and so, in one sense, he has "read the stars"—meaning that he has interpreted Weston's motivations correctly, according to the way the world and cosmos actually work.

These examples give just a small taste of Lewis's use of nuance and subtlety in language. As we read through the trilogy, I hope you will start to notice these little veins of starlight tucked inside otherwise "unimportant" sentences, just waiting for readers to consider.

---

3 *Silent Planet*, 24.

4 Ibid., 29.

6

THE HEAVENS DECLARE

Ransom's Revelation

> His headache was gone: he felt vigilant, courageous and magnanimous as he had seldom felt on Earth. Gradually he dared to raise his eyes to the skylight. Steel shutters were drawn across all but a chink of the glass, and that chink was covered with blinds of some heavy and dark material; but still it was too bright to look at.
>
> "I always thought space was dark and cold," he remarked vaguely. (Lewis, *Out of the Silent Planet*)

Chapters four and five of *Out of the Silent Planet* present us with a pivotal shift in both Ransom's perception of the cosmos and his own character and attitude. One might argue (as I would!) that these two chapters reveal the main purpose and focus of the entire trilogy: Lewis's desire to reintroduce us to the imaginative and emotional power of the medieval way of looking at the heavens.

In the first lines of chapter four, Ransom is terrified though he doesn't understand *why*: "At the moment he was unconscious of everything except his fear. He did not even know what he was afraid of: the fear itself possessed his whole mind, a formless, infinite misgiving."[1] Weston has just told him that the planet he saw from the space-ship window is, in fact, the Earth. The terror Ransom feels in response to this information is all-consuming, yet vague and unfocused. But then we see one of the sources of his fear. "'You mean we're—in space.' Ransom uttered the word with difficulty as a frightened child speaks of ghosts or a frightened man of cancer."[2] The very concept of being in "space"—in the cold, dead, black vacuity that the modern mind associates with that word—is enough to terrify Ransom. Anyone who has watched a "space" movie (that is, a movie set in outer space) can relate to this feeling. When I was younger, I hated movies that featured NASA expeditions or space shuttles—the idea of a vast expanse of nothingness was terrifying to me (and still is!).

Yet, as we have already discussed, this feeling is different than the feeling inspired by the medieval cosmos. As Lewis says in *The Discarded Image*, "This explains why all sense of the pathless, the baffling, and the utterly alien—all agoraphobia—is so markedly absent from medieval poetry when it leads us, as so often, into the sky [...] He is like a man being conducted through an immense cathedral, not like one lost in a shoreless sea."[3]

But Ransom's assumptions about space are quickly turned upside down, as his observations reveal:

---

1 *Silent Planet*, 27.

2 Ibid.

3 *Discarded Image*, 99.

> The light was paler than any light of comparable intensity that he had ever seen; it was not pure white light but the palest of all imaginable golds, and it cast shadows as sharp as a floodlight. The heat, utterly free from moisture, seemed to knead and stroke the skin like a giant masseur: it produced no tendency to drowsiness: rather, intense alacrity. His headache was gone: he felt vigilant, courageous and magnanimous as he had seldom felt on Earth. Gradually he dared to raise his eyes to the skylight. Steel shutters were drawn across all but a chink of the glass, and that chink was covered with blinds of some heavy and dark material; but still it was too bright to look at.
>
> "I always thought space was dark and cold," he remarked vaguely.
>
> "Forgotten the sun?" said Weston contemptuously.[4]

There are two things to note about this passage. First, Ransom's previous assumptions are treated as scientifically *backward.* Weston derides Ransom for having "forgotten the sun." Of course, we know that Ransom's prior thoughts about space are technically *true.* We have the empirical evidence to back it up. But here, it is *Ransom's* preconceptions that are to be upended. What he thought he knew about the universe is being shown to be false. But this is not to say that Lewis is himself arguing against our empirical evidence. He is writing fiction, after all. His endeavor in these books is something more complex than simply pushing for a rejection of the modern cosmology in terms of its physical layout. There are philosophical and imaginative repercussions that stem from the way we view the cosmos we live in,

4 *Silent Planet*, 31.

and it is these repercussions that Lewis wants to rid us of. For Ransom, this moment begins to reshape his imagination and emotions as he looks at the heavens and the worlds in those heavens. We will see more of this later on.

The second thing to note about this passage is Lewis's description of the light itself and the effect that this light has on Ransom. Remember that this is *sunlight.* It is coming from the Sun itself and is undiluted by any atmosphere. Hence Ransom experiences the pure, translunar influence of the Sun's rays. Note the strong influence of Sol on this scene. If you will recall from chapter two, Sol produces gold in the Earth (here, the light is the "palest of all imaginable golds"), he makes men "wise and liberal"[5] (Ransom feels "magnanimous"), and by his rays, "mists are parted"[6] (Ransom becomes vigilant and feels an intense alacrity). Ransom not only witnesses the truth that space is *not* cold and dark, he also tastes the influence of Sol himself, an influence that he comes to treasure as a "severe delight."[7]

In chapter five, Lewis gives a more detailed description of what the heavens are truly like, and Ransom's ideas about space are even further dismantled. The heavens are full of light and life and color. Lewis says that Ransom "found it night by night more difficult to disbelieve in old astrology: almost he felt, wholly he imagined, 'sweet influence' pouring or even stabbing into his surrendered body."[8] Ransom makes the connection between his unexpected experience and the "old astrology," meaning medieval cosmology. On the very next page, we get the culmination of his mental transformation, the total falling off of his previous mindset:

5 *Discarded Image*, 106.

6 "The Planets" in *Poems*, 13.

7 *Silent Planet*, 33.

8 Ibid.

> A nightmare, long engendered in the modern mind by the mythology that follows in the wake of science, was falling off him. He had read of "Space": at the back of his thinking for years had lurked the dismal fancy of the black, cold vacuity, the utter darkness, which was supposed to separate the worlds. He had not known how much it affected him till now—now that the very name "Space" seemed a blasphemous libel for the empyrean ocean of radiance in which they swam. He could not call it "dead'; he felt life pouring into him from it every moment. How indeed should it be otherwise, since out of this ocean the worlds and all their life had come? He had thought it barren: he saw now that it was the womb of worlds, whose blazing and innumerable offspring looked down nightly even upon the earth with so many eyes—and here, with how many more! No: space was the wrong name. Older thinkers had been wiser when they named it simply the heavens—the heavens which declared the glory[9]—the
>
> "*happy climes that ly*
> *Where day never shuts his eye*
> *Up in the broad fields of the sky.*"[10]
>
> He quoted Milton's words to himself lovingly, at this time and often.[11]

If there is one paragraph that could be said to be the most important in the entire trilogy, it would be this one. This is the point of Lewis's project—to encourage this sort of imaginative conversion in his readers, to reawaken a me-

---

9 Psalm 19:1

10 From John Milton's poem *Comus.*

11 *Silent Planet*, 34.

dieval imagination as we view our entire cosmos and the heavens in particular. The mental switch from seeing "space" to seeing "the heavens" when we look up at the night sky is what Lewis wants for his readers. He tells us this in the last chapter of *Out of the Silent Planet*, when Ransom explicitly states the primary reason for chronicling and publishing these stories of his adventures:

> [...] what we need for the moment is not so much a body of belief as a body of people familiarized with certain ideas. If we could even effect in one per cent of our readers a *change-over from the conception of Space to the conception of Heaven*, we should have made a beginning.[12]

Lewis makes it clear that a desire for this recovery motivated his writing of the Ransom Trilogy—a recovery of an "old mode" of looking at the cosmos. He wrote to one reader that "the substitution of heaven for space...is my favourite idea in the book."[13] Lewis saw that the modern scientific cosmos had led to a loss of essential imaginative and emotional experiences that were the strongest features of the Medieval Model. No, we don't need to accept the old *science*. Lewis isn't arguing that we reject everything we have learned about what space actually is like. Rather, he wants us to recover the image of the cosmos as living, breathing, Word-spoken. In our reduction of the cosmos to the material, we no longer experience wonder, awe, praise, or the bottom-heavy security of those who look up into a vast well of starlight. And it is this sense that he seeks to reawaken.

---

12 *Silent Planet*, 152, emphasis mine.

13 Lewis to Mrs. Stuart Moore, Oxford, October 29, 1938, in *Collected Letters*, 2:235.

7

STRANGE FICTION

H. G. Wells and the Sci-Fi Genre

> Is any man such a dull clod that he can look up at the moon through a good telescope without asking himself what it would be like to walk among those mountains under that black, crowded sky? The scientists themselves, the moment they go beyond purely mathematical statements, can hardly avoid describing the facts in terms of their probable effect on the senses of a human observer. Prolong this, and give, along with that observer's sense experience, his probable emotions and thoughts, and you at once have a rudimentary science fiction. (Lewis, *Of This and Other Worlds*, "On Science Fiction")

No discussion of the Ransom Trilogy would be complete without talking about the influences on Lewis's writings that are about as far removed from medieval thought as they could get. In a number of places, including his letters and a note at the beginning of *Out of the Silent Planet* itself, Lewis makes plain the debt he owes to the work of various sci-fi writers: H. G. Wells, David Lindsay, and the like. In his essay "On Science Fiction," he admits that he was fond of the science fiction genre before it was popular and became even more fond of it as its popularity sparked greater proficiency in the genre itself.

In Lewis's view of literary criticism, he says that the critic has to *like* and even *love* the work before he can be trusted to criticize it. Someone who hates the genre of science fiction will not do it any justice as a critic. Lewis himself says that he generally dislikes detective stories and all of them look alike to him. "[I]f I wrote about them I should therefore infallibly write drivel."[1] However, Lewis enjoyed science fiction as a genre. He was an avid reader of both high and low-brow fiction. But this does not mean that he was in any way blind to the faults of the genre. In fact, his enthusiasm for science fiction qualifies him to explore how certain sub-species simply do not work as well as others.

Lewis describes several of these sub-species, two of which he has no taste for. We will explore these sub-species briefly because they will shed light on the Ransom Trilogy and how Lewis categorized it within the sci-fi genre. Lewis believes that the first of these sub-species isn't actually science fiction at all. This is where the author "leaps forward into an imagined future when planetary, sidereal, or even galactic travel has become common,"[2] and in this setting proceeds to tell any kind of story he chooses: spy fiction, romance, detective story, etc. The so-called "science fiction" is mere backdrop and the story itself contains nothing dis-

1 "On Science Fiction" in *Of This and Other Worlds*, 81.

2 Ibid., 82.

tinctively belonging to that genre. The setting is *incidental* rather than a character in the story. The *Star Wars* films are a perfect example of this sub-species of sci-fi.

The second sub-species is a legitimate choice, Lewis says, but one for which he has little liking. This is what he calls the "fiction of Engineers." These stories are "written by people who are primarily interested in space-travel, or in other undiscovered techniques, as real possibilities in the actual universe."[3] The interest of these stories is found in speculating on technological advancements. Lewis calls himself too "uneducated scientifically"[4] to find any real pleasure in technical details.

The third sub-species is more speculative. Science may tell us that thus-and-such a planet likely has thus-and-such a climate or condition—but it doesn't tell us what standing on the planet would be *like*. Speculative sci-fi attempts to answer this question. This sub-species has regaled readers and listeners for centuries, for men have always asked this question about places they have never been or to which they can never go: what would it be *like*?

This brings us back to what we discussed in chapter three, the element that Lewis most excels at: *atmosphere*. This is what he is interested in, not all the cogs and wheels and how a space-ship could actually fly. Once we got there, *however* we got there, what would the surface of the Moon be *like*? What would it smell like and how would it feel? The memorable atmosphere is what he praises about H. G. Wells's *First Men in the Moon*. The book is not annoyingly scientifically accurate; if it were, it would fall under the second category and so lose most of its appeal for Lewis. Instead,

3 Ibid., 84.

4 Ibid.

Wells is primarily concerned with the *emotional impact* of this lunar experience. He wants to give his readers a glimpse into this other world—the "unveiled airless sky, the lunar landscape, the lunar levity, the incomparable solitude, then the growing terror, finally the overwhelming approach of the lunar night."[5]

The fourth sub-species Lewis calls the Eschatological. It is somewhat similar to the first sub-species, but rather than simply introducing a new "what if" by displacing a figure in time and telling a "normal" story, the imagined future itself plays a particular role. Lewis cites Wells's *Time Machine* as an example of this genre.

The fifth and final sub-species is the one into which the Ransom Trilogy falls. Lewis doesn't give this sub-species a clear name. We might call it "fantastical sci-fi" or even "mythical sci-fi." This is where the realms of fantasy and science blur together until the science is really just a means or mode of conveying what is, in essence, a *fairy tale*. Fairy tales, myths, and fantasies have always been told about the distant and remote, the foreign or unexplored realm. As we explore and settle our planet, places once mysterious and strange lose an element of magic. And so our gaze turns to the heavens as the next great frontier, a place relatively unexplored, a world wholly *other*.

In these types of stories, the reader is not looking for *scientific* discoveries or the possibility of using those discoveries to accomplish *technological* advancements. The science is simply a means to an end. It is a prop. Lewis references the Ransom Trilogy in order to explain the flavor and goals of this sub-species, starting by explaining his decision to change Ransom's mode of transportation from the first to

5 "On Science-Fiction", 86.

the second books. In *Out of the Silent Planet*, Ransom travels by space-ship, a space-ship whose mechanics Lewis conspicuously refuses to explain, because they are not the point. In *Perelandra*, Lewis has Ransom conducted by the Oyarses (angels) straight to Venus, because by now Lewis knew better what he was trying to accomplish:

> I took a hero once to Mars in a space-ship, but when I knew better I had angels convey him to Venus. Nor need the strange worlds, when we get there, be at all strictly tied to scientific probabilities. It is their wonder, or beauty, or suggestiveness that matters. When I myself put canals on Mars I believe I already knew that better telescopes had dissipated that old optical delusion. The point was that they were part of the Martian myth as it already existed in the common mind.[6]

Many of the sci-fi stories that Lewis enjoyed had deplorable worldviews and philosophies, which Lewis detested. (In fact, he used these philosophies and ideologies to form the motivations for the character of Weston.) However, Lewis noted the particular ability of sci-fi to carry the great weight of worldview, philosophy, and cosmology, and *still be enjoyable.* Wells was enormously influential, though his philosophy was rubbish. Lewis was inspired, not by Wells's worldview, but by what Wells was able to do to promote that worldview through his science fiction. Wells kindled in Lewis a love for the "whole interplanetary idea as a mythology," and made Lewis wish to "conquer for my own (Christian) point of view what has always hitherto been used by the opposite

6 Ibid., 91.

side."[7] And so Lewis wrote the Ransom Trilogy, in which he turned Wells's philosophy on its head.

Despite his philosophical disagreements with H. G. Wells, Lewis owed much to this great pioneer of the science fiction genre, and he was not afraid to let everyone know it. Readers of the Ransom Trilogy may imagine that Lewis must have disliked Wells's books, even as works of fiction. But the truth is the opposite—Lewis heartily approved. And that is exactly why he sets out to *redeem* the entire genre.

---

7 Lewis to Roger Lancelyn Green, The Kilns, December 28, 1938 in *Collected Letters*, 2:237.

8

LEARNING TO RE-SEE

Imaginative Training and the Cosmos

> His whole imaginative training somehow encouraged him to associate superhuman intelligence with monstrosity of form and ruthlessness of will. (Lewis, *Out of the Silent Planet*)

We have all heard the phrase "you are what you eat." But an even more accurate saying would be "you are what you read." We are created by a story-loving, story-writing, story-creating God and we are made in His image. We will therefore inevitably tell stories, hear stories, read stories. Have you been born into this world? Then you are surrounded by stories and storytellers and you are a storyteller yourself. That is non-negotiable. The other non-negotiable is that we *will be shaped* by these stories. The stories we are told when we are young, the books we feast on, the tales we steep in, will shape us. Stories form our loyalties and catechize our imagination. They have a profound impact on how we see the world and how we interact with it. The real question is this: *which* stories will we consume?

This is a frequent theme in Lewis's writings: what kinds of stories are we *living* on? Here is an example from the Chronicles of Narnia. In *The Lion, the Witch, and the Wardrobe*, shortly after entering Narnia together for the first time, the Pevensie children come across a robin that tries to get them to follow him. The children have a brief discussion about whether or not it is safe to trust the robin. Peter is in favor of following the bird, arguing that robins are "good birds in all the stories I've ever read."[1] His sisters accept this as a legitimate argument. It is only Edmund (who has already succumbed to the White Witch's magic) who raises any objections. By Peter's reasoning, robins are good birds in *stories*; therefore, we are safe to trust this particular robin. What is the premise behind Peter's claim? It is that there is a correlation between *stories* and *real life*. In other words, fiction instructs us about the actual world. Stories teach us wisdom. Stories train our instincts and our loyalties.

Another example occurs in *The Voyage of the* Dawn Treader. Eustace has not had proper training and is decidedly unprepared for what he encounters in Narnia. He stumbles upon a dead dragon and ducks into its cave in order to escape the rain. Lewis explains: "Most of us know what we should expect to find in a dragon's lair, but, as I said before, Eustace had read only the wrong books. They had a lot to say about exports and imports and governments and drains, but they were weak on dragons."[2] Eustace had subsisted on the

---

1 C. S. Lewis, *The Lion, the Witch, and the Wardrobe* (New York: HarperCollins, 1950), 61.

2 C. S. Lewis, *The Voyage of the* Dawn Treader (New York: HarperCollins, 1952), 87.

wrong stories. This is a large part of his spiritual problem in the first half of the book. His imaginative training had not prepared him to deal with dragons—and so he becomes one.

We don't often consider imaginative training when we think about what stories we should read or let our children read. But as Lewis argues, our imaginations are *always* being trained by what we read and watch. We are enrolled in imaginative boot-camp whether we like it or not. And so, we must pay attention to what kind of training we put our imaginations through. *Which* boot-camp are we going to choose? In the same way that Eustace had not been prepared to encounter dragons, Ransom's training has left him ill-equipped to deal with the world in which he finds himself in *Out of the Silent Planet.* He flees the strange creatures on Mars because all the stories he read have led him to expect "aliens" to be cruel and ruthless. He has no category for an intelligent, sentient being that is not human and yet simultaneously compassionate and kind.

This is because Ransom grew up reading the wrong stories—the sort of modernistic, materialistic sci-fi stories that also shaped Weston, one of the villains. The first book of the trilogy focuses heavily on re-training Ransom's entire imagination and re-baptizing him into the medieval cosmology. As we saw earlier, Ransom's previous perception of the cosmos—both its architecture and personality—weakens the second he awakes in Weston's space-ship. Everything he *thought* he knew is instantly rewritten. And because our cosmology profoundly affects the way we interact with the world, Ransom's cosmological shift ultimately upends his entire life and every part of his being: his emotions, his imagination, even his identity. The cosmos, as he formerly knew it, has changed. And so has his own place in it.

This is a theme that we will touch on in a number of following chapters. It gets at the Ransom Trilogy's central issue. If we miss this, we miss much of what Lewis intended for us to gain: the shift from a conception of space back to a conception of the *Heavens*—Heavens that are abundantly personal because they were created by and exist to glorify a *personal* God. What do we see and think and feel when we look up at the night sky? Does it inspire awe and wonder and joy, or fear and abhorrence? A sense of belonging, or a sense of meaninglessness?

If we see the cosmos as we ought, then we will see a place teeming with life and light and love, all things moving because of the love of the great Mover. All things are joined together in the Great Dance, praising their Creator and serving Him by doing what they were created to do. Because of the Fall, we have faltered and are out of step. We are out of tune with the Great Song. Through repentance and salvation and sanctification, we will slowly relearn the steps that we have forgotten, and we will remember the tune that echoes in the back of our memories so that we can rejoin the Dance and the Song. This world, the Silent Planet, the one that has been cut off from the rest of the cosmos because of our sin and rebellion, will be silent no longer.

So how does this *story* change the way we look at our everyday lives? Will it change anything at all? Oh, but it will change everything. Our point, our purpose, our place in the cosmos—all of it will affect how we view our lives, our neighbors, our families. Everything. Good and true storytelling is far more than mere entertainment or escapism. Good storytelling tells the truth about the way the world is. And that truth will reshape every part of our lives—starting with our imaginations.

Throughout the Ransom Trilogy, we see the beginning of the end of the silence that entombs our fallen world. That end starts with one man, Ransom, and the rebirth of his imagination through his adventures on Malacandra and beyond. Ransom is thus a picture of the glorification that awaits our entire planet—when it turns back to the truth.

9

GREY-EYED & KEEN

The Martial Influence

> There was something in the air he now breathed, or in the society of the *hrossa*, which had begun to work a change in him. [...] Something long sleeping in the blood awoke in Ransom. (Lewis, *Out of the Silent Planet*)

As I have alluded to before, Lewis's love for the planetary characters and their imaginative and emotional influence is not limited to the atmosphere of the trilogy alone. Throughout *Out of the Silent Planet*, Ransom's *character* itself is molded by the Martial influence. He spends this entire first book not only on Mars but in *becoming* Martial. He comes under the power of Malacandra himself—the god of war, of "sturdy hardiness," of masculinity and hammered iron.[1]

1 *Discarded Image*, 106.

As we move through the book, we will be paying close attention to Ransom's personal transformation. And one of the most important truths to keep in mind is that *none of what we read occurs in a vacuum*. Remember that Lewis attacks materialism every chance he gets (and materialism's sister, reductionism). In other words, place matters. Personality matters. Creation matters. And in this case, the location in particular *matters*.

Lewis doesn't randomly pick Mars as the location, as if any alien planet would do. No, he chooses Mars for a reason, and an enormous part of that reason is to mold Ransom into a Martial character. Ransom is on *Malacandra*. Place matters.

The Martial quality as defined by medieval cosmology is much broader than our modern understanding of what it means to be *martial* (with a lowercase *m*). Today, *martial* is used simply to mean anything pertaining to war or a warrior, descriptive of military life, etc. But for the medievals (and for Lewis), to be Martial (with a capital *M*) is much, much more. What is someone under the influence of Mars *like*? Keep in mind that the planets are first and foremost personalities. Therefore, their influence is going to be uniquely personal. The words *personality* and *personal* both come from the same root, the Latin *persona*, meaning "mask or character." The meaning of this word has shifted over time. We still use the word *persona* to refer to a put-on act or character taken on by a performer. But the word *person*, however, is considered synonymous with *human*. And *personality* is that combination of characteristics that work together to make a unique individual. Personalities are inherently personal. They have to do with the distinctions and variations that make every human being the way that they are. And we have these personalities because we are created in the image of a personal God, an infinitely personal God.

If there is one thing that Lewis emphasizes again and again it is this fact: the planets have *dynamic personalities*, personalities that, as discussed earlier, we need to know as we would know people rather than facts.

> The truth which emerges from this is that the planetary characters need to be seized in an intuition rather than built up out of concepts; we need to know them, not know about them, *connaître* not *savoir*. Sometimes the old intuitions survive; when they do not, we falter. Changes of outlook, which have left almost intact, and almost one, the character of Venus, have almost annihilated Jupiter.[2]

The unique personal qualities that the planets possess are potent and powerful. This is why they are able to exert such an influence on the Earth. To circle back to Mars, this means that the way we use the word *martial* to simply refer to anything that has to do with warfare or battle is not the way that a medieval man would have used the word and it is not the way that Lewis uses it in his writings. The word would have been impossible for the medieval to separate from the weight of the myth, legend, and *atmosphere* connected to that word. And Lewis doesn't separate it either.

Perhaps the best description of this Martial spirit is found in Lewis's alliterative poem "The Planets."

> MARS mercenary, makes there his camp
> And flies his flag; flaunts laughingly
> The graceless beauty, grey-eyed and keen,
> Blond insolence—of his blithe visage
> Which is hard and happy. He hews the act,

2 *Discarded Image*, 109.

The indifferent deed with dint of his mallet
And his chisel of choice; achievement comes not
Unhelped by him—hired gladiator
Of evil and good. All's one to Mars,
The wrong righted, rescued meekness,
Or trouble in trenches, with trees splintered
And birds banished, banks fill'd with gold
And the liar made lord. Like handiwork
He offers to all—earns his wages
And whistles the while. White-feathered dread
Mars has mastered. His metal's iron
That was hammered through hands into holy cross,
Cruel carpentry. He is cold and strong,
Necessity's song...[3]

On Earth, Mars is known as *Infortuna Minor* (literally the "lesser unfortunate," second to Saturn's *Infortuna Major*) because here in the sublunar realm, where sin holds sway, Mars's influence is easily corrupted. Mars leads readily to "Martial cruelty, trouble, haughtiness, gracelessness, mercenaries, insolence, coldness."[4] Martial men can be heartless, cruel, and tyrannical.[5] But *above* the orbit of the Moon, in the sphere of Mars himself, there is nothing bad or corrupt *per se*. The Martial virtues—strength, justice, keenness, courage, helping the weak, laughter in the face of danger—can be found on Earth as well but, due to the Fall, are never encountered in their purest form as they appear on Mars himself.

These are the characteristics that we encounter on Malacandra. In fact, Ransom comes under the effects of Mars's personality before he even leaves Earth, for his ad-

3 "The Planets", 13.

4 *Planet Narnia*, 78.

5 We see an example of this in King Miraz's character in *Prince Caspian.*

ventures are set in motion due to his own *Martial* determination to keep his word to Henry's mother. He is faced with both the obstacle of the hedge and his own unwillingness to put himself out any further on her behalf, yet his promise compels him to proceed. In breaking through the hedge, he is unknowingly setting the whole adventure in motion, for there he runs into Weston and Devine.

Yet despite his perseverance to save Henry, Ransom is hardly the Martial paragon throughout the beginning of the book:

> The bellicose[6] mood was a very rare one with Ransom. Like many men of his own age, he rather overestimated his own courage; the gap between boyhood's dreams and his actual experience of the War had been startling, and his subsequent views of his own unheroic qualities had perhaps swung too far in the opposite direction.[7]

Ransom is a philologist out on a walking holiday, and not too strenuous a walking holiday at that. He is not physically intimidating or dominant. He does not easily resort to physical violence or force. He likes his peace and quiet. Even his experience in the First World War has only served to prove to him that he is not so heroic as he imagined he would or could be! But now he has entered the sphere of Mars and we already see its influence at work. Ransom is deeply afraid at the prospect of meeting "monsters," the extraterrestrial beings that he assumes are horrific because

6 The use of this word *bellicose* is no accident. Bellicose comes from the Latin *bellum* meaning "war." As an English speaker, you don't have to know Latin to feel (even unconsciously) the weight of this root word; it resonates with centuries of significance and reinforces Mars's martial influence within the scene.

7 *Silent Planet*, 38.

of the stories that have shaped his imagination. Thinking of these monsters, he pragmatically ponders the fact that his knife will be able to "pierce other flesh as well as his own"[8]—a thought that startles him, for it is a more Martial observation than he is accustomed to making.

One of the most important scenes of transformation occurs in chapter thirteen when Ransom joins the *hrossa* in hunting the *hnakra*. Here, we see the influence of the Martial air on Ransom's perspective. He is "growing up."

> [This action] was necessary, and the necessary was always possible. Perhaps, too, there was something in the air he now breathed, or in the society of the *hrossa*, which had begun to work a change in him.[9]

> Something long sleeping in the blood awoke in Ransom. It did not seem impossible at this moment that even he might be the *hnakra*-slayer; that the fame of *Hmān hnakrapunt* might be handed down to posterity in this world that knew no other man.[10]

> He was one with them. That difficulty which they, accustomed to more than one rational species, had perhaps never felt, was now overcome. They were all *hnau*. They had stood shoulder to shoulder in the face of an enemy, and the shapes of their heads no longer mattered. And he, even Ransom, had come through it and not been disgraced. He had grown up.[11]

---

8 *Silent Planet*, 38.

9 Ibid., 79.

10 Ibid., 80.

11 Ibid., 81-82.

The Martial spirit of Malacandra has worked changes down into Ransom's bones. He began fearful of everything. But by the end of the book, he is willing to die should the Oyarsa proclaim it necessary. He is not the same man that he was at the beginning. He has come a long way from the wandering Pedestrian following a light over the hill. And as we will see in the second book, Ransom's transformation continues during his next adventure on Perelandra, where he becomes a true Martial prophet.

10

THE LOST POETS

Memory and Pleasure

A pleasure is full grown only when it is remembered. (Lewis, *Out of the Silent Planet*)

If we were to go by the number of words spent discussing a particular topic, one of Lewis's favorites would be that of pleasure and enjoyment. These are themes that he repeatedly comes back to in both his nonfiction and fiction writing. But what *is* pleasure according to Lewis? Is it different or the same as simple enjoyment? If it is different, how? What is its relationship to memory and the recollection of past pleasures that have faded?

Lewis doesn't shy away from addressing these types of questions in the Ransom Trilogy. In fact, this could be one reason why we might find ourselves struggling through the book—we signed up for a sci-fi adventure and got a bit more philosophy than we expected! But these discussions, though they seem tangential and disconnected at first glance, are just one of the many reasons the trilogy is so rich and layered with meaning. And because of the fictional setting, Lewis is able to talk about many subjects in a way that would be impossible in a non-fiction essay.

A prime example of this is Ransom's interactions with the different races of beings who inhabit Malacandra. While on Malacandra, Ransom encounters three different kinds of *hnau* (sentient beings). Of these three races, the *hrossa* are the ones that he comes to know and understand the best. He spends time living among them and learns the language (Old Solar) from them. During the course of his interactions with these beings, Ransom is confronted by several stark differences between the *hrossa* and mankind. Ransom's discussions with the *hrossa* concerning these differences serve to highlight problems within his own worldview which Lewis uses to represent the typical modern view of the world and cosmos. Two men could have the same discussions that Ransom has with Hyoi—discussions about philosophy, poetry, pleasure, war, morality, customs, etc. But having these same conversations between two men would not have the same impact. Hyoi (Ransom's *hross* friend) accepts his own views of reality to be as true and unbending as Ransom has always considered his own views. But the sense of *otherness* that pervades their interactions lends a compassionate aura of understanding. They both seek to understand the other's position because it is so utterly foreign and unfamiliar. We see this type of thing occasionally among our own race in interactions between people of different ethnic backgrounds. We cannot change someone's mind or position on a topic unless we first understand their position and why they hold it. The best apologetic is the one that seeks to first get into the mind of those they are trying to influence. Likewise, Hyoi and Ransom are simultaneously kind and compassionate to one another as they seek to understand the other's perspective, and yet they are firm in their own positions. Both of them are surprised at the thoughts of the other, as they are questioning things that it had never occurred to them to question before.

One such conversation between Ransom and Hyoi begins when Ransom tries to discover if there were ever any wars between the three different *hnau* on Malacandra. This conversation eventually winds to the topic of pleasure, but first, let me take a brief detour to talk about Ransom's difficulty with the language barrier. He has trouble phrasing the question about war because he "knew no word for war."[1] This is particularly surprising due to the fact that they are on *Mars*, and Mars is the god of war. How could there be no word for *war* in the Old Solar language when they are on the planet of the god of war himself?

The answer to this lies in the fact that the virtues bestowed by the influence of the planets are often muddied and distorted in the fallen realm below the Moon. On our silent planet, the Martial spirit is indeed frequently seen in the warlike machinations of men. But in the realm above the Moon, the pure, translunar Martial spirit need not display itself in military prowess. The *hrossa* have not experienced war, but they exhibit many *Martial* characteristics. The hardy courage typified by the Martial spirit is seen in many other ways, none of which involve killing or battle.

In any case, Ransom has to make do with other ways of describing what he means when he inquires after the relations between the different *hnau* or species on Malacandra:

1 *Silent Planet*, 73.

> "If both wanted one thing and neither would give it," said Ransom, "would the other at last come with force? Would they say, give it or we kill you?"
>
> "What sort of thing?"
>
> "Well—food, perhaps."
>
> "If the other *hnau* wanted food, why should we not give it to them? We often do."
>
> "But how if we had not enough for ourselves?"
>
> "But Maleldil will not stop the plants growing."
>
> "Hyoi, if you had more and more young, would Maleldil broaden the *handramit* and make enough plants for them all?"
>
> "The *séroni* know that sort of thing. But why should we have more young?"
>
> Ransom found this difficult.[2]

Here we see the conversation return to the matter at hand: pleasure. As their conversation progresses, Ransom realizes that the *hrossa* have a vastly different view of taking pleasure in good things than many humans. Hyoi is working under entirely different assumptions about the very nature of pleasure itself.

Sin distorts everything, including our view of pleasure. Fallen man is in bondage to pleasure. When we experience something we enjoy, we want to do it again and again. We do not realize that there are greater joys and deeper pleasures to be had by not seeking out the *same* pleasure *ad nauseam*. Repetition does not necessarily bring progress or growth.

For example, Ransom mentions sexual pleasure, and tells Hyoi that some people want this pleasure multiple times and so end up with more children than they can actually support. This idea is foreign to Hyoi because the *hrossa* do

2 *Silent Planet*, 73.

not approach sexual pleasure in this way at all. They see the entire process—from courting to sex to begetting to childrearing—as one whole, unique pleasure. And after this pleasure, with all of its diverse parts, has ended, the *remembering* of each part of that process engenders yet another, deeper pleasure that springs out in song and poetry and wisdom. Hyoi goes on to explain:

> A pleasure is full grown only when it is remembered. You are speaking, *Hmān*, as if the pleasure were one thing and the memory another. It is all one thing. The *séroni* could say it better than I say it now. Not better than I could say it in a poem. What you call remembering is the last part of the pleasure, as the *crah* is the last part of a poem. When you and I met, the meeting was over very shortly, it was nothing. Now it is growing something even as we remember it. But still we know very little about it. What it will be when I remember it as I lie down to die, what it makes in me all of my days till then—that is the real meeting. The other is only the beginning of it. You say you have poets in your world. Do they not teach you this?[3]

Ransom, as a member of a race that has become fixated on the pleasures of an instant and the immediate gratification of countless desires, has a difficult time understanding how anyone could be content to experience a pleasure only once and then be happy simply *remembering* it.

Lewis uses this conversation to give us a fresh perspective on a topic that has perhaps grown commonplace to us. He intends for us to rethink our definition of plea-

3 Ibid., 74.

sure and what it means to taste things deeply and fully, not merely as commodities readily available whenever we have an itch. Lewis believes that a true, deep, lasting pleasure is to be found not simply by revisiting things that please us over and over again, but in the *maturation* of the full story of that pleasure's life—from experience to memory. Pleasure is a seed. From expectation to enjoyment, to the growth of beauty and maturity that the pleasure gains from being remembered, pleasures *grow*. The joy is not found just in the act of plucking and eating the fruit, but in the planting, the watering, the harvesting, the feasting, and finally in the remembering of the whole experience.

Many of us have experienced this, perhaps without realizing it or analyzing it in these terms. Think of a moment in your life when you were perfectly happy. In remembering, you are not necessarily trying to recreate that moment. If you did try to recreate it, you would most certainly be disappointed. But what happens when you *remember* it? Every time you travel back in your mind to that time and place, your pleasure grows. It is a different type of pleasure than the one you experienced in the moment. It is fuller, more robust, more mature. It shapes you and becomes something *more* in you. What in the moment is enjoyable, over time becomes a treasure of far greater value.

The title of my chapter here is "The Lost Poets" and you may be wondering, what do poets have to do with pleasure and memory? As Hyoi explains to Ransom, it is the *poet's* job to teach this sort of thing to others. In the society of the *hrossa*, poets (and poetry) hold more of an instructive role than they do on Earth. Ransom, from a race that has been cut off from the music of Deep Heaven for millennia, has no category for this particular function of poetry.

To quote Lewis himself, "It's all in Plato, all in Plato: bless me, what do they teach them at these schools!"[4] Plato presents a starting point for a brief philosophical excursion to explore Lewis's thoughts on poetry and the poets. Plato himself is well-versed in many forms of literature, including poetry. However, somewhat surprisingly, he bans poets from his plan for the ideal city and denies that poetry is an art. In Lewis's magnum opus *English Literature in the Sixteenth Century*, he gives two reasons for Plato's condemnation of poetry. First, he is guarding against the common error of "mistaking art for science and treating Homer as an encyclopedia."[5] While poetry does instruct, there was a temptation in the ancient world to treat poetry as true *per se*. If Homer said that the entrance to the underworld was on the corner of 3rd and Jackson Street, the Greeks would pull out their shovels and start excavating.

The second reason is metaphysical. Remember that in Plato's philosophy, nature, the physical world that we interact with on a daily basis, is itself merely a copy of the "real and supersensuous world."[6] Poetry, as an art that merely imitates nature, leads us away from Plato's ideal world of the Forms.[7] All art is a "copy of a copy.[8] Regardless of Plato's views on the matter, poetry has always had close ties to philosophy and so even he could not ignore it.

4 C. S. Lewis, *The Last Battle* (New York: HarperCollins, 1956), 195.

5 *English Literature in the Sixteenth Century*, 319.

6 Ibid.

7 Plato's philosophy proposed that there was an ideal, spiritual realm where there existed the perfect "form" of every object and that earthly things are only themselves in so far as they partake of that ideal form. Every tree partakes (in some measure) of the form of "treeness" and so on.

8 *English Literature*, 319.

In Lewis's discussion of the "Golden" poetry of sixteenth century England which began with Sidney and Spenser and led to such genius as Shakespeare and Marlowe, he contends that Sir Philip Sidney's defense of poetry is rooted in a certain view of mankind's place in the natural universe. Man's superiority over the created order is *why* poetry is both possible and necessary:

> Nothing shows both [Man's] superiority and its loss (*de facto*) by the Fall so clearly as poetry. For in it we produce what surpasses Nature; our 'erected wit' still enabling us to conceive perfection though our 'infected wil' hinders us from achieving it in action.[9]

Poetry is a sign of man's dominion on Earth and over creation. Truly great poetry is not merely written: "it is created, presented, so as to compel our imaginations."[10] Poets imitate their Creator by using the written word to instruct and train both our imaginations and emotions, and verse is peculiarly suited to this task.

"Let me make the songs of a nation and I care not who makes its laws."[11] There was a time when poets were prophets, teachers, the best that a country had to offer. Look at the state of a nation's poets and the state of the nation is not far behind. The poets are the first fruits of a people. Today, our best poets are found in the recording studios and sound booths. Music, rather than poetry, is king. Singers and songwriters are the new prophets of our time and they accurately reflect the culture that they are speaking to. Poetry, and its

9 *English Literature in the Sixteenth Century*, 344.

10 Ibid., 329.

11 Often attributed to Andrew Fletcher, the official origin is unknown and the quote appears in many variations.

sister music, have a power and a potency all their own. Good poetry and good music combine truth, goodness, and beauty in a way that pierces deep and true, sometimes past our defenses. Like a well-honed blade slipping cleanly between chinks in a suit of armor, poetry is a powerful tool which has largely become rusty outside the realm of popular music.

We have lost poetic giants, men who saw farther and deeper than others and were able to put it in "golden" verse. That ability to speak truth and goodness and beauty to a culture obsessed with death and destruction has become a thing of the past. If any power remains, it can be found on the radio or our favorite music streaming app or perhaps in our Twitter feed. *That* is where we will find the reigning philosophies of our day. And though the great poets of the past may be lost, they are not entirely forgotten. Poetry itself *cannot* be forgotten. Because poetry has been knit into our bones from the beginning:

> In the beginning God created the heaven and the earth. And the earth was without form, and void; and darkness was upon the face of the deep. And the Spirit of God moved upon the face of the waters. And God said, Let there be light: and there was light (Genesis 1:1-3, KJV).

> And Adam said, This is now bone of my bones, and flesh of my flesh: she shall be called Woman, because she was taken out of Man (Genesis 2:23).

> In the beginning was the Word, and the Word was with God, and the Word was God.
> The same was in the beginning with God.
> All things were made by him; and without him was not any thing made that was made.
> In him was life; and the life was the light of men.

> And the light shineth in darkness; and the darkness comprehended it not (John 1:1-5, KJV).

God *spoke* the world into existence in the very beginning using poetry in its purest, most powerful form—a poetry that created everything from nothing. And then, God created Eve, woman, a helpmeet to Adam. And like his Creator, our first father's first recorded words are *poetry*: "Bone of my bone, flesh of my flesh." Jump forward millennia, over thousands of years of men and women speaking poetry, echoing creation, and pointing forward to something even greater: a new Adam, a new creation. That Word, that *true* Poetry, who was there in the beginning, became flesh and dwelt among us (John 1:14).

Maybe the poets are lost. But, to quote one of the greatest of their number:

> Whatsoever from one place doth fall,
> Is with the tide unto another brought:
> For there is nothing lost, that may be found if sought.[12]

Our planet is silent, our ears dull and accustomed to the lack of sound. But it is to this planet that God sent His Son, the incarnate Word. And in a world like this, there *must* be poets.

12 Edmund Spenser, *The Fairie Queene*, bk. 5, canto 2.

11

STRANGE COUNSEL

Maleldil and the Great War

[...] and we know no more of that planet: it is silent. We think that Maleldil would not give it up utterly to the Bent One, and there are stories among us that He has taken strange counsel and dared terrible things, wrestling with the Bent One in Thulcandra. But of this we know less than you; it is a thing we desire to look into. (Lewis, *Out of the Silent Planet*)

When Ransom meets the Oyarsa of Malacandra, the Oyarsa tells him the story of the Fields of Arbol before the fall of Satan. He tells him of the Great War, the fight between the angels and the demons when Satan was cast out of Deep Heaven. This history is a perfect example of how Lewis deftly uses his fictional works to make old tales new. We all know this story from the Bible, but when the Oyarsa tells it, using different terminology and coming from an alternate perspective, we feel almost as if we had never heard it before.

And then Oyarsa utters that phrase that is more than a little familiar: "It is a thing we desire to look into." Where else have we heard this?

> To them it was revealed that, not to themselves, but to us they were ministering the things which now have been reported to you through those who have preached the gospel to you by the Holy Spirit sent from heaven—*things which angels desire to look into.* (1 Peter 1:12, emphasis mine)

About a page later, the Oyarsa uses the same phrase again: "For that, as I have said, is a thing we desire to look into."[1] While there are innumerable biblical allusions in the Ransom Trilogy, Lewis does not often use such a *direct* quotation from the biblical text. By doing so here, Lewis is writing in big block letters: "THIS IS IMPORTANT." In case anyone missed what the Oyarsa is talking about, in case we didn't realize *exactly* who Maleldil is (God) and who the Bent One is (Satan) and what all this new terminology is pointing towards, Lewis tells us through the Oyarsa. This is the Gospel story. The "strange counsel" and the "terrible things" that Maleldil has done, the things that all the angels desire to look into, is the Gospel of Jesus Christ: the Incarnation, birth, death, and resurrection of the Son of God.

That God became man, that He took on our feeble human flesh and died on the cross for sins, is a thing too great and glorious and terrible for us to truly understand. And yet, as men, *we* somehow understand it more than the

1 *Silent Planet*, 121.

angels, as only people who have been redeemed by this astounding act can understand it. It has been revealed to *us*. The Gospel has come to us, fallen and sinful men that we are. And the *angels* desire to look into it. How often do we take the Incarnation for granted?

The Incarnation did not affect mankind alone. It changed the shape of *reality*, the entire cosmos. God entered into His own creation. The Infinite Son of the Father now has ten fingers and ten toes. Eternal Truth once dwelt on Earth in our temporal reality in a particular place. Such an earth-shattering event cannot occur without completely overturning the old order and causing a new creation to spring up in its place. The ripples of the Incarnation on the structure of the entire medieval cosmos and man's place in it will be a subject that pops up frequently in both the trilogy and the rest of this book.

While salvation is, and must be, an incredibly personal, individual thing, it does not and cannot remain so. The salvation of mankind is the salvation of *all creation*. Earth awaits the revealing of the sons of man (Romans 8:14) and the day the barrier will be broken. She longs for it—for the silence to end and the glory to awaken. When God took on human flesh and dwelt among us, there was a fundamental shift. Remember that in the Medieval Model of the cosmos, the central position of Earth indicates its relative *unimportance*. The center was the lowest, the humblest, the drain where the dregs of the cosmos swirled down and down into nothingness until at the very center of all, as Dante shows us, they find their final place in Hell. Earth is the sump pump of the universe, not its crown.

> Nor was it generally felt that earth, or Man, would lose dignity by being shifted from the cosmic centre.

> The central position had not implied pre-eminence. On the contrary, it had implied, as Montaigne says [...] "the worst and deadest part of the universe", "the lowest story of the house", the point at which all the light, heat, and movement descending from the nobler spheres finally died out into darkness, coldness, and passivity. The position which was locally central was dynamically marginal: the rim of being, farthest away from the hub.[2]

So what does this mean for the doctrine of the Incarnation? On the one hand, it makes the Incarnation all the more remarkable to the medieval man. God not only took on our human flesh, but He did so while entering into the lowest part of the cosmos, the farthest removed (short of Hell) from the Heaven of Heavens. At the same time, as we will discuss later, the Incarnation introduces a strange tension between mankind's *unimportance* in the cosmos and the *importance* granted to mankind in the Incarnation. But like I said, more on this later.

We have seen that the Gospel has cosmic ramifications. Here, in this conversation with the Oyarsa of Malacandra, Ransom gets a unique glimpse of the Incarnation from the *outside*. He sees how wonderful it appears to these other sentient, rational beings. It is as if Lewis peels back a layer of reality and gives us a glimpse into "heavens too big to see."[3] Like Elijah's servant in the Old Testament, we are given a look at the flaming army, the host of heaven who look down upon the Earth and, rather than pity, they marvel. The Incarnation is a crucial event (in more than one way) in the history of not just our world, but all worlds. Lewis is by no means

2 *English Literature in the Sixteenth Century*, 3.

3 C. S. Lewis, "On Being Human" in *Poems*, 35.

subtle here, yet he is still frequently misunderstood. When *Out of the Silent Planet* was first published, many readers had no clue who Maleldil really was. As in the parables of Christ, the truth is clear for those who have ears to hear and eyes to see. To those steeped in Scripture, like Lewis himself, these biblical allusions and quotations leap off of the page, flashing like Mercury, binding together "thing with thought."[4]

4 "The Planets", 12.

12

DEVILS IN DISGUISE

Hell on Malacandra

"For the first question, Oyarsa, I have come here because I was brought. Of the others, one cares for nothing but the sun's blood, because in our world he can exchange it for many pleasures and powers. But the other means evil to you. I think he would destroy all your people to make room for our people; and then he would do the same with other worlds again. He wants our race to last for always, I think, and he hopes they will leap from world to world...always going to a new sun when an old one dies...or something like that." (Lewis, *Out of the Silent Planet*)

We return once again to *The Divine Comedy*. As we saw early on, Dante's influence on Lewis's life and writings is almost as impossible to overstate as the influence of the planets themselves. Dante's works shine like the rays of the sun through Lewis's writings, fostering "soul in secret."[1]

In the three canticles of *The Divine Comedy*, Dante the Pilgrim travels through the realms of Hell, Purgatory, and Paradise, one realm per canticle. We might easily jump to the conclusion that Lewis has Ransom do the same throughout the three books of the trilogy, but looking closer, we see Lewis did nothing so simple as that.

The trajectory of the Ransom Trilogy both parallels and *contrasts* with Dante's *Comedy*. While each book brings Ransom closer to Earth according to the medieval order of the planets—first Mars, then Venus, then Earth itself—he brings Deep Heaven with him until Paradise itself arrives on the Silent Planet. But at the same time, each book *feels* increasingly hellish as the conflict between good and evil intensifies. Ransom's movement throughout the trilogy is both opposite of Dante's and yet the same, for he is moving towards Heaven and Hell *at the same time*. Heaven and Hell each grow thicker as Ransom comes closer to Earth, until the two realms finally meet face to face.

Keeping this trajectory in mind, there are certainly parallels between *Out of the Silent Planet* and *Inferno*. We've already explored the opening scene in another chapter—how Ransom is first introduced to us as "the Pedestrian" (echoing Dante's Pilgrim), first appearing in a Dantean dark wood, "midway along the journey of life."[2] But parallels in the literary structure continue. Dante falls unconscious before being taken across the river Lethe and wakes up on the opposite side, having been transported into an other-

1 "The Planets", 12.

2 *Inferno*, 1.1.

worldly realm while asleep. Ransom likewise is drugged and comes back to consciousness only after he has been taken aboard the space-ship, and so wakes up having been brought into another realm himself.[3]

A stronger similarity is found in Ransom's and Dante's spiritual journey. Both men spend the first part of their journey learning to re-see the universe, particularly in terms of the sinfulness of mankind. Ransom's experiences on Malacandra put him into contact with other races of intelligent beings which presents a rare opportunity to see mankind under a sort of microscope. He is forced to learn a new language, one that limits his ability to communicate, which means he must find creative ways to explain the human race. Ransom has several moments of shameful clarity. In explaining a fallen race to unfallen creatures, he has to own up to man's perverse and twisted nature.

There are three quotations that serve to highlight the progression of Ransom's thought in terms of his awareness of the greatness of Man's depravity. Let's look at each one in turn.

> At last it dawned on [Ransom] that it was not [the *hrossa*], but his own species, that were the puzzle. That the *hrossa* should have [monogamous] instincts was mildly surprising; but how came it that the instincts of the *hrossa* so closely resembled the unattained ideals of that far-divided species Man whose instincts were so deplorably different? What was the history of Man?[4]

3 For a deeper exploration of the similarities between *The Divine Comedy* and the Ransom Trilogy, see *Reflecting the Eternal: Dante's* Divine Comedy *in the Novels of C. S. Lewis* by Marsha Daigle-Williamson.

4 *Silent Planet*, 75.

In this first instance, Ransom is still struggling under the weight of his preconceived notions about "extraterrestrial" non-human creatures—that because the *hrossa* are more primitive in their technologies they are thus somehow less intelligent or less moral in their culture than mankind. He is still assessing the *hrossa* as he would a species of animal—in terms of their *biological* makeup, and that *this* is the reason for their monogamous traditions. Ransom is thus behaving in accordance with the assumptions of all the typical science fiction stories in Lewis's day:

> In modern stories of what the Americans call 'scientifictional' type—stories about unknown species who inhabit other planets or the depth of the sea—these creatures are usually pictured as being wholly devoid of our moral standards but as accepting our scientific standards. The implication is, of course, that scientific thought, being objective, will be the same for all creatures that can reason at all, whereas moral thought, being merely a subjective thing like one's taste in food, might be expected to vary from species to species.[5]

Ransom then has a bit of a revelation. In viewing this species as animals, he is operating under the assumption that the *hrossa* just happened to attain (as a biological fluke) a human moral ideal (monogamy) that mankind has consistently striven toward, yet repeatedly fallen short of. This assumption, driven by Ransom's imaginative education up to this point, is not only strange but incredible. He becomes aware that the instincts of the *hrossa* are not biologically driven, as with animals and dumb beasts, but are in fact a

5 C. S. Lewis, "De Futilitate" in *Christian Reflections* (Grand Rapids: Eerdmans, 1995), 61.

result of the lack of sin and a fallen nature on Malacandra. Thus Ransom moves away from the reductionistic, materialistic mindset that pervades the scientific community, the mindset that led him, no matter how subconsciously, to assume that any creature not as scientifically advanced as man must somehow be *less* than man. He comes to a way of looking at the world that is oriented towards and deeply aware of spiritual realities. This includes a realization of the extent of mankind's sin.

> They were astonished at what he had to tell them of human history—of war, slavery and prostitution.[6]

In this second scene, Ransom is speaking with the *seroni* and telling them about the Earth. He resolves from the first to be candid about the darkness of humanity. He will not shy away from the sordidness and the sinfulness. But the reason that he gives in his own mind for this honesty is interesting: because anything less would not be *hnau.* Up to this point, the word *hnau* has meant an intelligent being with a soul, but now Ransom suddenly attaches a moral element to it. Lying or deception, or even avoiding telling the entire truth, would not be *hnau.* In other words, it would not be appropriate for a *creature with a soul* to lie or tell half-truths. Ransom has come to a knowledge of what it actually means to be *hnau.* It is not mere intelligence, sentience, or ability to speak. To be truly *hnau* is to be a moral agent who acts in accordance with the way the worlds were created. Mankind are bent *hnau.* And although we are still *hnau*, we are no longer what we were created to be. We have been created in the image of God, but that image has been disfigured.

---

6 *Silent Planet*, 102.

> "[Weston] does not know there is any Maleldil. But what is certain, Oyarsa, is that he means evil to your world. Our kind must not be allowed to come here again. If you can prevent it only by killing all three of us, I am content."[7]

In the third and final scene of Ransom's transformation, he meets with the Oyarsa of Malacandra. Here Ransom expresses his complete understanding of the wickedness of mankind and its ability to corrupt the as-yet-unfallen Malacandrians and potentially other planets as well.[8] He is willing to submit himself to execution in order to preserve the planet he has come to love. This is hardly an emotionless decision, but neither is Ransom being melodramatic. He understands his own bent nature, and the Oyarsa agrees. Even though Ransom has not committed the treacheries that Devine and Weston have purposed, he is still bent, and for this alone he deserves death. Oyarsa denies Ransom's offer, saying that when Ransom has "grown a little braver" he will be "ready to go to Maleldil."[9] If the men were under *his* jurisdiction, Oyarsa would execute them for their bent deeds and for violating the laws of the cosmos. And Ransom accepts and understands this judgement.

Significantly, the word *Hell* itself occurs only once in the entire book, and it is in this scene. Weston and Devine are captured and brought before the Oyarsa, and so all three men—Ransom, Weston, Devine—are present. Weston tries and fails, amid much shouting and butchering of the language, to communicate with the Oyarsa. But he is so bent that he sees only through his preconceived notions of a

---

7 *Silent Planet*, 122.

8 Foreshadowing of the next book, *Perelandra*.

9 *Silent Planet*, 122.

"savage" people, of unlearned and uncultivated ignorance. While the *sorns*, the *hrossa*, the *pfifltriggi*, and even the *eldila* are laughing at Weston's outrageous behavior, their noise sounds like a terrible roaring that frightens him. He finally realizes his approach isn't working, and Devine, in an outburst of frustration and anger, exclaims, "Oh, Hell!"[10]

First, notice the rather obvious play on words with Devine's name. When you say it out loud, it sounds like the word *divine*. The irony of this is made clear as we see the sort of man that Devine really is. And then the spelling of the word tips us off that he is more *devil* than angel.

Second, notice the capitalization of "Hell." Capitalization in exclamations is usually reserved for proper names. "Hell" thus appears as a proper place, even as an expletive.

Third, and most important, look at the *context* of this exclamation. Weston is so bent and stuck in his own mind, so glued to his dead philosophies, that he is willing to die for them. Devine, on the other hand, knows nothing but his own greed. He will say anything he needs to just to save his own hide. Where Weston will die for a philosophy he loves and a humanity that he hates, Devine's only love is *himself*, and thus he cannot die for it. To die would be antithetical to the self-preservation which is the driving force behind his self-love. Hell is the ultimate giving over of a being to the *self*. Hell is constant gnawing and self-devouring. Hell is where Devine has really been all along. Lewis says it best in this scene from *The Great Divorce*:

> "That is what mortals misunderstand. They say of some temporal suffering, 'No future bliss can make up for it,' not knowing that Heaven, once attained,

---

10 Ibid., 128.

> will work backwards and turn even that agony into a glory. And of some sinful pleasure they say 'Let me have this and I'll take the consequences': little dreaming how damnation will spread back and back into their past and contaminate the pleasure of the sin. [...] And that is why, at the end of all things, when the sun rises here and the twilight turns to blackness down there, the Blessed will say, 'We have never lived anywhere except in Heaven,' and the Lost, 'We were always in Hell.' And both will speak truly."[11]

Thus, the scene that Lewis paints is a sort of Hell out of which Devine and Weston are both incapable of rescue, especially Devine. The Oyarsa specifically says of Devine: "[...] this Thin One who sits on the ground [the Bent One] has broken, for he has left him nothing but greed. He is now only a talking animal and in my world he could do no more evil than an animal. If he were mine I would unmake his body for the *hnau* in it is already dead."[12] Devine has become so broken that he is past any repair the Oyarsa can offer. He is trapped in fear and deluded by greed. He has created a Hell for himself out of which there is no escape. Furthermore, he does not *want* to escape. If he did, he would be able to do so.

Lewis makes a fascinating point about human history in *That Hideous Strength*, speaking through Dr. Dimble:

> "Have you ever noticed," said Dimble, "that the universe, and every bit of the universe is always hardening and narrowing and coming to a point? [...] Good is always getting better and bad is always

11 C. S. Lewis, *The Great Divorce* (New York: Macmillan, 1946), 67.

12 *Silent Planet*, 138.

> getting worse: the possibilities of even apparent neutrality are always diminishing."[13]

This observation can be aptly applied to the Ransom Trilogy as a whole. Throughout the three books, good and evil grow starker. The ability to ride the middle disappears. In *Out of the Silent Planet*, what first appears to be a private conflict between Ransom and his two kidnappers is revealed to be a war of cosmic proportions, a war that dominates the next two books. We see a hint of this war in the Oyarsa's farewell to Ransom, where he issues a warning and a command:

> "[...] you must watch this Weston and this Devine in Thulcandra if ever you arrive there. They may yet do much evil in, and beyond, your world. From what you have told me, I begin to see that there are *eldila* who go down into your air, into the very stronghold of the Bent One; your world is not so fast shut as was thought in these parts of heaven. Watch those two bent ones. Be courageous. Fight them. And when you have need, some of our people will help."[14]

This conflict is not private. It cannot remain between individuals, for there has been a breach in the barrier between Deep Heaven and the sublunar realm—the Silent Planet, the "very stronghold of the Bent One." The perennial divide has been broken. This breach changes everything. The conflict introduced on Malacandra will thicken as it moves to Perelandra, and from there to Thulcandra, where the Silent Planet itself will ring with the sounds of a cosmic battle. The wall between the worlds has been broken down and nothing can be the same as it was before.

---

13 C. S. Lewis, *That Hideous Strength* (New York: Scribner, 1945), 181.

14 *Silent Planet*, 142.

13

THE OCEAN OF ETERNAL NOON

Ransom's Imaginative Transformation and the Final Chapter

> He knew [...] that unrecorded death in the depth of space would almost certainly be the end of their adventure. But already it had become impossible to think of it as "space." Some moments of cold fear he had; but each time they were shorter and more quickly swallowed up in a sense of awe which made his personal fate seem wholly insignificant. (Lewis, *Out of the Silent Planet*)

In the penultimate chapter of Ransom's adventure, we see his transformation come full circle. His fear during his journey at the beginning of the book was extreme. He experienced terror and horror until the rays of the Sun exerted their influence to calm him. On the return journey to Earth, his fear is significantly less. Even before the Sun's rays have begun their work, he has only "moments of cold fear."[1] He is not terrified, even though he is fairly certain that they shall never make it back to Earth.

And as he falls more under the Sun's "sweet influence,"[2] he comes to understand what dying in "space" would actually mean. He has not simply outgrown much of his fear of death, he has outgrown fear of this *kind* of death in particular. His conception of space as a dead, cold expanse of nothingness has now itself been cast into empty darkness. Ransom finds it *impossible* to think of it as "space." If he were to die in this place, it would not be because it is dead and empty, but it would be from the "excess of its vitality."[3] In other words, Ransom is not *alive enough* to survive a place so teeming with life.

This is an example of what some scholars call Lewis's "Christian Platonism," though I would argue it is more *anti*-Platonism than anything else. Plato believed in the realm of the Forms—an unearthly, immaterial realm containing the perfect form of everything. It is a rational, spiritual, nonmaterial realm. Everything that we see down here in the earthly realm is merely a distorted version, a poor imitation of the perfect form that exists in the sky. Platonism views the material world as imperfect *because* it is material. Thus, to become perfect, to become like the flawless realm of the Forms, we must shed our material bodies. Death is all about becoming more spiritual and less physical.

In his writings, Lewis repeatedly pushes back against the Platonic view. Plato's rejection of the material realm as inherently corrupt is contradicted by the Christian view of

---

1 *Silent Planet*, 145.

2 Ibid., 33.

3 Ibid., 145.

the cosmos. God created matter and when He did, He called it all "very good." The world's corruption is not a result of possessing a material nature. Rather, the material nature has been corrupted by the Fall and the introduction of sin and death into the world. According to Lewis, the problem with this fallen world is not its materiality. The problem is that it isn't material *enough*. It is not real or solid or physical *enough*. The Fall has weakened and thinned creation. We live in the shadowlands, a world of ghosts who no longer remember what having real bodies was actually like. When God creates the new earth, it will be *more* solid and *more* real than the one we experience now.

To see what Lewis means by this, let's look at an example from another of his books. In *The Great Divorce* we get a vivid image of what that type of world could look like, with grass like shards of glass and raindrops like stones.[4] The people visiting from Hell are gray and ghostly, unable to make any dent or mark on this world of granite and marble. Lewis says that after Christ's resurrection He repeatedly proved to His disciples that He was not a ghost.[5] Christ could walk through walls after His resurrection not because He was ghostly and the wall was real and solid. Christ has just finished demonstrating to His disciples that He is in fact real and not a ghost at all, eating food, showing them His hands and side, having Thomas poke His ribs. *He* is no ghost. But the *wall* is. Christ's resurrected body was so much more real than the wall that He could pass through it. We may live in the shadowlands now, but we look forward to a more physical, more solid world.

---

4 *Great Divorce*, 27.

5 C. S. Lewis, "What Are We to Make of Jesus Christ?" in *God in the Dock* (Grand Rapids: Eerdmans, 1998), 159.

This is what I mean when I say Ransom realizes he would die not from the *emptiness* of space, but from its *excess of vitality*. The unfallen, translunar realm would simply crush him. It is more real than he is. He is traveling through the "ocean of eternal noon."[6] He is in a place more alive and more real than any he has experienced. To think of the Heavens as the great outer darkness (as our modern minds often do) is to replace Heaven with Hell. Thinking this way restructures the imaginative layout of the cosmos and changes the way we look up at the sky at night. It rejects the view of thousands of years of prophets and poets in favor of listening to science, without entertaining the idea that perhaps there are realities that are deeper than the material and that we are not yet real enough to see them.

To die *here*, in this Heaven, Ransom thinks, would be no great terror, no casting out into a silent void. The bliss he felt traveling through this radiance the first time is magnified tenfold on his return, for he now knows the truth. He is "convinced that the abyss was full of life in the most literal sense, full of living creatures."[7] Ransom's *imaginative* transformation is complete. Throughout the rest of the series, though we see him growing spiritually in a number of other ways, we never see him struggle again with his conception of the cosmos.

The overhaul of Ransom's imaginative assumptions may be complete, but what about the readers'? Near the end of the final chapter, we encounter what could be called Lewis's manifesto: "If we could even effect in one per cent of our readers a change-over from the conception of Space to the conception of Heaven, we should have made a beginning."[8] And yet, when I flip my copy of the book over, right

6 *Silent Planet*, 145.

7 Ibid.

8 Ibid., 152.

there emblazoned on the front cover are the words "FIRST IN THE CELEBRATED SPACE TRILOGY." Now, I can't necessarily fault them for referring to this series using its popular name, "the Space Trilogy." But my point is that Lewis was *clearly not heavy-handed*, because people still miss what he was doing, both casual readers and scholars alike. Readers still approach the books as "outer space adventures," not realizing that Lewis's whole project was to re-awaken the medieval idea of the cosmos—a living, breathing, integrated structure, created and organized, crafted and filled with light and music, dynamic and personal and blazing with glory, a cosmos animated by love for God and imitation of the One who set the whole thing in motion.

In the final chapter of *Out of the Silent Planet*, Lewis inserts himself as a character in the book, writing the adventures of Ransom as a sort of biographer. We also learn that the name *Ransom* is a pseudonym. The character of Lewis stumbles across a strange term (*Oyarses*) in the writings of the twelfth-century Platonists and writes a letter to Ransom to ask him about it. Ransom in turn invites Lewis over for a weekend and tells him the whole story we have just read. We then get a prophetic warning of the dangers yet to come, dangers that are "not planetary but cosmic, or at least solar" and "not temporal but eternal."[9] These dangers will make up the main plot structure of the next two books.

The postscript is comprised of extracts from a letter that Ransom writes to Lewis the character. In this postscript, we get a further description of Malacandra and a crescendo in Lewis's use of donegality to communicate the Martial spirit. You could almost view the final chapter as a didactic *exposition* of the medieval cosmology, and the postscript as

9 Ibid.

the living, breathing *application* of his use of that cosmology. Ransom describes the Malacandrian smells and the *hrossa* singing "a warm, dark noise."[10] In Ransom's detailed descriptions of the living, breathing world of Malacandra, we get another glimpse of the Medieval Model as Lewis truly intended to use it. It drives the emotion of his writing, but in such a way as to almost escape detection, lingering in the background like a smell we cannot quite place or a memory on the edge of thought that we can't quite grasp.

An important paragraph to note is the one where Ransom talks about his knowledge of the *hrossa*. Earlier, we spoke of Lewis's anti-Platonism—how he rejects the notion that matter is inherently corrupt and instead sees the physical universe as not real enough. The true earth, the one that we sometimes dream of when we see things so beautiful that they hurt, *that* earth is more solid and more real than this one, not less. At the same time, Lewis is not a materialist. In fact, a driving theme behind the whole trilogy is Lewis's *rejection* of materialism, the idea that all true reality is *just* matter. Remember that materialism sees spiritual realities, including things like morality, religion, and faith, as results of chemical processes. This view can also be referred to as "materialistic reductionism" in the sense that the entire cosmos is "reduced" to the merely material. This worldview is ultimately inconsistent as it leads logically to a rejection of the rational arguments that are used to support it. If our thought processes are "merely chemical reactions," then why should we base our entire view of reality on those chemical reactions? In our previous discussion, we saw that it also leads to a rejection of any moral code or ethic or epistemology, because all of these things are immaterial in nature.

---

10 *Silent Planet*, 154.

Ransom tries to tell Lewis (the character) what living with the *hrossa* was like. Those simple, quiet days are "the main thing that happened," he says.[11] Yet he realizes that simply telling Lewis random facts about what he and the *hrossa* did during those weeks will not add up to what *actually* happened.

> I know them, Lewis; that's what you can't get into a mere story [...] But what can one do with these scraps of information? I merely analyse them out of a whole living memory that can never be put into words, and no one in this world will be able to build up from such scraps quite the right picture.[12]

Ransom can list all of these physical details about the *hrossa*—their internal temperature, their mating customs, and other purely scientific, biological details gained by empirical observation. But all these facts cannot bring Lewis (the character) even close to understanding the *relationship* Ransom had with *hrossa*. He had a spiritual relationship, a friendship. We can describe the physical features of our best friend (blue eyes, brown hair, etc.) so accurately that a stranger could recognize them on the street. But does that mean they *know* the person? Can they claim the same friendship?

Materialistic reductionism would attempt to boil such a relationship down to chemical reactions. Ultimately, however, reductionism cannot *explain* the relationship; it robs the relationship of its soul. In fact, reductionism cannot *explain* anything. Truth cannot always be charted and graphed and dissected and measured using scientific data. In Ransom's relationship with the *hrossa*, we see, at its very center, *personal-*

11 Ibid.

12 Ibid.

ity. Lewis's rejection of materialism means that the cosmology affects more than just the physical layout of the universe. It has spiritual as well as material repercussions. As we discussed earlier, Ransom was on *Mars*. And this means that he formed specific relationships and became a certain sort of person because of his time there. All of these things *matter* because we are not just atoms bumping into one another. Everything *means* something.

To illustrate this even more clearly, Lewis closes the book with an extended introduction to the most important character of the entire trilogy: Jupiter.

> There is a glow like moonrise on the *harandra*. *Ahihra*! cries Hyoi, and other baying voices answer him from the darkness all about us. And now the true king of night is set up, and now he is threading his way through the strange western galaxy and making its lights dim by comparison with his own. I turn my eyes away, for the little disk is far brighter than the Moon in her greatest splendour. The whole *handramit* is bathed in colourless light; I could count the stems of the forest on the far side of the lake; I see that my fingernails are broken and dirty. And now I guess what it is that I have seen—Jupiter rising beyond the Asteroids and forty million miles nearer than he has ever been to earthly eyes [...] Glundandra (Jupiter) is the greatest of these and has some importance in Malacandrian thought which I cannot fathom. He is "the centre," "great Meldilorn," "throne" and "feast." They are, of course, well aware that he is uninhabitable, at least by animals of the planetary type; and they certainly have no pagan idea of giving a local habitation to Maleldil. But somebody or

> something of great importance is connected with Jupiter [...][13]

But somebody or something of great importance is connected with Jupiter. Who or what does Ransom see? Which person or what thing of great importance is connected with Jove, the greatest planet? Ransom sets out to "read every old book on the subject"[14] in order to learn as much as he can about Jove, the one who connects, bridges, and binds together.

Jove has been active throughout *Out of the Silent Planet,* for it is *by Jove* that the book's adventures are set in motion. Now, as we turn to *Perelandra,* we will see Ransom becoming Jovial himself.[15] And it seems, by *Perelandra* at least, he has a very good idea of just what (or who) is connected with Jupiter, the planet whose influence ultimately shapes Ransom into the man he is meant to become.

---

13 *Silent Planet,* 157.

14 Ibid., 158.

15 Michael Ward was the first scholar to explore this idea at length in *Planet Narnia.*

Discussion Questions

Introduction & Out of the Silent Planet

1. How does cosmology affect the imagination and emotions? How are the effects of different cosmologies evident in literature and art?

2. Look at Lewis's use of the word "tingling" or "consider" in *Out of the Silent Planet.*[1] Discuss the significance of Lewis's use of these symbolic words in those passages.

3. How does *Out of the Silent Planet* as a whole express the Martial characteristics? What specific imagery or symbolism helps towards this goal? How does Mars influence Ransom's experiences and character throughout the book?

4. Describe the "imaginative transformation" that Ransom undergoes. How does his transformation point to Lewis's purpose in writing the Ransom Trilogy?

1 See pages 18, 24, 29, 57, 118, and 153 in *Out of the Silent Planet.*

PART II:

Perelandra

SUMMARY

Ransom, having returned to Earth from his adventures on Malacandra at the end of the previous book, is now sent to a different planet: Perelandra (Venus). Because of his time on Malacandra, he has learned Old Solar (the language of Deep Heaven) and so has been given a task to perform on Perelandra. He is not entirely sure at first what this task will be, though he knows it will consist of preventing an attack by the enemy.

Upon arriving on Perelandra, Ransom discovers an unfallen world in which there are only two inhabitants: the Green Lady (Tinidril) and her husband, Tor. When Ransom meets the Green Lady, she has been separated from her husband, and she remains so for much of the book. Shortly after Ransom meets the Green Lady, Weston lands on Perelandra in his space-ship. Weston has been dabbling with dark powers and is possessed by a devil. Throughout the story, he becomes less and less like the Weston we met in the first book, and earns the name "the Un-man."

The middle section of the novel is mostly comprised of conversations between the Green Lady, the Un-man/Weston, and Ransom. It becomes clear to Ransom that his purpose in being sent to Perelandra is to prevent the Green Lady from obeying the Un-man's temptations and falling into disobedience. For many pages, Ransom's fight against the Un-man is purely argumentative, until he realizes that he must fight the Un-man *physically*.

After many blows and a terrible journey across Perelandra's oceans to a subterranean cave, Ransom finally smashes the Un-man's head in with a stone. Ransom himself has sustained a terrible wound to his heel. After his victory, Ransom makes his way up the mountain to a glorious, paradisal place: Tai Harendrimar, the Hill of Life. There he meets the Oyerésu of Malacandra and Perelandra, as well as Tor and Tinidril themselves. Having saved Perelandra from a Fall like that of Earth, Ransom is sent back to Earth to complete the defeat of the enemy, this time on the Silent Planet itself.

14

WORLD FROM BEYOND THE WORLD

The Medieval Principles of the Triad and Plenitude

> It was dark enough but that might be due to the fog and the trees. It wasn't the dark I was afraid of, you understand. We have all known times when inanimate objects seemed to have almost a facial expression, and it was the expression of this bit of road which I did not like. (Lewis, *Perelandra*)

Heading into the second and third books of the trilogy, we encounter two more key medieval concepts: those of the Triad and Plenitude. When introducing these principles, Lewis says that they are "really the same principle."[1] We will see how that is true in this

1 *Discarded Image*, 43.

discussion. Both of these principles play a large part in the trilogy and we have already seen them at work in the first book. However, they take a more central role in the second and third books. Having read *Out of the Silent Planet*, we will not find these ideas so strange. We've already been exposed to them, even if we weren't aware of what Lewis was doing.

The medieval man deeply loved order and organization. That is one of the sources of the beauty and joy he found in the Medieval Model of the cosmos. Everything is arranged, organized, and seamless. As Lewis says: "There was nothing which medieval people liked better, or did better, than sorting out and tidying up. Of all our modern inventions I suspect that they would most have admired the card index."[2] The Medieval Model can perhaps be considered the pinnacle and culmination of this "tidying" mentality. The Model is a catalog of the universe. Everything has a place, and the final product is a vision of the cosmos in which a mind can rest in ordered awe and wonder without the pathless wandering of our modern picture.

In keeping with this "ordering" mentality, a recurring theme in medieval thought is that of the Triad. The Triadic Principle is simply the concept of *threes*. Lewis gives us Plato's definition of the Triadic principle from the *Timaeus*: "It is impossible that two things only should be joined together without a third. There must be some bond in between both to bring them together."[3] In other words, if you have two things joined together, you must have a third thing that does the joining.

The Triadic Principle saw its heyday in medieval scholastic thought. One particular example of this is how the

2 *Discarded Image*, 10.

3 Ibid., 43.

medievals viewed the interactions between God and man. As Lewis says, "[...] god does not meet man. They can encounter one another only indirectly; there must be some wire, some medium, some introducer, some bridge—a third thing of some sort—in between them."[4]

This idea was not new, even in Plato's day, and indeed it has biblical support. Throughout the Old Testament, no one could see God face to face, hence the need for priests and mediators. Even the priests themselves hardly ever entered the Holy of Holies—only the High Priest, once a year, and a rope was tied to his ankle so that he could be pulled out if God struck him dead. When Moses interceded with God on behalf of the Israelites, he had to cover his face with a veil to hide how his visage was transformed by this interaction. Prophets and priests were the bridges between the people and the Lord of Hosts; they were the *third thing*, the bond. In the New Testament, we still have a Mediator, the Son of God Himself, Jesus Christ, who continually makes intercession for us to the Father (Hebrews 7:25). We now have direct access to the Father through the Son, but this idea of the Triad remains.

In medieval thought and literature, we see these third things taking the shape of a variety of creatures—creatures that the medieval men called *Daemons*, also known as the *Longaevi* (literally, those who live long lives). Now, it's important to take note that while we do get our word *demon* from these creatures, *not all Daemons are demons.* In other words, all demons are Daemons, but not all Daemons are demons. Make sense? The word *demon* is now synonymous with *devil*, but this was not always the case. Daemons were simply the

4 Ibid., 44.

in-between beings, neither mortal like men nor immortal like God and the angels.

So we have the Triadic Principle. What about the Principle of Plenitude? Remember that Lewis said these two ideas are basically the same idea. Here is how.

As we have already seen, the medieval cosmos was simply teeming with life, filled with creatures that we cannot see with the naked eye. In fact, the cosmos *must* be inhabited. This is what the Principle of Plenitude posits. The physical structure of the universe, in accordance with the Triadic Principle, is made up of *three* basic components: earth, air, and aether. The physical globe of Earth is made up of (you guessed it) earth. Above the Earth is air which extends to the border of the Moon. Beyond the Moon, in the rest of the spheres, we find the element of aether. Each of these areas is inhabited by pure necessity. "If between aether and Earth, there is a belt of air, then...*ratio* [reason] herself demands that it should be inhabited," Lewis explains; for according to the medievals, "The universe must be fully exploited. Nothing must go to waste."[5] The cosmos teems with beings because no space must go unfilled.

The *Longaevi* are important to understand as we read the Ransom Trilogy. We have already encountered creatures that are in close kinship with them. The *eldila* are very similar to *Longaevi*, though they are not quite the same because *eldila* dwell in the realm of aether and are unfallen and uncorrupted. In contrast, the bent *eldila* (what we might call devils or demons now) do fall into the category of *Longaevi*, since they dwell in the realm of air between earth and aether. Other examples of *Longaevi* include fairies (various kinds), elves, nymphs, and so on. These are the magical folk, neither mortal nor immortal, that flit on the edges of the old stories

5 *Discarded Image*, 44.

like the leaf-shadows between forest and field. It is the very nature of the *Longaevi* to defy facile description.

Lewis was intrigued by this characteristic of being *in between*. He was fascinated by the elusive nature of the beings that dwell in the air between earth and aether, filling that third space in order to satisfy both the Triadic Principle as well as the Principle of Plenitude. Lewis gives a whole chapter in *The Discarded Image* to the discussion of the *Longaevi* and, as he says in the first paragraph of that chapter, this isn't necessarily because they are the most important. In fact, the reason is almost the opposite:

> [...] their unimportance is their importance. They are marginal, fugitive creatures. They are perhaps the only creatures to whom the Model does not assign, as it were, an official status. Therein lies their imaginative value. They soften the classic severity of the huge design. They intrude a welcome hint of wildness and uncertainty into a universe that is in danger of being a little too self-explanatory, too luminous.[6]

Once again, we come back to Lewis's love for the imaginative value of the Medieval Model, only this time, he speaks about an aspect of the Model that is perhaps less orderly and organized than the rest, something that gives it wildness and mystery. The very existence of these disorderly creatures is due to the *orderliness* of the Model. The Triadic Principle led to the belt of air between earth and aether, and the Principle of Plenitude means that this air needs to be inhabited by creatures. But the creatures themselves are surprising, unexpected, and untamed.

6 Ibid., 122.

So, why talk about this now, right at the beginning of *Perelandra*? Because in chapter one we encounter, along with the character of Lewis, the existence of these creatures on our own planet for the first time. On Malacandra, Ransom encountered the three earthly types of *hnau* (*hrossa*, *séroni*, and *pfifltriggi*) and he also met the *eldila* and the Oyarsa of Malacandra. These, as Augray the *sorn* explains, are all creatures though they have different types of bodies. This is a difficult concept for Ransom to grasp, but he does have the thought that even on our world there is a "recurrent human tradition of bright, elusive people sometimes appearing on the Earth"[7] and that these may actually be some of the beings with different bodies that Augray is speaking of. And he is right.

In the first chapter of *Perelandra*, Lewis the character has received a wire from Ransom asking him to come down and see him. Lewis is on his way to meet Ransom, and it is from his perspective that we are given a brief synopsis of the happenings in the first book to orient us. His journey to meet Ransom, which should be a very simple matter of a train journey and a walk down a country lane, turns into something much more sinister. Lewis hardly knows why or how, but doubts are sown into his mind: doubts about Ransom's story, his trustworthiness, and this meeting.

Lewis's doubts soon turn to terror. The road is dark and disturbing. A little empty house has windows boarded, "staring like the eye of a dead fish."[8] Lewis, in the end, has to fight his way to the house—not against any *physical* threat, as we might understand it, but he feels as if he is "walking

7 *Silent Planet*, 95.

8 C. S. Lewis, *Perelandra* (New York: Scribner, 1944), 13.

against a headwind"[9] and in the end he really has no idea how he gets into the house:

> At all events, I *can't* really describe how I reached the front door of the cottage. Somehow or other, despite the loathing and dismay that pulled me back and a sort of invisible wall of resistance that met me in the face, fighting for each step, and almost shrieking as a harmless spray of the hedge touched my face, I managed to get through the gate and up the little path. And there I was, drumming on the door and wringing the handle and shouting to him to let me in as if my life depended on it.[10]

As it turns out, Lewis is nearly thwarted in his attempts to reach Ransom's house by the Tellurian *eldils*, that is, by *devils*. These are creatures of our world that dwell in the air and are under the sway of the Bent One. They know what Ransom is being sent to do, and they want to stop it. They understand, even if Ransom himself doesn't quite yet, what is at stake in Ransom's mission.

And so we, with Ransom, have come to the next battlefront in the cosmic conflict. Perelandra is the stepping stone that will lead to the confrontation in the last book. What happens in the end of *That Hideous Strength* could not happen if Ransom had not been sent on this mission first, and so the evil powers of the air are striving to prevent this from happening.

In the end, the only way Lewis makes it to Ransom's cottage is the only way he ever could, the only way that this whole series of events happened in the first place: by Jove.[11]

---

9 Ibid., 11.

10 Ibid., 14.

11 Ibid., 19.

15

FOREKNOWLEDGE & MISSION

Ransom the Prophet

"It's not Malacandra I'm being sent to. It's Perelandra."

"That's what we call Venus isn't it?"

"Yes."

"And you say you're being sent?"

"Yes." (Lewis, *Perelandra*)

The second book of the Ransom Trilogy begins rather differently than the first. Far from being abducted and coerced into his interplanetary journey, this time Ransom is a willing traveler, looking forward to another adventure among the stars. He remembers Malacandra with fondness and longing. There could be no higher joy or pleasure than to return. But now Ransom has been given a task. He has a new role to play, one that brings him closer to the man he is meant to be, introduces him to more splendid joys than he could ever imagine, and transforms him in order that he may perform an even greater role in the future.

Ransom is told by the Oyarsa of Malacandra that the Bent One is planning an attack on Perelandra, something that we glimpsed at the end of *Out of the Silent Planet.* The danger introduced at the beginning of *Perelandra* is directly connected to the one found in *Out of the Silent Planet.* This much Ransom knows. He also knows that he has been chosen to perform some task which he assumes (correctly) involves somehow preventing this attack.

But why has *he* been chosen for this job? Ransom admits that it is not for any extraordinary virtue that he possesses in himself. The reason is a much more pragmatic one. Quite by accident, it would seem, Weston *chose* his own nemesis. By kidnapping Ransom, Weston and Devine unknowingly sowed the seeds of their own destruction: they brought Ransom to Malacandra where he *learned Old Solar* and where his conception of the cosmos was transformed. Because of this transformation, Ransom is given a special role in the second book.[1] Ransom, because he stumbled across Devine and Weston *by Jove*, was given a unique opportunity to learn this ancient, universal language and is thus equipped to take on the task that is being asked of him now: that of traveling to Perelandra and communicating with the Green Lady, protecting her from the Un-man, and opening her eyes to more of the cosmos.

Ransom's role in *Perelandra* demonstrates his growth from a simple pilgrim into a Martial prophet. Everything he learned on Malacandra—from the language to the Martial influence—has prepared him to take up the prophetic mantle.

Now, what do I mean when I say *prophet*? Ransom's mission, from the beginning, is left purposefully vague. As he tells Lewis the character, "No idea at all what I'm to

1 *Perelandra*, 22.

do. There are jobs, you know, where it is essential that one should *not* know too much beforehand...things one might have to say which one couldn't say effectively if one had prepared them."[2] In having *less* foreknowledge, Ransom's prophetic role is strengthened rather than weakened. Prophets throughout the Old Testament and Apostles in the New were occasionally sent out with prepared words, but most of the time the Word of the Lord was given to them as they declared it. We can hardly begin to understand the closeness and intimacy of the relationship that these men had with the Most High God, but Ransom's experience may give us a glimpse.

Later in the book, at the moment of crisis, when everything seems to be going wrong, Ransom is confronted with the hard truth of what it means to be a prophet: to have a task that, regardless of success or failure, *must* be attempted:

> He was no longer making efforts to resist the conviction of what he must do. He had exhausted all his efforts. The answer was plain beyond all subterfuge. The Voice out of the night spoke it to him in such unanswerable fashion that, though there was no noise, he almost felt it must wake the woman who slept close by. He was faced with the impossible. This he must do: this he could not do.[3]

Words and foreknowledge are given to Ransom at the *right* time—and not always when he wants them. Even in the very first chapter, there is a hint of the knowledge he has been given, though he himself doesn't recognize it. As he tells Lewis the character about his upcoming mission, he says: "I've no particular reason to suppose I shall come back wounded. But just in case—if you can find a doctor whom

2 Ibid., 23.

3 Ibid., 124.

we can let into the secret, it might be just as well to bring him with you when you come down to let me out."[4] Ransom does indeed return injured—in his heel.

Ransom arrives on Perelandra as a man who, in some ways, still has much to learn. There are times in his conversations with the Green Lady that he feels like a small child at the knee of his mother; times when he is humbled by his interactions with an unfallen woman and an unfallen world; times when the sin of his own world and race shames him. That said, he is also approaching Perelandra and the Green Lady as a *man*, a human. And as such, there is another sense in which he takes up the prophetic mantle. Prophets throughout the Old Testament reveal and instruct those with the ears to hear. Ransom, in his role as prophet on Perelandra, reveals things to the Green Lady that she can only wonder at. Just as he told the Oyarsa of Malacandra about the "strange counsels" of Maleldil in the first book, so he holds this knowledge on Perelandra. Ransom, though he frequently feels inferior to the Green Lady in many ways, has knowledge that he possesses *by virtue* of being a fallen man.

Here again we see the power of the Incarnation.

Man's place in the cosmos has shifted. Before Christ came to Earth, mankind occupied the lowest place in the cosmos. But as we have already discussed, the entire order of creation was turned on its head when God became a man. This leads to a great mystery. Ransom as a *sinful* man is unworthy to speak to Tinidril in her sinless purity, and yet Ransom as a *man* is part of the human race into which our Lord Himself was born as a baby. Ransom, in Christ, is therefore Tinidril's equal. Ransom, in Christ, has been chosen for this task. And Ransom fulfills his task *in Christ.*

---

4 *Perelandra*, 25.

Ransom has taken on a crucial role in this second book of the trilogy. But even still, this role is but a stepping stone on the way to something greater. Even after his task on Perelandra is completed, Ransom is far from finished with his journey and with his job. "For whoever has, to him more will be given, and he will have abundance; but whoever does not have, even what he has will be taken away from him" (Matthew 13:12). Or, as Lewis says in *The Horse and His Boy*: "If you do one good deed your reward usually is to be set to do another and harder and better one."[5]

Remember that Jupiter, the greatest of the planets, is the one who bridges and binds things together. He is the one who connects Ransom's tasks in each book. Each task is given in order to shape and mold Ransom into the person he needs to be in the final book when the cosmic conflict comes to a head. As I've mentioned, this second stage of Ransom's journey shows clearly that the conflict that was introduced on Malacandra is growing more concentrated, more heated, and ever closer to Earth. Venus is *spatially* nearer Earth according to the medieval cosmos, but that is not the only closer kinship it shares. Tinidril, the Green Lady, whom Ransom meets there and the Eve of that world, is nearer in both form and nature to mankind than any of the inhabitants of Malacandra. While Ransom recognizes that Perelandra has its own history that is quite separate from ours, he understands the parallels, unable to resist comparison with the story of our own Temptation and Fall. The desperate attempts of the enemy on Perelandra are but a foretaste of what is coming on Earth, and while Ransom successfully completes his prophetic calling, he will soon be called to an even more important part to play on the Silent Planet itself.

---

5 C. S. Lewis, *The Horse and His Boy* (New York: HarperCollins, 1954), 146.

16

THE END OF SILENCE

Principalities and Powers

"For we do not wrestle against flesh and blood, but against principalities, against powers, against the rulers of the darkness of this age, against spiritual hosts of wickedness in the heavenly places" (Ephesians 6:12).

At the beginning of his journey, Ransom is an Everyman. He is not particularly special or important and has no one to miss him when he is kidnapped. He is somewhat cowardly and physically weak. He is not especially impressive. And Ransom himself would be the first person to admit this. As we discussed in the last chapter, Ransom is not given this mission to Perelandra out of any particular merit. He was simply in the right place at the right time and was given the opportunity to learn Old Solar, leaving him peculiarly equipped for this next task. He knows he's an "ordinary" person, to whom extraordinary things, through no design of his own, have happened.

At the beginning of *Perelandra*, when Ransom is explaining his task to Lewis the character, he addresses Lewis's interpretation of Ephesians 6:12:

> "I know!" said [Ransom] with one of his singularly disarming smiles. "You are feeling the absurdity of it. Dr. Elwin Ransom setting out single-handed to combat powers and principalities. You may even be wondering if I've got megalomania."[1]
>
> "I didn't mean that quite," said I.
>
> "Oh, but I think you did. At any rate that is what I have been feeling myself ever since that thing was sprung on me. But when you come to think of it, is it odder than what all of us have to do every day? When the Bible used that very expression about fighting principalities and powers and depraved hypersomatic beings at great heights (our translation is very misleading at that point, by the way) it meant that quite ordinary people were to do the fighting."[2]

Ransom says that the common interpretation of the idea of fighting principalities and powers is to see it as a purely moral conflict. Of course, he does not deny that there is a *difference* between facing moral conflict and physical conflict. However, he does not believe that the passage need be about only one *or* the other. If ordinary men and women are called upon to fight in one way (morally), it is not proud or self-aggrandizing to think that they may be called upon to fight in another way (physically).

---

1 Megalomania: "A mania for great or grandiose performance."

2 *Perelandra*, 21.

Once again, Ransom shows his own foresight, even if he doesn't know *how* he will embody the very opinions that he is stating now. When the time actually comes, as we will see, it is much harder than he has anticipated to follow through with what he here claims he believes. It is one thing to say that you believe a fight might become physical—it is another to strike the first blow.

So *does* Ransom have megalomania? Far from it. He is an ordinary man, true, yet as an ordinary man he is also one of the most extraordinary things in creation. As Lewis says elsewhere:

> There are no ordinary people. You have never talked to a mere mortal. Nations, cultures, arts, civilizations—these are mortal, and their life is to ours as the life of a gnat. But it is immortals whom we joke with, work with, marry, snub and exploit—immortal horrors or everlasting splendors.[3]

It is not megalomania to believe what God promises in His word: that He chooses the weak things of the world to confound the things which are mighty (1 Corinthians 1:27, KJV). God regularly uses ordinary means to accomplish His extraordinary purposes. He uses weak, broken, human vessels to carry out His will.

Furthermore, it is not megalomania for Ransom to believe that he, a *human*, a Son of Adam, would be chosen for a grand task. God made man in His image: the crown of creation. He gave us immortal souls with dignity and honor. And none of this is eradicated by the Fall. In His grace, His image was marred but not erased. As Lewis says in *Prince*

---

3 C. S. Lewis, *The Weight of Glory and Other Addresses* (New York: HarperCollins, 1949), 46.

Caspian: "You come of the Lord Adam and the Lady Eve... And that is both honour enough to erect the head of the poorest beggar, and shame enough to bow the shoulders of the greatest emperor on earth."[4] And then, beyond the hope of even the darkest mutterings of old, He sent His Messiah, God Incarnate, Man Divine. Jesus Christ took on our frail human flesh and nature. And when He died and rose again, we rose with Him. All is made new.

These *ordinary* men and women play vital roles in the battle between good and evil, the conflict that has existed since the Fall. And, as Ransom says, the current spiritual struggles could very well be but one phase in this ongoing war. When you are in one phase, you "get into the habit of thinking and behaving as if it was going to be permanent," Ransom warns Lewis.[5] Up to this point in human history, ordinary men have not had to confront the dark *eldila* (the spiritual forces of darkness) in any way *except* in a psychological or moral form. This is one result of being in the "phase of the great siege," as Ransom describes it.[6] Earth has been sealed off and silent. But, as we've already discussed, that phase is coming to an end. The siege has been broken. What then? In this next phase, Ransom says, "It may be anyone's job to meet [the dark *eldila*]...well, in some different mode."[7] Any normal human being may be called to confront evil in a way far different than we are accustomed to.

Ransom himself hardly knows what this mode will be exactly. But he will soon find out. Throughout the rest of *Perelandra*, in all of his interactions with the Un-Man, Ransom

---

4 C. S. Lewis, *Prince Caspian* (New York: HarperCollins, 1951), 233.

5 *Perelandra*, 22.

6 Ibid.

7 Ibid.

confronts him as a physical being. Ransom has moral and spiritual struggles, but his enemy has taken a physical body and it is this kind of confrontation that Ransom has been called to partake in. He may well be a Martial prophet, as we saw in the last chapter. But, in the end, what qualifies him for this particular fight is his very ordinary humanity. He comes to cast off his habit of thinking of "spiritual warfare" as a purely mental or moral exercise. He is forced to step up and simply throw a punch. Or two. Or more. The conflict is heating up and more is at stake than philosophies and ideologies. As we will see in the third and final book, it is this kind of conflict that reaches its boiling point on Thulcandra itself. The siege has ended and all men will be called to the fight.

17

ALONG THE BEAM

Enjoyment, Contemplation, and Love

"I have never done it before—stepping out of life into the Alongside and looking at oneself living as if one were not alive. Do they all do that in your world, Piebald?" (Lewis, *Perelandra*)

One of the first things to strike Ransom shortly after meeting the Green Lady is her lack of self-awareness. She is not self-conscious in any way. She is genuinely *unconscious* of her *self*. This lack of self-awareness is a major theme throughout the book. While speaking with Ransom, her revelations often revolve around the theme of self-knowledge, and when the Un-man steps in, he frequently tempts the Green Lady using a twisted version of the same theme.

Before we consider this theme, we need to make an important distinction about knowledge in general. It is a distinction called to mind because of the language that the Green Lady uses concerning the idea of looking at oneself. She notably uses the phrase "stepping out of life into the Alongside."[1]

This wording echoes an essay that Lewis wrote titled "Meditation in a Tool-shed." In that essay, Lewis explores the differences between what he calls Enjoyment and Contemplation. He uses the picture of standing in a dark tool shed with a single crack at the top of the door through which there comes a sunbeam. *Contemplation* is what he is doing when he is looking at that beam of light. "From where I stood that beam of light, with the specks of dust floating in it, was the most striking thing in the place. Everything else was almost pitch-black. I was seeing the beam, not seeing things by it."[2] But when he moves so that the beam falls on his eyes, when he looks *along* the beam, he can actually see outside the tool shed: "green leaves moving on the branches of a tree outside and beyond that, ninety-odd million miles away, the sun. Looking along the beam, and looking at the beam are very different experiences."[3]

When you look straight at the beam, you see only the beam; you experience Contemplation as you admire the beam as itself. But when you look along the beam, you can no longer see the beam; rather, you see everything else *by* it. You have stepped into Enjoyment—personal and particular knowledge in which you are full to the brim with *experiencing* rather than merely *thinking* of yourself experiencing.

It is this type of Enjoyment that has made up the entirety of the Green Lady's experience to this point. The thought

1 *Perelandra*, 52.

2 C. S. Lewis, "Meditation in a Toolshed" in *God in the Dock* (Grand Rapids: Eerdmans, 2014), 230.

3 Ibid.

of Contemplation, of stepping outside of the beam of light and actually looking at it from the "Alongside," is utterly new to her. This sort of awareness of the Self that seeks to step outside is strange. Contemplation entails "abstract, external, impersonal, uninvolved knowledge"[4] and this practice is utterly foreign to her.

The idea of looking at oneself may be new, but it is not unpleasant or evil in itself. As part of his prophetic role, Ransom has been introducing the Green Lady to new concepts ever since he arrived, and she is growing older. She was always meant to grow older, to learn new things, to mature. There is a place for both Enjoyment and Contemplation, and we can often learn from one what we cannot learn from the other.

For example, thanks to this new way of looking at herself, Tinidril begins to see the true nature of her obedience and what it means to be a distinct created being:

> "I thought," she said, "that I was carried in the will of Him I love, but now I see that I walk with it... It is a delight with terror in it! One's own self to be walking from one good to another, walking beside Him as Himself may walk, not even holding hands. How has He made me so separate from Himself? How did it enter His mind to conceive such a thing? The world is so much larger than I thought. I thought we went along paths—but it seems there are no paths. The going itself is the path."[5]

Ransom introduces Tinidril to a beneficial kind of self-knowledge. To paraphrase a great theologian, to truly

4 *Planet Narnia*, 17

5 *Perelandra*, 60.

know ourselves we must know God, and to truly know God we must know ourselves.[6] There is a genuine good to be had from learning to step outside of our own experience and actually look at ourselves, to contemplate our own being. In doing this, we learn more about who we are as creatures and thus who God is as our Creator and Redeemer.

That being said, self-contemplation has its pitfalls. We see this explicitly in the way the Un-man tempts the Green Lady. He ultimately tries, like the serpent of old, to get the Green Lady to disobey her Lord and spend the night on the Fixed Land. However, in order to get her to that point of disobedience, he must first work on her perception of love and of obedience itself. And the gate where he launches the great force of his attack is called Vanity.

> [The Un-man] appeared to be telling, with extreme beauty and pathos, a number of stories, and at first Ransom could not perceive any connecting link between them. They were all about women, but women who had apparently lived at different periods of the world's history and in quite different circumstances [...] At last it dawned upon him what all these stories were about. Each one of these women had stood forth alone and braved a terrible risk for her child, her lover, or her people. Each had been misunderstood, reviled, and persecuted: but each also magnificently vindicated by the event. The precise details were often not very easy to follow. Ransom had more than a suspicion that many of these noble pioneers had been what in ordinary terrestrial speech we call witches or perverts. But that was all in the background. What

6 John Calvin, *Institutes of the Christian Religion*, ed. John T. McNeill (Louisville: Westminster John Knox Press, 2006), 35.

> emerged from the stories was rather an image than an idea—the picture of the tall, slender form, unbowed though the world's weight rested upon its shoulders, stepping forth fearless and friendless into the dark to do for others what those others forbade it to do yet needed to have done.[7]

The two-edged sword of the Un-man's temptation plays on the natural love and affection of Tinidril for her King and for Maleldil, and seeks to plant the tiny but destructive seeds of vanity in her heart. He tries to corrupt her good self-awareness (the Contemplation that Ransom awakened in her) into full-fledged vanity. From Ransom's first meeting of the Green Lady, he has been struck by her regal splendor tempered with an almost childlike naiveté. Pride and vanity had no place in her countenance. In the Un-man's attempts to sow vanity, he dresses her and shows her how to see her own reflection in a pool of water. Vanity is one step in the temptation, a slippery slope leading to pride and ruin.[8]

As the quote above shows, the Un-man mixes a dangerous cocktail of *physical* and *moral* vanity. He tells stories of women who allegedly made great sacrifices for those they loved, some even dying for their beloved. He paints these

---

7 *Perelandra*, 107-108.

8 Note the similarities and differences between this scene of Tinidril and that of Milton's Eve in *Paradise Lost.* In telling the story of the creation of Eve, Milton pictures her waking up alone in a forest glade. One of the first things she sees upon waking is her own image in a pool. The parallels to Tinidril's glimpse of her reflection are striking. But where Tinidril is frightened and startled, Eve is entranced. She is mesmerized by her own beauty and if a voice from heaven had not called her away, she may have stayed an eternity, gazing at her own reflection in that paradisal pool. When she sees Adam, she isn't very impressed: after the vision of her own beauty, she finds his masculine form not so pleasing in comparison. But where Milton introduces Eve's vanity into her character from the start, Lewis has vanity implanted in Tinidril by the Un-man.

stories in a tender, tragic light. As Ransom realizes, of course, these women were *not* the misunderstood saints the Un-man is making them out to be, but rather monstrous and wicked. The Un-man is putting forth every effort to stir the Green Lady's emotions, to bring about a desire to put herself on the same stage, to be in the same spotlight, like *these* women.

Not only does he want Tinidril to be aware of her physical beauty, but he wants her to see herself *in the role of savior.* This is where he almost succeeds. Mixed in with the Green Lady's response of genuine love and concern for the beloved, there is "the faintest touch of theatricality, the first hint of a self-admiring inclination to seize a grand rôle in the drama of her world. It was clear that the Un-man's whole effort was to increase this element."[9] The self-awareness that was first introduced in a beneficial way by Ransom is being distorted by the Un-man. Now Tinidril knows what it is like to *look at herself*, to see herself from the Alongside. And the Un-man wants this self-awareness to be all-consuming, for the ego to become the focal point while maintaining the lie that her disobedience would actually be in the beloved's best *interest.* The Un-man presents the action of staying the night on the Fixed Land (the one thing she was forbidden from doing) as noble and sacrificial: the two concepts which have been introduced by the Un-man in such a way as to be tainted by a deadly hint of vanity.

The other edge of the Un-man's attack seeks to distort Tinidril's love for her husband and for Maleldil. He knows that her love is too strong to be utterly broken, too true to be undone completely, too pure to be eradicated in an instant. But it can be twisted, corrupted, and *used.* Her new self-awareness will put her, for the first time, in a *story.* She

---

9 *Perelandra*, 113.

begins to see herself as a character on a grand stage with an important role to play. To her credit, it is her love that drives her to inquire further, to make sure that there is "no great deed" that needs to be done. As the temptation goes on, Tinidril's main concern is still chiefly for her love for the King. "Shall I go and rest and play," she asked, "while all this lies on our hands? Not till I am certain that there is no great deed to be done by me for the King and for the children of our children."[10] The "all this" that Tinidril refers to is the idea the Un-man has now successfully planted in her imagination: the idea that there is some essential duty that the Green Lady must perform herself for the *good* of her husband and any future progeny.

This leads us to ask a question: why does the Un-man focus on the element of vanity and self-awareness in his two-pronged attack? Why not simply focus on deluding Tinidril into thinking that her love (already strong and obedient) demands that she sleep on the Fixed Land? Because the Un-man is far more subtle, and his subtlety is far more effective and deadly. He cannot urge flat disobedience immediately and obviously. Instead, he introduces vanity into her love—the belief that there is some great thing that *she* must overcome in order to achieve true nobility. Once again, this temptation hinges on a corrupted view of the self. "The external and, as it were, dramatic conception of the self was the enemy's true aim."[11] The Un-man attempts to make the idea of sacrifice more attractive by introducing a *self*-focus. This warped focus is what enables the suggestion that Maleldil actually *desires* Tinidril's disobedience to become believable. The fundamental lie that He expects her

10 Ibid., 112.

11 Ibid., 118.

to disobey in order to achieve a sort of noble self-sufficiency sticks *because* of the vanity and twisted self-knowledge that have now crept in to her understanding. Yet in all of this, the core of true love is essential—it is the engine that drives the temptation. Using her own strength against her, trying to turn her greatest virtue into the means of her destruction, is far more cunning and deadly than a full-frontal assault. The Devil is a deceiver, the father of lies.

As soon as vanity and self-admiration enter the picture, Tinidril's desire for the beloved's good becomes slightly blurred. It is now entangled with her own desire to be *seen* as sacrificial, a desire tainted by vanity. There is no longer a pure desire for the loved one's happiness, but a desire mixed with something else. For example, we might see how the love of a mother for her children can quickly become suffocating and destructive. The mother sees *herself* in her children and lives vicariously through them, trying to mold them into her own image, acting as their god, demanding complete and utter submission at every turn, and all in the name of "love" and "affection." And if a child expresses a desire for change, the charge of "you don't really love me" flies from her lips like a bullet. This is self-love *masquerading* as other-love. Sacrifice is a tool often used to entangle others in feelings of debt and to increase feelings of superiority. The martyr card is played frequently. And in the end, when all the objects of love have fled the suffocating grasp of this demanding tyranny, this mother will use her own self-pity and her knowledge of this "ill-treatment" as a balm in her self-inflicted isolation.

Where vanity has made a habitation, true love will have shallow roots. Loving others as ourselves does not mean loving them *as if they were us*. Because they aren't—they are other. But as in the example of the mother above, love that seeks to control and stifle at every turn, love that tries to make others into versions of our own selves, is not true love. True love for others requires knowledge of *their* desires, *their* nature, *their* personalities. Love for others does often require sacrifice, but it should be the true sacrifice of desiring the loved one's good even when that means sacrificing our own desires. A "sacrifice" that masquerades as setting aside our own desires while simultaneously trampling over the happiness of others is no true sacrifice at all.

This is the "sacrifice" that the Un-man is tempting the Green Lady to make: a sacrifice that comes from self-admiration and vanity. This kind of sacrifice constantly parades in front of a mirror so that it can see how noble it looks while serving others, and places the will of the self over and above the will of God. As the Un-man's temptation tactics display, the seeds of vanity quickly sprout thick roots that supplant the foundation of true obedience. True obedience is not always glamorous or attractive. It doesn't always turn you into the hero of an epic drama. It's rarely grand enough to be the main theme of novels and legends. Rather, true obedience often means *forgetting* ourselves. What would God have us do? What would He have us do even if no one is around to see it? And if we follow vanity into a hall of mirrors, is it any wonder that we never see anyone but ourselves?

This is the particular fall from which Ransom saves the Green Lady. And, in the end, it is also the one from which he himself is delivered. Remember in the very beginning when Ransom told Lewis that he was sure Lewis thought he suffered from megalomania, the desire to perform some great act. He told Lewis that in the end it would actually be very ordinary men and women who would do the fighting. His words are then put very much to the test on Perelandra. Ransom, just like Tinidril, just like every human being from the creation of the world, is tempted towards an egocentric mindset. And because he is tempted to put his own self and his own actions at the center of the story, this is why he nearly gives up. He thinks this job is too much for *him*, too great for *him* to handle. Ransom's focus, when he comes closest to despairing, is all inward, all towards himself. He has forgotten to have the right kind of self-awareness. He has forgotten that this is the job he has been sent to do, and the high likelihood of failure is no excuse for not trying.

Ransom and the Green Lady must both learn how to see Alongside in the right way, to love and to obey, to walk in God's will. Viewing ourselves rightly, not with vanity, but with sober-minded obedience, is not only a guard against temptation, but also the path to true joy.

18

LADY OF LOVE

The Influence of Venus

> The sky was pure, flat gold like the background of a medieval picture [...] the ocean was gold too, in the offing, flecked with innumerable shadows. The nearer waves, though golden where their summits caught the light, were green on their slopes: first emerald, then lower down a lustrous bottle green, deepening to blue where they passed beneath the shadow of other waves. (Lewis, *Perelandra*)

In this chapter, I am going to explore how the imagery and influence of Venus work together to shape the unique donegality and, indeed, the entire story arc of *Perelandra*. Even as Mars influenced not just the atmosphere of *Out of the Silent Planet*, but also the events themselves and the effect of those events on Ransom as a person, so Venus influences the atmosphere and events of *Perelandra*, and their effect on Ransom.

As we saw in the introduction to this book, Venus is also known as *Fortuna Minor* and stands second only to Jupiter in beneficence.[1] She produces copper in the earth. This is largely due to her connection with the island of Cyprus, for the goddess Venus, or Aphrodite, is known as the Lady of Cyprus, an island famous for its copper mines. Venus's influence produces beauty and amorousness in mortals. She is the goddess of fertility and pleasure. There is a playfulness and levity to her influence, for she is "laughter loving" and "partly a comic spirit."[2] Think of richness, warmth, maternity, settled joy and laughter, verdant fruitfulness. As Lewis describes:

> In grass growing, and grain bursting,
> Flower unfolding, and flesh longing,
> And shower falling sharp in April[3]

Now let's see Venus's influence at work. The first impression that Ransom gets of Perelandra is a "golden or coppery" light followed by a "great green darkness."[4] Both of these colors are closely associated with Venus and they dominate the Perelandrian scenery. Ransom then begins to experience all the delights and pleasures that Perelandra has to offer. There is a "delicious coolness"[5] washing over him. The water of the ocean is drinkable like fresh water. "It was almost like meeting Pleasure itself for the first time."[6] Everything is "rich and dim"[7]:

---

1 *Discarded Image*, 107.

2 C. S. Lewis, *The Four Loves* (New York: Harcourt, 1960), 99.

3 "The Planets", 13.

4 *Perelandra*, 31.

5 Ibid.

6 Ibid., 32.

7 Ibid.

> The very names of green and gold, which he used perforce in describing the scene, are too harsh for the tenderness, the muted iridescence, of that warm, maternal, delicately gorgeous world. It was mild to look upon as evening, warm like summer noon, gentle and winning like early dawn. It was altogether pleasurable. He sighed.[8]

The rich colors, the mellow and yet poignant tastes and feelings and sensations that Lewis describes, the fruitfulness and soft voluptuousness—the entire atmosphere is saturated with an overwhelming sense of bewildering pleasure, knit together with the sensation that Ransom is in the middle of experiencing something that has been lost. Even the fact that the planet is made up of vast oceans with soft, floating islands is an effect of Venus's influence, for Venus herself was born out of the sea, the womb of the world.

How do all of these details work together to create a distinct donegality? To start, it is inevitable that *pleasure* should be a large and even central theme in the book. Ransom experiences delights on Perelandra that are beyond any he has ever experienced on Earth or could even imagine. Because these pleasures take place in a completely different sphere than Earth, to even speak of them in earthly terms is difficult. As fallen, sublunar creatures, we can hardly imagine any pleasure so great that is not sexual in nature. But this is what Lewis goes through great pains to emphasize.

"It was like a discovery of a totally new *genus* of pleasures, something unheard of among men, out of all reckoning, beyond all covenant."[9] The pleasures that Ransom experiences are not merely sensual. They are what he calls

---

8 Ibid.

9 Ibid., 37.

trans-sensual, using the original definition of the prefix *trans-* to mean "beyond" rather than "across." Think of the word *transcend*, going beyond and above a prior state. In his essay "Transposition," Lewis talks about this sort of thing as he compares physical pleasures to spiritual or emotional pleasures. The spiritual pleasures transcend the physical, and yet we can really only talk about them using physical metaphors. The emotional pleasures we get from spiritual experiences often manifest themselves in physical sensations, and thus give those physical sensations more than one meaning. Lewis explains this by comparing our limited physical sensations to a small vocabulary, or a piano adaptation of an orchestral piece:

> If you are to translate from a language which has a large vocabulary into a language that has a small vocabulary, then you must be allowed to use several words in more than one sense. If you are to write a language with twenty-two vowel sounds in an alphabet with only five vowel characters, then you must be allowed to give each of those five characters more than one value. If you are making a piano version of a piece originally scored for an orchestra, then the same piano notes which represent flutes in one passage must also represent violins in another.[10]

In our earthly bodies, we are limited in our "vocabulary" in terms of our means of experiencing pleasure. The emotional pleasures we get from spiritual experiences often manifest themselves in physical sensations, and so give those physical sensations more than one meaning. Lewis goes on

10 C. S. Lewis, "Transposition" in *The Weight of Glory* (HarperCollins: New York, 1976), 99.

to say that since we already experience pleasures on different planes, what is to keep there from being an even higher plane whose pleasures have an even larger vocabulary? This is what is meant by *trans-sensual*—pleasure that is above and beyond any physical sensation we can experience and even beyond the emotional/spiritual sensations we experience that are *communicated* to us by the physical. When Ransom meets these pleasures, he can hardly sustain them.

> The smells in the forest were beyond all that he had ever conceived. To say that they made him feel hungry and thirsty would be misleading; almost, they created a new kind of hunger and thirst, a longing that seemed to flow over from the body into the soul and which was a heaven to feel [...] If he had any fear now, it was a faint apprehension that his reason might be in danger. There was something in Perelandra that might overload a human brain.[11]

As we've seen several times, Lewis rejects any form of the belief that the material world is inherently evil or sinful. On the contrary, he continuously celebrates the goodness and wonders of creation and nature, while still recognizing that nature has been corrupted by the Fall. Remember his inverted Platonism, where he argues that the problem is not that the material world is physical but that it is not physical *enough.* The world was created by God and though it has been corrupted by the Fall, yet it too shall be redeemed and remade—including its pleasures. God created pleasure. He created *physical* pleasure. He created a rich, fruitful garden and gave it to those that He made in His image. He told

11 *Perelandra*, 37.

them to tend it and keep it, to make it fruitful and to be fruitful themselves. All that is good and lovely and pleasurable was given to us by His hand. "Every good gift and every perfect gift is from above, and comes down from the Father of lights" (James 1:17).

On Perelandra, Ransom is given a taste of the glory of a world where no disobedience has entered in. He is given a glimpse of what pleasures could have been like for our first parents before the corruption introduced by the Fall twisted those good gifts. Whereas last time he became Martial on Malacandra, here he is taken up to the Morning Star herself and, under the influence of Venus, relearns everything he thought he knew about pleasure and joy. And that joy and pleasure, for a fallen son of Adam, often goes hand in hand with pain—pain that, as with the greater Ransom, leads to even more glory.

19

THE TREE & THE FIXED LAND

Real Loss and the Consequences of the Fall

> As [Ransom] stood looking down on her [the Lady], what was most with him was an intense and orphaned longing that he might, if only for once, have seen the great Mother of his own race thus, in her innocence and splendour. "Other things, other blessings, other glories," he murmured. "But never that. Never in all worlds, that. God can make good use of all that happens. But the loss is real." (Lewis, *Perelandra*)

As I've mentioned previously, Ransom's mission on Perelandra is to prevent the fall of that world. Perelandra is an unfallen planet—a new, innocent world where the Green Lady and her husband Tor are the only two members of their race thus far, the Adam and Eve of that people. Many of the parallels between the story of the first few chapters of Genesis and *Perelandra* are immediately apparent. Ransom himself makes many observations on the similarities. He does this so regularly that he has to remind himself that the situation on Perelandra, while similar, is *not* the same as the Genesis story. God never tells the same story twice. Perelandra is not Earth, Tinidril is not Eve, and the whole course of these events is taking place after something cosmically important occurred, something that changed and shaped the course of history for the entire cosmos—the Incarnation. This story is happening in a cosmos where God became man, where the ultimate price has already been paid for the sins of an entire race. This will be discussed at length in later chapters, but notwithstanding this crucial cosmic shift, the parallels and similarities to our own story are worth noting and serve to place the differences in even higher relief.

Let's approach this comparison like a play. First, we will set the scene. Ransom compares Perelandra in numerous places to Paradise, to Eden. He calls it "the garden of the Hesperides,"[1] which in ancient mythology was the goddess Hera's garden in the far west of the world. In this garden there is a tree with golden apples that grant immortality to whomever eats of them. And, just as in the Garden of the Hesperides, in Perelandra there is a red-gold dragon curled around a tree "loaded with yellow fruits and silver leaves."[2] Ransom feels as if he has stepped into a myth, into that ancient past. As we saw in the last chapter, the joys that he encounters give him a glimpse into a world untainted by sin, a true look at Eden. But he himself is sinful and so many of these joys nearly crush him. He is unequipped to handle the sheer weight of that glory. He is

1 See chapter twenty of this book: "Garden of the Hesperides: True Myth".

2 *Perelandra*, 40.

not *real* enough yet. But, in the end, Ransom says: "I have lived in Paradise."[3] And so we have our backdrop: a vision of Paradise and a mirror of Eden.

Let's move on to the next element of the play: the cast. As in Genesis, we have the first man and the first woman of this race of beings. We also have the Satan figure in the form of Weston/the Un-man. But we quickly diverge from Genesis as the story unfolds. In Genesis, Adam must not have been too far away from Eve since she offers him the fruit to eat, and many believe that Adam was actually present *with* Eve during the Serpent's temptation. In *Perelandra*, by contrast, the Adam figure is conspicuously absent throughout most of the book. Tor does not appear on stage until the very end of Ransom's adventures. When Ransom first meets the Green Lady, she has been separated from her husband. And this will make perfect sense if we consider another very important character throughout the series—the character of Maleldil himself.

Maleldil is the Old Solar name that Lewis gives to the triune Christian God of all creation. As Lewis hinted at in *Out of the Silent Planet*, Maleldil is associated with Jove, the one who has orchestrated the events of the story thus far. Maleldil, "upholding all things by the word of His power" (Hebrews 1:3), orders the story from beginning to end. He is the ever-present, all-pervasive character. Now, as I've mentioned, the trilogy could be summed up as the story of Ransom becoming more and more *Jovial* or, said more simply, more like the image of Christ. In this sense, Ransom remains the "Everyman" that he was on the first page of *Out of the Silent Planet*—he is doing what all of us are meant to do, being molded and shaped into Christ's image. But

3 Ibid., 129.

we also learn, as Ransom does throughout the trilogy, the cosmic significance of the Incarnation. God took on human flesh. God became man, Emmanuel, God with us. This event, this specific thing that happened at a specific time in history, granted *importance* to mankind, an importance that is difficult to comprehend. We must be humbled and awed by this deep mystery of the Incarnation, by what God did to accomplish the salvation of the human race. The Incarnation shifted everything, refocusing the eyes of heaven upon Earth in a new way. Everything is different. This is now a cosmos where God became *man*.

And so, this is why Tor is conspicuously absent. Ransom, in his role as prophet on Perelandra, also takes on a Christological role—Ransom is the Adam of this story. If Tor were present, then he would, by default, act as the new Adam. So we see that Ransom, in the spirit of Maleldil, is standing *in loco viri*, in place of the husband. This, too, is a role that prepares him for the next job, the next responsibility.

So much for the stage and cast. Now we need the plot points, most of which are very similar to those in the Genesis account. We have a prohibition: Tor and Tinidril are not to spend the night on the Fixed Land, the land that, unlike the floating islands, does not move. This is the parallel to the forbidden fruit. Like the fruit of the Tree of the Knowledge of Good and Evil, this is the point at which Satan launches his attack. "Has God indeed said…?" In addition, we see that the prohibition regarding the Fixed Land is meant to be temporary. The Fixed Land is ready to be inhabited. It will not remain empty forever, but the Green Lady is not yet ready to inhabit it. First, she must grow up.

And this is where the book diverges from the Genesis story, for Ransom *does* prevent the Fall of this new world. His combat with the Un-Man is at first only verbal and spiritual, battling for Tinidril's attention. But eventually, the fight turns to physical blows. Ransom fulfills his prophetic and Christological role, bashing the Un-Man's head in with a rock and suffering an injury to his heel—an injury that cannot be healed until he returns to Perelandra at the end of the third and final book. But the struggles that Ransom has to undergo in his own soul before he can finally bring himself to fight the Un-Man are almost more painful than the physical difficulties he sustains. For many pages, he is at war with himself. The Martial temperament he learned on Malacandra fails at the thought of a physical battle with the Un-man. It seems impossible. He considers backing out. He makes excuses and tries to explain away his cowardice. Then, amid his internal battle, he hears the voice of Maleldil himself: "It is not for nothing that you are named Ransom," said the Voice [...] "My name also is Ransom."[4] And Ransom realizes that if he fails and Perelandra falls, then this world too will be redeemed. *He* might not be the one to save it, but it will be saved nevertheless. Should he fail, should Tinidril give way to temptation, should sin enter Perelandra as it did our own world, then Maleldil will dare things more terrible still on its behalf:

> So *that* was the real issue. If he now failed, this world also would hereafter be redeemed. If he were not the ransom, Another would be. Yet nothing was ever repeated. Not a second crucifixion: perhaps—who knows—not even a second Incarnation...some act of even more appalling love, some glory of yet deeper humility...if Venus fell, her evil would be a cube—her Redemption beyond conceiving. Yet redeemed she would be.[5]

4 *Perelandra*, 125 and 126.

5 Ibid., 126.

The same story is never told twice. At the end of *Perelandra* we get a glimpse, shadowy and imperfect, of what glories were lost in our first mother and father's Fall—glories that stem from obedience, from fighting temptation, from defeat of the Serpent. The last chapter of *Perelandra* is the crescendo, a sweeping symphony that resembles the very circling of the heavens in its rise and fall. Lewis pours every ounce of his genius into crafting this great, final hymn which echoes and resounds with allusions to the last lines of Dante's *Paradiso*. Ransom has been through Purgatory—he's arrived in the Garden at last. Glorious blessings are showered upon Tor and Tinidril and their future offspring. The Earth lost such a scene when it fell, and Ransom feels the loss deeply:

> I have never before seen a man or a woman. I have lived all my life among shadows and broken images. Oh, my Father and my Mother, my Lord and Lady, do not move, do not answer me yet. My own father and mother I have never seen. Take me for your son. We have been alone in my world for a great time.[6]

The redemption that God has worked on the Earth is a wondrous mystery, one which angels desire to look into. It is a glory that we can hardly comprehend; a terrible charity; an "appalling love."[7] And yet...the *loss* is real. Ransom tastes, feels, touches, and sees a glimpse of a real, true glory that was really and truly lost in our Fall. And it nearly unmakes him. To pretend that there was no real good or glorious future lost when Adam and Eve ate of the fruit is to down-

6 *Perelandra*, 176.

7 Ibid., 126.

play the immensity of the sin and thus the immensity of the redemption. The loss is *real.*

This is a crucial point in Ransom's response to the Un-man's arguments. The Un-man tries to use the great *good* that is God's redemption of the world to justify Tinidril's disobedience:

> "There is more. [Ransom] has not told you that it was this breaking of the commandment which brought Maleldil to our world and because of which He was made man. He dare not deny it."[8]

Ransom is stuck at first. He cannot deny it. He cannot lie. He cannot even skirt the truth or evade it in the slightest. And yet, the way the Un-man is twisting this truth to justify disobedience for the sake of some "greater good" is sickening. The Un-man uses the truth to present a dangerous falsehood lurking beneath the surface of his words. Ransom doesn't know how he can answer such a thing. Everything the Un-man says is *true*. Then Ransom's struggle ends, and we come to one of the greatest paragraphs in the trilogy, worth quoting at length here:

> "I will tell you what I say," answered Ransom, jumping to his feet. "Of course good came of it. Is Maleldil a beast that we can stop His path, or a leaf that we can twist His shape? Whatever you do, He will make good of it. But not the good He had prepared for you if you had obeyed Him. That is lost for ever. The first King and first Mother of our world did the forbidden thing; and He brought good of it in the end. But what they did was not

8 Ibid., 103.

> good; and what they lost we have not seen. And there were some to whom no good came nor ever will come." He turned to the body of Weston. "You," he said, "tell her all. What good came to you? Do *you* rejoice that Maleldil became a man? Tell her of *your* joys, and of what profit you had when you made Maleldil and death acquainted."[9]

The true joy of redemption, the deep aching joy, can be truly felt only if we reckon the cost all the way down—from beginning to end. But we cannot. Not fully. This is a joy that knows that something truly was lost, a true price paid, a true good gone forever. But God turns all of this loss into a greater glory—a different glory, but a greater one. A glory that has known loss and sorrow, a joy "beyond the walls of the world, poignant as grief."[10]

---

9 *Perelandra*, 104.

10 This is J. R. R. Tolkien's definition of *eucatastrophe*, which is his word for a great and stunning rescue after terrible darkness. Eucatastrophe, by definition, is possible only after some sort of *fall*. Hence, it is the perfect word to describe the concept Lewis is after here: of glory restored after sorrow and ruin. See "On Fairy Stories" in *The Tolkien Reader* (New York: Ballantine Books, 1966), 68.

20

GARDEN OF THE HESPERIDES

True Myth

> Round the base of the indigo stem was coiled a small dragon covered with scales of red gold. [Ransom] recognised the garden of the Hesperides at once. "This is the most vivid dream I have ever had," he thought. [...] He remembered how in the very different world called Malacandra—that cold, archaic world, as it now seemed to him—he had met the original of the Cyclops, a giant in a cave and a shepherd. Were all the things which appeared as mythology on earth scattered through other worlds as realities? (Lewis, *Perelandra*)

Picking up on the Garden of the Hesperides mentioned in the last chapter, *Perelandra* is the most obviously *classically* influenced book of the trilogy, in that it contains the highest concentration of classical mythological references. To the reader familiar with Homer, Vergil, and Greek and Roman myths, *Perelandra* is full to the brim with allusions and reflections. But more than that, Ransom finds that he has in fact entered a *myth* himself. The world that he has entered is true, living myth. How is this possible? Isn't myth, by definition, untrue? To understand what Lewis does with all of the mythological references in *Perelandra*, we must first understand his view of myth itself.

What is myth? A quick search of the term will give us multiple definitions that all distinguish myth from historical fact. The idea of falsehood has been intricately intertwined with the word itself. I have no problem with this definition *per se*. Myths are lumped in with legends or tall tales and there isn't anything necessarily wrong with this categorization.

That said, a story can have a deeper truth than that of being *historically accurate*. We get a taste of this when we encounter truly great stories. As we saw in an earlier chapter, we can know that stories are fiction while also recognizing that they are instrumental in training our imaginations.

Lewis once told Tolkien that myths were "lies breathed through silver."[1] He said this prior to his conversion when he was wrestling with how to reconcile the beloved truths he had encountered in literature with his beliefs about the world and God. He struggled because he *loved* the old myths. These myths presented him with archetypes and models and themes that enchanted him. Even before he was close to accepting Christ as his Lord and Savior, Lewis had encountered the "dying god" motif over and over throughout his classical studies. He had fallen in love with things that he believed were simply untruths—utterly "mythical" in every *usual* sense of the word.

1 Humphrey Carpenter, *J. R. R. Tolkien: A Biography* (Boston: Houghton Mifflin, 2014), 151.

Tolkien corrected Lewis's assumption about the nature of myth by means of a poem, "Mythopoeia," wherein Tolkien crafted a direct answer to Lewis's claim that myths are simply "lies breathed through silver." Tolkien argues that everything we see or touch or experience is in fact a *myth* in the sense that it is more than the sum of its parts. There is more truth in the world than can be measured, weighed, touched or observed with the naked eye. Myth need not be historically *accurate* in order to be *true*. A tree is true myth, not just because it exists but because its existence points to the very nature of the universe and the One who created it. When we look at that tree or a sunset or the stars, we see far more than the material that they are made up of. Tolkien says it beautifully:

> He sees no stars who does not see them first
> Of living silver made that sudden burst
> To flame like flowers beneath the ancient song,
> Whose very echo after-music long
> Has since pursued. There is no firmament,
> Only a void, unless a jewelled tent
> Myth-woven and elf-patterned; and no earth,
> Unless the mother's womb whence all have birth.[2]

The form that a story takes (and myth is one of those forms) cannot itself be true or false. It is simply the *vehicle* used to communicate. Hence, the fact that a story is told as a myth does not necessitate its truth or falsity one way or the other. Yet, in order to be a myth at all, a story must be archetypical. An archetype is a recurring image or figure that is loaded with meaning: a cross, the youngest of three sons,

---

2 J. R. R. Tolkien, "Mythopoeia" in *Tree and Leaf* (New York: HarperCollins, 2012), 87.

bread and wine, an olive branch, a lost city, a king in exile, a broken sword. Archetypes include symbols and story tropes which have accumulated the dust of centuries. Myths echo with the sound of a thousand thousand tales told using the same figures and repeating symbols. A myth is fundamentally built using archetypes—and those *archetypes* themselves can be true or false.

So how can we say that something is *true myth*? It comes down to this: does it actually tell the *truth* about the world? More than names and dates, more than facts and figures, myths can carry truths that run all the way down to the roots of the world. Myths, in this sense, are often truer than our most accurate history books.

This is exactly how Ransom realizes that he is living a true myth. Everything he sees and experiences is archetypical, pointing to deeper realities and truer truths than any he has ever experienced. He comes to see that the division or separation between truth, myth, and fact is contrived and was, perhaps, really never meant to be at all. The event that brings this realization to mind is Ransom's growing conviction that his battle against the Un-man must and will become a *physical* one. This conviction is pressed upon him from something, or Someone, outside himself.

Ransom fights against this idea with all his being. He is disturbed by it, in part because of his lingering assumptions about the fundamental division between soul and body. He is still holding on to remnants of gnostic thought that cling to the corners of Christianity: the idea that the physical body is somehow crude and inherently less holy than the soul and spirit. He still thinks that spiritual warfare should only occur within the realm of *spirit.* To make this conflict physical would be to degrade it or lessen its importance.

> [...] no such crude, materialistic struggle could possibly be what Maleldil really intended. Any suggestion to the contrary must be only his own morbid fancy. It would degrade the spiritual warfare to the condition of *mere mythology*. But here he got another check. Long since on Mars and more strongly since he came to Perelandra, Ransom had been perceiving that the triple distinction of truth from myth and of both from fact was purely terrestrial—was part and parcel of that unhappy division between soul and body which resulted from the Fall. Even on earth the sacraments existed as a permanent reminder that the division was neither wholesome nor final. The Incarnation had been the beginning of its disappearance. In Perelandra it would have no meaning at all. Whatever happened here would be of such a nature that earth-men would call it mythological. All this he had thought before. Now he knew it. The Presence in the darkness, never before so formidable, was putting these truths into his hands, like terrible jewels.[3]

In this moment, Ransom is forced to actually know, in an enfleshed way, what has been lingering in his thoughts this whole time. The idea that spiritual warfare, by its very definition, excludes any physical component is an unbiblical distinction. It is this distinction that he needs to cast off in order to accomplish his mission, and it is this distinction that is closely connected to his view of myth. And, as with the other grand mysteries of the cosmos, the Incarnation is where these ideas come together. The Incarnation is, itself, a sort of myth. Just as myth transcends brute fact, so Incarnation transcends myth. It is myth made tangible. As Lewis

3 *Perelandra*, 122, emphasis mine.

says elsewhere about the Incarnation: "By becoming fact it does not cease to be myth. That is the miracle."[4] Ransom can bash in the Un-man's head with a rock and still call it spiritual warfare, because he is taking part in a true myth. Serpents' heads always get crushed by rocks and Ransoms are always bruised in their heels. *This is the way the world works.* On top of that, Ransom is able to take part in this true myth, because Christ did it first—Christ the Greater Ransom, paid once for all.

4 Lewis, "Myth Became Fact," in *God in the Dock*, 59.

21

THE LANGUAGE OF PARADISE

Poetry on Perelandra

> Ransom was hunting him with the fish and they would not cease to follow. He laughed aloud. "My hounds are bred out of the Spartan kind, so flew'd so sanded," he roared. (Lewis, *Perelandra*)

As mentioned in the last chapter, Lewis's writings are full of allusions to many other great works of literature that played an integral part in his thought and imagination. This is one of the reasons we have books like the one you are currently holding—there are such depths to be found in Lewis's writing that the exploration has kept scholars and writers busy for decades.

In addition to subtler influences and allusions, Lewis also occasionally throws direct quotations into his writings. Sometimes the quote will be familiar enough that the average reader knows exactly where it comes from. Other times, it is not so obvious. Lewis's genius can be seen in the fact that the quotes are not distracting but they flow seamlessly, intertwined with the narrative. This gives them an unseen strength. Readers don't stop reading when they see the quotation marks to puzzle out exactly what Lewis is quoting and why. It just *fits*. However, that doesn't mean that identifying the source of the quotations is a waste of time.

In *Perelandra*, we come across more direct quotations than the other two books in the trilogy. In *Out of the Silent Planet*, Ransom spent most of his time either terrified, or trying to learn a new language and understand the world he'd been brought into. And in *That Hideous Strength*, as we'll see, we do not get inside Ransom's head like we do in the first and second books. It is *Perelandra* that shows us a different side to Ransom. Though he is still very frightened at times, the Martial influence from Malacandra has not worn off, and he is excited at the prospect of visiting another planet. In addition, the rich atmosphere of Perelandra is one in which his mind rests. This change in Ransom's circumstances and disposition from the first book gives rise to a relaxed *context* that is more suited for direct quotations of poetry. Not only does Ransom's mindset allow him to recollect poetry more easily, but the atmosphere of Venus demands it.

Before considering a few particular quotations, I want to briefly discuss why it is more than just suitable—in fact, almost *necessary*—that there be a higher concentration of poetic quotations and allusions in this book. As we saw in our discussion of myth, Perelandra is a picture of Paradise. The rich, sensual environment is free from any stain or impurity or imperfection (besides that which Ransom brings with him). So what other language could be spoken *besides* poetry? Poetry is our most exalted form of language. To quote Samuel Taylor Coleridge, poetry is "the best words in the best order."[1] Poetic verse is prose condensed and glorified. Where common speech may stumble, poetry soars.

As we discussed in an earlier chapter on poetry, Lewis believed that one of the functions of poetry is to train and instruct as well as to delight, following in the footsteps of Sir Philip Sidney. In Lewis's presentation of Sidney's *Defense of Poesie*, he first relates Sidney's opinion that poetry is meant to inspire men to virtue:

> This is [poetry's] share in the common function of all learnings, which is 'to lift up the minde...to the enjoying of his owne diuine essence'. To that end she is set free from Nature, not 'captived' like history to the trueth of a foolish world' but licenses to create 'things either better than nature bringeth foorth, or quite anew, forms such as never were'.[2]

Poetry lifts the mind to transcend nature and to the enjoyment of man's "own divine essence." In addition, poetry imitates God in creating new worlds rather than being bound to the actual events of a fallen world. In response to the accusation that the things created by poetry are not in fact *real*, Lewis goes on to outline Sidney's two answers to this objection:

> What matters most about anything is not its reality in the sense demanded but its idea. [...] And secondly, in so far as poetry makes its readers enamoured of virtue and thus modifies their behaviour, poetry does produce results in the historical world.[3]

1 Samuel Taylor Coleridge and Henry Nelson Coleridge, *Specimens of the Table Talk of the late Samuel Taylor Coleridge* (London: John Murray, 1851), 48.

2 *English Literature in the Sixteenth Century*, 345.

3 Ibid.

On Perelandra, Ransom eats, drinks, and breathes *poetry*. The entire unfallen world to which he has traveled has been instructing him in virtue since the moment he felt the touch of its warm waters and floating islands. Pleasure, purity, virtue, and mythology all work together to make this a world knit together by living, tangible poetry. Thus it is fitting that poetry spills through his mind at random moments, and that he uses strands of memorized verse to keep himself sane while pursuing the Un-man.

This idea of poetry being the language of Paradise does not come out of thin air. It is grounded in both the nature of language and poetry itself and in the Bible. We have an incredible gift that we almost always take for granted: that of having on record the first words ever spoken by a man to a woman, by one member of the human race to another member of the human race. The first words spoken by a husband to his wife—when the world was pure and fresh as the morning and God still walked with man in the Garden—were poetry. If poetry truly is the "best words in the best order," then where else could we find the most perfect poetry but in the perfection of Paradise?

Now we will go through a few of the poetical quotations in *Perelandra* and consider their context and significance.

1) "…die of a rose in aromatic pain," Alexander Pope, "An Essay on Man: Epistle I"[4]

Alexander Pope's poem "An Essay on Man" is rich with allusions to medieval cosmology, the Edenic garden, and Milton's *Paradise Lost*, all of which make it an appropriate poem to quote on Perelandra. To borrow the words of Milton's self-stated goal, Pope seeks to "justify the ways of

---

4 *Perelandra*, 42.

God to man." His approach, however, is more philosophical than theological or poetical. "An Essay on Man: Epistle I" is a philosophically optimistic take on God's sovereignty and man's limited knowledge, two concepts that Ransom himself ponders at great length.

2) "Sober certainty of waking bliss," John Milton, *Comus (A Mask Presented at Ludlow Castle, 1634)*[5]

The first thing to note is that this is the second time that Lewis has directly quoted Milton's *Comus* in the trilogy. The first time was in a key passage in *Out of the Silent Planet*, when Ransom had his first major revelation regarding the true nature of the heavens. However, the use of a quote from this poem here, on Perelandra, is even more striking. *Comus* is about a young woman traveling through the wood with her brothers. When her brothers leave her to rest while they seek food, she is kidnapped by Comus, a wicked and debauched god. The majority of the poem relays the debates between the young lady and Comus who tries to tempt her out of her temperance and chastity into gluttony and sexual impurity. The whole poem serves as a metaphor for the war between the lusts of the flesh and godly virtue. This is a fascinating poem to quote in such a book as Perelandra. The quote above is spoken by Comus when he first hears the lady singing. He names a list of ethereal, beautiful sounds that he has been accustomed to hearing and yet:

> "Such a sacred, and home-felt delight,
> Such sober certainty of waking bliss
> I never heard till now"[6]

5 Ibid., 44.

6 John Milton, *Comus*, lines 262-264.

Pleasure and virtue have met in this moment. Comus takes true, waking pleasure in a pure sound, one that he enjoys all the more for the fact that there is no magic or delusion in it. Whatever arguments he makes for giving in to *carnal* lusts throughout the rest of the poem, in this one moment he sees and experiences something truly good, an experience that Ransom also participates in on Perelandra.

3) "'Tis not in mortals to command success," Joseph Addison, *Cato*, I.2[7]

Written in 1712, *Cato* takes place during the last days of Marcus Porcius Cato Uticensis, a renowned Stoic who resisted the tyrannical rule of Julius Caesar and became a figurehead of liberty and virtue. The play became highly popular throughout England and the New World, and many credit it with being a great literary inspiration for the American War for Independence.

The significance of Lewis's quotation is not *immediately* apparent. Ransom is in the midst of making excuses for himself; he desperately wants to avoid a physical confrontation. He performs all sorts of mental gymnastics to avoid doing what he must do. All he can do is his best, right? And God will "see to the final issue."[8] Ransom uses this quote from *Cato* as part of his self-justification for avoiding this physical conflict.

The interesting fact about the context of this quote, however, is that Portius (Cato's son) is speaking to Sempronius of his intent to go rally the troops, to "animate the

7 *Perelandra*, 120.

8 Ibid.

soldier's drooping courage." Where Portius uses this line to inspire courage, Ransom uses it to excuse cowardice.

4) "...fallings from him, vanishings," William Wordsworth, "Intimations of Immortality"[9]

"Intimations of Immortality," written while Wordsworth was returning to orthodox Christianity, is one of his more solid works of poetry. It presents the loss of innocence and idyllic peace as a very real *loss*, and yet one that leads to deeper, richer glories. Unlike many Romantic poets, here Wordsworth does not treat innocence and childlike naivete as a loss that is to be mourned as if it were the loss of a highest good, but as the loss of a *particular good* that leads to deeper truths and higher joys. In this poem, he rejects the typical flawed Romantic view of man as naturally pure and innocent and embraces instead the biblical perspective that sees maturity as greater than the loss of childhood. The "fallings from him, vanishings" are the doubts and questions that come from being a creature: a finite, limited being. But the poet is grateful for these things and he raises a song of "thanks and praise" for those "blank misgivings of a Creature."

Ransom, likewise, is going through a spiritual struggle. A flurry of doubts and questions are plaguing his mind and he himself struggles with those "blank misgivings of a Creature." He knows, as the Presence tells him, that he is only wasting time—and yet the doubts continue to bombard him and he distracts himself with these questions to avoid facing the real issue, the thing that needs to be done.

9 Ibid., 123.

5) "Once he was actually astride the [Un-man's] chest, squeezing its throat with both hands and—he found to his surprise—shouting a line out of *The Battle of Maldon*: but it tore his arms so with its nails and so pounded his back with its knees that he was thrown off."[10]

6) "My hounds are bred out of the Spartan kind, so flew'd so sanded," William Shakespeare, "Midsummer Night's Dream"[11]

7) "[Ransom] recited all that he could remember of the *Iliad*, the *Odyssey*, the *Æneid*, the *Chanson de Roland*, *Paradise Lost*, the *Kalevala*, the *Hunting of the Snark*, and a rhyme about Germanic sound-laws which he had composed as a freshman."[12]

I have grouped these three passages together because I believe that they serve a similar purpose. Ransom yells out a line from *The Battle of Maldon*, an Old English battle poem written about a battle occurring in 991, during his fight with the Un-man; he shouts out Shakespeare as he pursues the Un-man across the waves; and he proceeds to recite all that he can from a variety of different works in order to keep himself from going mad while he waits for the dawn so he can make sure that the Un-man is really dead.

These quotations have a few key elements in common. First, Ransom says them *out loud*. Up to this point, his poetic quotations have all occurred inside his head. Secondly, they all take place in the context of Ransom's physical strug-

10 *Perelandra*, 132.

11 Ibid., 134.

12 Ibid., 148.

gle with the Un-man. And finally, they are all Martial: *The Battle of Maldon*, hunting hounds, the Trojan War, Odysseus's adventures, Aeneas' battle in Italy, Roland's last stand, the battles of the *Kaleval*. Ransom, shaped and formed by the Martial spirit in the first book, has finally grown into a Martial prophet, facing and defeating the Un-man in physical combat. And how does he express this Martial spirit? In the language of Perelandra, of Paradise—in *poetry*. Mars and Venus have met indeed.

22

A FIT RECEPTACLE

Weston as the Anti-Ransom

> "Guided," [Weston] said. "Chosen. Guided. I've become conscious that I'm a man set apart. Why did I do physics? Why did I discover the Weston rays? Why did I go to Malacandra? It—the Force—has pushed me on all the time. I'm being guided. I know now that I am the greatest scientist the world has yet produced. I've been made so for a purpose. It is through me that Spirit itself is at this moment pushing on to its goal." (Lewis, *Perelandra*)

Weston comes to Perelandra like Satan. He arrives on this new, unfallen world in a space-ship as a second Lucifer falling from the sky like a shooting star out of heaven,[1] and Ransom quickly discovers that something dark and dreadful has happened to the great scientist. Weston, at first seeming mostly unchanged (if a bit more radical in his ideals), has in fact been possessed by a devil, quite likely *the* Devil himself. Weston has walked dark paths since we met him last and they have led him to his final undoing. Soon, very soon, Weston the man is no longer there at all.

One of the most striking characteristics of Weston's first conversation with Ransom on Perelandra is the similarity that he bears to Ransom himself. If we compare this conversation with the one between Ransom and Lewis at the beginning of the book, some glaringly obvious similarities jump out. And yet no two viewpoints could be more opposed than theirs. And throughout the rest of *Perelandra*, we see Weston, or the Un-man, become more and more clearly an anti-Ransom, the photo-negative of everything Ransom is there to do and be.

Let's consider the similarities between the two men. Weston, like Ransom, has apparently been "chosen" for a role. He sees everything that he has done up to this point as part of a greater purpose, with a powerful "spirit" behind it. Ironically—he is exactly right. Weston was chosen as the means by which Ransom would come to Malacandra and learn to speak Old Solar. He was chosen to be the tipping point that broke the barrier between the sublunar and translunar realms. He set more and greater things in motion than had occurred to him in his wildest dreams.

1 "Then, quite involuntarily, [Ransom] added in English, 'By Jove! What was that?' She also had exclaimed. Something like a shooting star seemed to have streaked across the sky, far away on their left, and some seconds later an indeterminate noise reached their ears" (*Perelandra*, 65-66).

However, the language that Weston uses when he talks about his role is decidedly different from the language Ransom uses when he tells Lewis about the job he has been given. Ransom is fully aware he might come across as egotistical and self-centered, so he makes efforts to assure Lewis that he knows that he was not chosen on account of any particular greatness about himself. Weston is the polar opposite. Weston doesn't try at all to hide the fact that he considers *himself* to be the greatest scientist in all history and that he feels he has been chosen based on his particular qualities and abilities. He is entirely consumed by his own self. He rejects any distinction "between me and the universe."[2] While Ransom acknowledges that he, Ransom, is an ordinary man given an extraordinary job, Weston abhors the thought of being considered ordinary in any way. His pride and vanity are all-consuming, just one of the many reasons he is a prime target to be taken over by a devil.

Another contrast between Weston and Ransom is that Weston is shown to be an *anti-prophet.* He comes to Perelandra claiming to bring knowledge, revelation, and instruction. Like Satan himself, he often weaves thick tapestries out of truth and lies and twists them together so intricately that it becomes difficult to separate them or tell them apart. The power behind the Un-man's deceptions is truth, and this drives Ransom into corners that seem nearly impossible to get out of. The Un-man seeks to open Tinidril's eyes, to show her "greater" things than what she has learned from Ransom. In many respects, the Un-man is a formidable opponent with a better-stocked armory than Ransom, a threat which Ransom feels keenly. This is one of the reasons that the fight finally comes to physical blows. Ransom sees the

2 *Perelandra*, 82.

Un-man's arguments weakening the Green Lady. He sees the trajectory of their discussions. And he decides it cannot go on: he cannot win the arguments, but he *must* win the war.

Weston, again in contrast to Ransom, continually seeks to downplay the antithesis between God and the devil, between flesh and spirit, between the individual and the cosmos, between light and dark. As Weston says:

> "[...] all my life I had been making a wholly unscientific dichotomy or antithesis between Man and Nature—had conceived myself fighting *for* Man against his non-human environment [...] I saw almost at once that I could admit no break, no discontinuity, in the unfolding of the cosmic process. I became a convinced believer in emergent evolution. All is one. The stuff of mind, the unconsciously purposive dynamism, is present from the very beginning."[3]

Weston pushes this rejection of antithesis as far as it can go, saying that God and the devil are one and the same thing, that "no real dualism in the universe is admissible."[4] He uses the word *dualism* here to refer to the very *fact* of twos—of different entities or things, of distinction of any kind. Ransom, on the other hand, has been preparing for a *conflict*, which necessarily presupposes an antithesis, a clash of twos. From the end of *Out of the Silent Planet* to the beginning of *Perelandra*, Ransom has become very much aware of the cosmic forces at work and of the battle that looms ahead. He knows that the time is coming when ordinary men and women will be called on to take a stand. He has already

---

3 *Perelandra*, 78.

4 Ibid., 80.

told Lewis that the two sides of good and evil are becoming *more*, not less pronounced. They "have begun to appear much more clearly, much less mixed, here on Earth, in our own human affairs—to show in something a little more like their true colours."[5]

The dark forces at work on Thulcandra are becoming more and more apparent. Neutrality is impossible. And one of those forces is already at work here on Perelandra, one that he was sent to deter. Ransom was well-formed by the Martial influence—he is now a Martial prophet, ready to take a stand, ready to fight. He, of course, has a long way to go and a lot to learn before he is finally ready to plunge into the fray. But he cannot stand by and take Weston's nonsense about there not being two sides or about the amorphous "oneness" brought about by mindless evolutionary processes. It is all nonsense—nonsense that often contains kernels of truth, nonsense that often seems sweet as honey—but nonsense nonetheless. Ransom knows that there are sides to be taken. He also knows that, whatever Weston may say, the Un-man knows it too. *The Un-man is on a side as well.* And the Un-man hates the *opposing* team with a vengeance. That is why he attempts to wear away the antithetical language—not so that there will be no more sides, but so that his side will win.

The final comparison to note between Ransom and Weston is Lewis's use of the term *bridge*. The first time we see the term is in the first chapter of *Perelandra*, in Lewis the character's own mind. He is concerned about Ransom. The dark *eldila* who are trying to turn him back sow all kinds of frightening thoughts into his mind. He worries that Ransom may be an "unwitting bridge" or "Trojan horse" that the

5 Ibid., 21

dark forces will use to launch an invasion into earth.[6] The irony here is that Lewis's fear is actually true: Ransom is indeed a bridge.

However, the reason for Ransom's transformation into a bridge is not to bring devastation on Earth but rather salvation. He does bring an invasion—but it is the invasion of a benevolent army into the stronghold held by the enemy for far too long, an invasion to free the captives and drive out the usurpers. It is D-Day for the Allies, not the German invasion of Poland. By the third book, Ransom has fully become this bridge.[7]

On Perelandra, Weston becomes a bridge as well. He becomes the "fit receptacle"[8] that he wished to be.

> Weston's body, travelling in a space-ship, had been the *bridge* by which something else had invaded Perelandra—whether that supreme and original evil whom in Mars they call The Bent One, or one of his lesser followers, made no difference.[9]

Weston is the complete antithesis to Ransom. He is the anti-prophet, the anti-bridge, the anti-Ransom. He sold himself, very literally, to the devil for his cause and, in the end, it is his undoing.

After killing the Un-man, Ransom takes the time and effort to carve a tombstone for Weston into the rock face. Why does he do this? He tells himself afterwards that it was a "tomfool thing to do."[10] But he defends his actions by telling

6 *Perelandra*, 12.

7 *That Hideous Strength*, 288.

8 *Perelandra*, 81.

9 Ibid., 96, emphasis mine.

10 Ibid., 161.

himself there ought to be some record of the man, and that Weston was a very great physicist, after all. But really, deep down, I think Ransom *knew.* He knew that Weston was not so very unlike himself. Weston, like Ransom, felt he had been *called.* He, too, was a man of great learning and conviction, but one who had started down a very dark path. And but for the grace of God, Ransom could have had a very similar fate.

23

KINDLING LOVE IN MAN

Purgatory for the Pilgrim

For better waters now, the little bark
Of my poetic powers hoists its sails,
And leaves behind that cruelest of the seas.

And I shall sing about that second realm
Where man's soul goes to purify itself
And become worthy to ascend to Heaven.
(Dante, *Purgatorio*, 1.1-6)

As we have already seen, Perelandra is Paradise, and so as we continue to compare the Ransom Trilogy to Dante's *Divine Comedy*, we might easily expect *Perelandra* to parallel *Paradiso*. Now, while certain similarities do exist, I would argue that *Perelandra* actually parallels *Purgatorio*. The key thing here is not the *setting* (Paradise) but rather Ransom's role, his struggles, and the things he embodies. So in this chapter, we will explore these parallels and see how fitting it really is that Purgatory find its place on the Lady of Love herself. These parallels with *Purgatorio* will serve to deepen our understanding of what Lewis is doing in the trilogy as a whole.

The purpose of Purgatory was two-fold: to purge away all fear and sinful desire, as well as to re-order every love. According to Dante, following in the footsteps of Augustine, all sins ultimately arise from distorted or disordered love, loving a thing out of proportion. Purgatory itself is located on an island mountain, reached by crossing a great sea, and at the top is found the earthly paradise. On Perelandra, Ransom's character undergoes his own personal Purgatory: he is completely tested, reshaped, and purified. As a Martial prophet his role is clear, but he is still purposed for greater things. His experiences on Perelandra prepare him for what lies ahead.

As Ransom fulfills his role as prophet, he is put through the intellectual, emotional, spiritual, and (finally) physical wringer. Ransom fights the Un-man in the deeps until finally he crushes his head in a fiery chamber and throws his body into the pit. His fight with the Un-man takes him from the lowest, deepest parts of Earth and up through the center of the mountain, at the top of which he finds the Eden of Eden, the garden at the center of the paradise that is Perelandra. From there Ransom passes from glory to glory until he arrives at the Holy Mountain. Ransom's purging tested his entire being—his body, his soul, and his faith.

Similarly, in *Purgatorio*, Dante's Pilgrim must cross an ocean in order to reach Mount Purgatory. And, perhaps most important of all, one of the first sights that the Pilgrim sees after he and his guide emerge from the depths of Hell is the planet Venus:

> The lovely planet kindling love in man
> Made all the eastern sky smile with her light,
> Veiling the Fish that shimmered in her train.[1]

Why Venus? If we remember anything at all from our study of the planets and their importance in the medieval mind, then we know this is no accident. Venus isn't just a planet. She isn't here for dramatic effect. She is here on purpose. Dante, like Lewis himself, is not simplistic in his use of symbolism or imagery. As Dante remarked about the *Comedy*, "Be it known that the sense of this work is not simple, but on the contrary it may be called polysemous, that is to say, *of more senses than one*."[2] This means that we can dig deep into the imagery of Venus and still discover more and more.

On one level, Dante uses this sighting of Venus as a beacon of hope. The Pilgrim is encouraged by the sight of the sky after so much time spent in the dark, and the light of Venus in particular lifts his spirits, as it is that planet which "kindles love in man."

But this love *itself* is a symbol, pointing to the even greater Love around which the whole poem revolves. Love is both the driving force behind Purgatory *and* Purgatory's end and purpose. Through the purging of all other loves and fears, one learns to love and fear the Author of all, the "Love that moves the sun and other stars."[3] Remember that one of the primary functions of Purgatory is the reordering of loves that have been misplaced or misused. Hence, it is fitting that Ransom's purging should occur on the Morning

---

1 Dante, *Purgatorio*, 1.19-21

2 Quoted by H. Flanders Dunbar in *Symbolism in Medieval Thought and Its Consummation in* "The Divine Comedy" (New Haven, CT: Yale University Press, 1929), ix, emphasis mine.

3 *Paradiso*, 33.145.

Star herself, the Lady of Love. His journey through Purgatory primarily involves a shaping and directing of his love.

Love is always directed at something—it has an object, a *telos*, a purpose. Love is not passive, but active, because love is the great mover. According to Dante (and all of medieval thought), the entire cosmos moves the way it does out of love for God. Motion, action, and direction are inescapable, but the ordering of our love matters. Remember how all of the Un-man's ploys to corrupt the Green Lady and cause her to disobey play upon love—her love for Maleldil, for her husband, and for herself. The Green Lady's love is true, but it can be misdirected and misused. The Un-man tries to influence her by telling her that the objects of her love will love her all the more for her disobedience, that what they really mean for her to do is disobey, and so forth. Love is a mover. It moves either towards or away from obedience, but it is always moving. Ransom's debate with himself is really the same debate that the Un-man has with the Green Lady—the same question that has deceived and twisted love from the beginning. "Has God indeed said…?" (Genesis 3:1). What is required and what will we do? How great is our love? Is it great enough to dare obedience? But most of all, where is it directed?

By the end of *Perelandra*, Ransom has changed drastically. His love, which drove him to accept the mission in the first place, has been directed and focused through his challenges. He has been tested, tried, and refined, and is now "worthy to ascend to Heaven." But these changes could not have occurred at all if it weren't for the changes that had already taken place in the first book. Each change has been a steppingstone, leading Ransom on to the man he is meant to be: one whose love has been reordered rightly.

"Discipline and freedom from anxiety"[4] are two primary characteristics of the Martial character that Lewis admired. If there were ever two things that Ransom learns on Malacandra and that he comes to embody on Perelandra, they are these. He reaches the point where his own physical well-being and safety are of little importance compared to his task. Ransom fulfills his role as Martial Prophet, undergoing both a physical and spiritual purgatory on Perelandra. Where he left Thulcandra a middle-aged scholar, he returns with his youth restored and a wound in his heel that can never be fully healed on Earth. He is now more than just a prophet or pilgrim. He draws the gaze of Heaven with him, closer and closer to Earth. Thulcandra has always been there, sitting at the bottom of the cosmos, beneath the eyes of Deep Heaven, an object of wonder and mystery, sequestered and silent beyond the boundary of the Moon. But her silence is coming to an end. For, at the end of all his purgation, Ransom returns to Thulcandra, bringing Deep Heaven in his wake.

4 Lewis to Sister Penelope CSMV, Oxford, January 31, 1946, in *Collected Letters*, 2:702.

Discussion Questions

Perelandra

1. Discuss the influence of Venus and how Lewis uses her characteristics to describe *Perelandra.* (E.g., use of color, texture, atmosphere, etc.)

2. How does Lewis's discussion of the Incarnation in a fictional setting and his portrayal of other species' commentary on it give you a new perspective? What is the benefit to this kind of fiction?

3. What is true myth? Why is it important for Christians in particular to understand true myth?

4. How does Lewis use the term "trans-sensual?" What are some ways that we glimpse this sort of thing on Earth?

PART III:

That Hideous Strength

SUMMARY

The third book of the Ransom Trilogy follows Mark and Jane Studdock who, in the beginning, are unhappy in their marriage. Mark is a senior fellow of sociology at Bracton College which is being taken over by an organization called the N.I.C.E. (National Institute of Co-ordinated Experiments) whose headquarters are at Belbury. The N.I.C.E. is attempting to re-create humanity in a culmination of Weston's philosophy from the earlier books.

Ransom (now known as the Director) has gathered a group of people at the village of St. Anne's in an attempt to thwart the plans of the N.I.C.E. Ransom knows that the people at Belbury are trying to get their hands on Merlin, who was buried under Bracton Wood and, as legend has it, is not truly dead. The company at St. Anne's seeks to find Merlin first and try to persuade him to join their cause.

Mark is slowly sucked into the workings of Belbury even as Jane joins the company at St. Anne's, finding protection from Belbury which wants to use her for her abilities as a seer. Ransom and his company manage to find Merlin first and the powers of Deep Heaven descend to the Silent Planet, filling Merlin with the power he needs to defeat Belbury.

In the end, Belbury falls. Their language is confused, and they are attacked by the beasts that were the subjects of

Belbury's experiments. Mark and Jane are reunited and their marriage is restored. Ransom is taken to his final resting place on Perelandra where the wound in his heel that he once received there can finally be mended.

24

MARS & VENUS

Mark and Jane Studdock

"Matrimony was ordained, thirdly," said Jane Studdock to herself, "for the mutual society, help, and comfort that the one ought to have of the other." (Lewis, *That Hideous Strength*)

The first word of *That Hideous Strength* is *matrimony*. As Michael Ward points out, this is an entirely appropriate beginning for the most Jovial book of the trilogy, as one of Jove's primary roles is to join or bring together.[1] Jove's role is much needed, because Mark and Jane are nowhere near a state of happily wedded bliss. In fact, you could say that *That Hideous Strength* is basically a story about marriage counseling.

1 *Planet Narnia*, 49.

The sins of Mark and Jane, specifically as they pertain to their relationship with each other, drive the plot. They have been married only six months, but they are equally unhappy in their relationship. They no longer understand one another, they get easily irritated at one another, and they both keep secrets from one another. They justify keeping these "small" things from each other by making excuses—the other person wouldn't understand, they have more important things on their minds, etc. But these seemingly insignificant secrets turn out to be pivotal issues in the coming conflict. Mark and Jane are swept up into joining opposite sides with very little resistance. They have already drifted apart emotionally, and for much of the book they are also separated physically. Mark spends most of the story at Belbury in the company of people from the N.I.C.E. while Jane ends up at St. Anne's in the company of those who are working with Ransom to prevent the N.I.C.E. from succeeding in their evil plans.

There are several reasons that Mark and Jane are at odds, but the central cause is the fact that they have both rejected their respective roles and turned away from the tasks given to them in the context of marriage. What is truly fascinating is that, in this final, Jovial book, these two characters are meant to embody the primary planetary characters of the first two books—Mars and Venus. Mark's name itself points towards this connection: *Mark* is the English form of the Latin *Marcus*, derived from *Mars*. Just as Ransom himself comes to embody the Jovial character, so Mark and Jane are clearly meant to incarnate the two planetary characters that we have come to know through the first two books of the trilogy. But both Mark and Jane are failing in these roles. Mark is far from the Martial hero willing to fight, bleed, protect, and lay down his life for his bride. And Jane rejects everything Venus stands for: fertility, softness, and femininity. This rejection not only causes the crumbling of their marriage but also has near-disastrous consequences for the larger conflict.

When we first meet Mark, he could not be more un-Martial. He is a soft, yielding man whose great fear is being left out and whose great desire is to *get inside*. He wants to belong, to be included, to be part of the elite club with the special knowledge. Being "in the know" is his obsession and his most excruciating thought is that he is somehow on the "outside."[2] Mark is not brave or fearless. He is easily led and manipulated and frequently goes along just so that he doesn't appear out of step. He doesn't question or think for himself. He is, as Lewis would say, a "man without a chest."[3] We will consider this idea at length in a later chapter, but Mark's natural human emotions have been stamped out again and again, first by his abysmal education and then by his abysmal work environment. Though his natural affections have not been entirely eradicated, and they consistently try to lift their heads, Mark repeatedly forces them down by thin rationalizations or excuses. Verging on pacifistic, Mark assiduously avoids conflict and confrontation, including any that may arise in his own marriage.

On the other side, we have Jane. Jane is the opposite of Mark. She does not understand Mark's desire to always get *in*—all she has ever wanted is to get *out*, to be respected as her own person, to be left alone. She has come to despise her husband. She despises his lack of spine, his willingness to give in, his inability to stand up for himself. At the beginning of the book, Jane is the anti-Venus. She has no desire to

2 See "The Inner Ring" in *The Weight of Glory and Other Addresses*, 141.

3 C. S. Lewis, *The Abolition of Man* (New York: Macmillan, 1955), 34.

have children: something that does not seem to be important at first, but eventually becomes a crucial issue. She rejects all of the typical house-wifely duties. She does not want to make a home for her husband, and the very idea of submission and obedience is abhorrent to her. She is sterile, hard, and quickly becoming brittle and bitter. Even so, we do get glimpses here and there of a softer Jane whose dreams and hopes were crushed by pragmatism and worldliness, which eventually led her to reject the biblical vision of womanhood and exchange it for…what? Definitely not a happy marriage.

The sins and issues that plague Mark and Jane as individuals lead to the wreckage of their relationship. They represent two sides of the coin that ultimately leads to destruction. Mark is *meant* to be Martial—to be strong and fierce, leading and protecting his wife and family, standing firm in the face of opposition. Jane is *meant* to be Venus—soft and beautiful, obedient to her husband and submissive, fruitful and glorifying everything she touches. The trajectory of the book follows Mark's and Jane's transformations. And as we will see, the triumph of their restored marriage flies in the face of everything that Belbury stands for.

The way that Mark and Jane are enabled to do this is no surprise. As with everything else in the trilogy, their transformation and restoration are accomplished *by Jove.*

25

JOY & JUBILEE

The Jovial Character

[...] Soft breathes the air
Mild, and meadowy, as we mount further
Where rippled radiance rolls about us
Moved with music—measureless the waves'
Joy and jubilee.
(Lewis, "The Planets")

We've made it through the first two installments of the Ransom Trilogy. As we dive into this last book, it is helpful to back up and look at the big picture once more. Why should we care about medieval cosmology? Why should we care about Jupiter or Saturn or Venus? And the most important question of all: *What does the Gospel have to do with Jove? What does Christ have to do with Jupiter?*

The ancient gods and demons, the principalities and powers, have lost the sway they once had and we often give them no thought whatsoever. Those dark, bloody gods speaking through twisted sages in cramped caves, if we believe in them at all, have been mythologized and placed in crusty anthologies for use in 4th grade unit studies. We give them as little thought as we give unicorns or dragons and, for many, this is the same amount of thought we give to trees or grass or blue sky—that is to say, we take them for granted and have ceased to see them for what they really are. Nature itself has been stripped of magic, of power, and of any interest besides the scientific. So what about myth and legend? We live in an entirely different world than the one medieval men inhabited, right?

What *does* Christ have to do with Jupiter?

Lewis's answer would be: *everything.*

Of all the planets, one stands out above the rest, not just in the hierarchy of the planets themselves, but in the central place that it clearly holds in Lewis's imagination—Jupiter, the kingly planet. Here is Lewis's description of the Jovial influence in *The Discarded Image*:

> Jupiter, the King, produces in the earth, rather disappointingly, tin; this shining metal said different things to the imagination before the canning industry came in. The character he produces in men would now be very imperfectly expressed by the word 'jovial', and is not very easy to grasp; it is no longer, like the saturnine character, one of our archetypes. We may say it is *Kingly*; but we must think of a King at peace, enthroned, taking his leisure, serene. The Jovial character is cheerful, festive yet temperate, tranquil, magnanimous. When this planet dominates we may expect halcyon days and prosperity. In Dante, wise and just princes go to

> his sphere when they die. He is the best planet, and is called The Greater Fortune, *Fortuna Major.*[1]

In Lewis's alliterative poem "The Planets," we get another view of the Jovial character:

> [...] Soft breathes the air
> Mild, and meadowy, as we mount further
> Where rippled radiance rolls about us
> Moved with music—measureless the waves'
> Joy and jubilee. It is JOVE's orbit,
> Filled and festal, faster turning
> With arc ampler. From the Isles of Tin
> Tyrian traders, in trouble steering
> Came with his cargoes; the Cornish treasure
> That his ray ripens. Of wrath ended
> And woes mended, of winter passed
> And guilt forgiven, and good fortune
> Jove is master; and of jocund revel,
> Laughter of ladies. The lion-hearted,
> The myriad-minded, men like the gods,
> Helps and heroes, helms of nations
> Just and gentle, are Jove's children,
> Work his wonders. On his white forehead
> Calm and kingly, no care darkens
> Nor wrath wrinkles: but righteous power
> And leisure and largess their loose splendours
> Have wrapped around him–a rich mantle
> Of ease and empire [...][2]

Lewis says that the Jovial influence is "not very easy to grasp."[3] This elusive quality is one of the forces that drives

1 *Discarded Image*, 106.

2 "The Planets", 14.

3 *Discarded Image*, 106.

Lewis's focus on Jupiter throughout his professional and personal writings. We struggle to understand Jove's influence because we have completely forgotten Jove himself. We live in a casual, fast-paced society. Qualities like solemnity and nobility and regal ceremony have all but faded away. This is a loss that Lewis mourned. He honors the Jovial influence in his writings because he desires to reawaken this knowledge that has been lost.

In contrast with Jove, Lewis believes that *Saturn* is all too familiar to us. Saturn, the "lord of lead" with his "melancholy complexion," connected with "sickness and old age," is far too beloved, especially among the poets of the early twentieth century who were born out of the world wars and fed by the cynical fallout. Perhaps, if you have ever attempted to write poetry yourself, you have experienced this. It is much easier to successfully write a sad, melancholy, or contemplative poem than a joyful or celebratory one. And so Lewis designated himself as Jove's "standard-bearer," deftly weaving the Jovial character throughout his writings in order to launch a sort of Jovial renaissance.[4]

The Jovial spirit is not simply being *jolly*, a word that does share origins with *joviality*. But while jolliness is indeed jovial, it is not synonymous with it. Joviality encompasses and moves beyond jollity. It possesses a depth and richness, a well of deep calm that reaches beyond the snap and sparkle of gaiety. It includes the jolly twinkle of rippling waters in the sunlight, but there are deep blue twilight pools underneath that give joviality its special quality. "Ease and empire," "calm and kingly," Lewis says in his poem. As he mentions in *The Discarded Image*, this kingliness is the quality of a king at peace, ruling in unbridled majesty and splen-

4 *Planet Narnia*, 44.

dor, not without joy and feasting but with a solemnity that deepens joy rather than eradicating it. Is it any wonder that this quality is difficult to find in our informal, superficial, modern culture?

In the Ransom Trilogy, Jove acts as a unifying force in more than one way. Remember that Jupiter bridges and binds. And in *That Hideous Strength*, Jove is embodied in the person of Ransom. Ransom has become a Christ figure, a priest-king. We will explore Ransom's role in this book in more depth in a future chapter, but one of his primary jobs is to bring about the reunion of Mark and Jane Studdock and the restoration of their marriage. If we've paid close attention to the role that Jove plays throughout the trilogy and Lewis's other works, this won't surprise us. Bridging and binding, joining together, connecting and holding—these are all things accomplished "by Jove."

Jove as priest-king is not a new image. Jove was the planet most closely associated with Christ. The red spot on Jupiter's side looks like a wound and in combination with the kingly place given to it in the medieval cosmology, the Christological connection is easy to see. Jove is the wounded priest-king who heals and binds, cures and connects. Jove is the King of Kings. He "tempers and transforms"[5] the qualities of the other planetary rulers with his own quality. He blends and unites all of the characters of the other planets and holds their number in harmony. Near the end of *That Hideous Strength*, in a chapter titled "The Descent of the Gods," Jupiter himself descends to Thulcandra. The relationship that Jove has with the other Oyéresu as well as with the cosmos is fundamental to understanding the Jovial spirit itself.

---

5 *That Hideous Strength*, 323.

> Suddenly a greater spirit came—one whose influence tempered and almost transformed to his own quality the skill of leaping Mercury, the clearness of Mars, the subtler vibration of Venus, and even the numbing weight of Saturn.[6]

But what is the Jovial influence *like*? Let's look at Jove's arrival on the Silent Planet:

> Before the other angels a man might sink: before this he might die, but if he lived at all, he would laugh. If you had caught one breath of the air that came from him, you would have felt yourself taller than before. Though you were a cripple, your walk would have become stately: though a beggar, you would have worn your rags magnanimously. Kingship and power and festal pomp and courtesy shot from him as sparks fly from an anvil. The pealing of bells, the blowing of trumpets, the spreading out of banners, are means used on earth to make a faint symbol of his quality. It was like a long sunlit wave, creamy-crested and arched with emerald, that comes on nine feet tall, with roaring and with terror and unquenchable laughter. It was like the first beginning of music in the halls of some King so high and at some festival so solemn that a tremor akin to fear runs through young hearts when they hear it. For this was great Glund-Oyarsa, King of Kings, through whom the joy of creation principally blows across these fields of Arbol, known to men in old times as Jove and under that name, by fatal but not inexplicable misprision, confused with his Maker—so little did they dream by how

6 *That Hideous Strength*, 323.

> many degrees the stair even of created being rises above him.[7]

So what *does* Jupiter have to do with Christ? Ultimately, the Jovial spirit that Lewis was so keen to see reawakened in our own day is Christian joy, Christian love, and Christian charity. It is *salvific joy*—the God who dies, the King who serves. Who is Jove? He is Aslan, the great Lion who melts a hundred years of winter into Christmas, who submits himself to be slain by the White Witch so that a Turkish-Delight-coated, envious traitor might be saved. Joyful boldness, deep gladness, solemn gaiety—these qualities have been slowly rubbed away, like gilding off a picture frame, by the cynicism and saturnine melancholy of our culture. But Lewis, with determined cheerfulness, pulls out his bottle of liquid gold, dips in his brush, and begins to paint—without restraint, and with unabashed, excessive, Jovial generosity, covering all the corners.

---

7 Ibid., 323-324.

26

MEN WITHOUT CHESTS

The Abolition of Man

> And all the time—such is the tragi-comedy of our situation—we continue to clamour for those very qualities we are rendering impossible. You can hardly open a periodical without coming across the statement that what our civilization needs is more 'drive,' or dynamism, or self-sacrifice, or 'creativity.' In a sort of ghastly simplicity we remove the organ and demand the function. We make men without chests and expect of them virtue and enterprise. We laugh at honour and are shocked to find traitors in our midst. We castrate and bid the geldings be fruitful. (Lewis, *The Abolition of Man*)

In the Preface to *That Hideous Strength*, Lewis says that the serious point behind the book is the same one that he has "tried to make in [his] *Abolition of Man*." The best way of really understanding this point is, simply, to just read that small book. So get to the nearest library or bookstore and read it! That said, my goal here is not to just give you a list of other resources to read, so to that end, I will provide a fairly brief introduction to a primary theme that can be found in *The Abolition of Man*. Still, it is no replacement for reading Lewis's book itself.

Before we head over to *Abolition of Man*, we will take a look at one of the main threads in *That Hideous Strength*. This thread is one that has been woven throughout the entire Ransom Trilogy, and the third book simply displays the fruit that comes from seeds that were first sown in *Out of the Silent Planet*.

In the first book, we were introduced to a certain philosophy of life, science, and mankind—that of reductionism and materialism. And Weston was the embodiment of this philosophy throughout the first two books. In *That Hideous Strength*, Weston is dead, but the men he influenced (including Devine, who returns as Lord Feverstone) and his ideology are very much alive. In *Perelandra*, we saw that Weston's philosophy had shifted substantially, even before the Un-man ultimately takes over his mind and body. And now, in the final book, we see how this philosophy has morphed into something resembling demon-worship. The materialistic and reductionistic philosophy that began by exalting reason and objective science as the only path to ultimate answers has degenerated into necromancy and dark magic. The philosophy that led Weston to reject the claims of human feeling and emotion in favor of unmoving, objective science and hard facts is now driving men to reanimate decapitated heads, level small villages, and take orders from dark spirits whose natures are far beyond what their hard "science" can explain. They left objective "facts" behind a long time ago.

In *Abolition of Man*, Lewis critiques a certain system of education, a system that leads, in the end, to this same madness and to men like Mark Studdock—men without chests. Classically, the chest was seen as the seat of "emotions organized by trained habit into stable sentiment."[1] In keeping with their belief in the importance of the Triad, medievals proposed that there must be a third element in man in addition to the stomach and the head. The seat of passions, desires, and animal appetites was the *stomach* (not much stranger than saying it is in the heart—just a different internal organ). Reason, logic, and knowledge, meanwhile, were located in the head. But humans cannot be ruled by reason alone (the head) or feelings/appetites alone (the stomach). There must be that third, essential thing to govern and rule both. As Lewis says, "It may even be said that it is by this middle element that man is man: for by his intellect he is mere spirit and by his appetite mere animal."[2] But what does this third thing, the *chest*, actually mean?

As moderns, we place the seat of the emotions and appetites together in the heart, little distinguishing the two. What is the difference between passion, appetite, and desire, and organized emotion that has been trained into "stable sentiment"?[3] Because we live in an age that has given supreme importance to the gratification of desire, the idea of training emotion seems foreign. But to the medieval man, this would have been a natural thought stemming from the fact that desire and stable emotion are *two different things*. Patience, self-control, love, loyalty, obedience, temperance—true virtue and the fruits of the Spirit would be found here, in

1 *Abolition of Man*, 34.

2 Ibid.

3 Ibid.

the chest, the seat of genuine human emotion that governs and tempers both appetite and head-knowledge. "Reason and appetite must not be left facing one another across a no-man's-land. A trained sentiment of honour or chivalry must provide the 'mean' that unites them and integrates the civilised man."[4] And so, the phrase "men without chests" is striking. It refers to men who have lost touch with those basic human emotions and instincts that lead us to operate like human beings, sometimes even in spite of ourselves.

Lewis argues that the modern system of education is in the business of creating the type of man who does not have this middle element: men without chests—that is, men who are completely governed either by cold reason or gluttonous appetites and desires. Rather than emphasizing *governing* emotions, modern education seeks to *extinguish* them: "By starving the sensibility of our pupils we only make them easier prey to the propagandist when he comes. For famished nature will be avenged and a hard heart is no infallible protection against a soft head."[5] This education leaves its students utterly incapable of either deep feeling or clear thinking; it is an education that strips men of their humanity by turning them either into mechanistic robots or slaves ensnared by their animal appetites.

Mark Studdock is a perfect example of the sort of man that is produced by this kind of education, an education that seeks to stamp out every natural human emotion and then bridle that element which should govern both mind and desire. The result is that Mark has absolutely no spine. He is led along by the loudest voice or the person with the most charismatic personality. He is utterly fearful of being

4 *The Discarded Image*, 58.

5 *Abolition of Man*, 24.

cast out, of being counted as part of the "uneducated" and "unenlightened" working class. Yet there is a deeper, more sinister problem that arises from removing the governing element from the chest of a man: Mark will, in the end, be governed entirely by either cold logic or animalistic appetite.

The people at Belbury who have infected Mark with this kind of education are the epitome of what this looks like. They start out by promoting pure reason, hard science, and a cold, sterile reality free from material or physical being, ideas driven solely by the *head*. But what they end up with is dark magic, necromancy, consorting with evil spirits, and taking orders from devils without question. In one way, they are getting what they wanted: they wanted a bodiless existence, a sterile world with no messy physicality or solid materiality. But those who make gods out of good, created things find, at last, that they lose both God and that very good which they idolized. Wither, the deputy director of the N.I.C.E., ends up doing just what his name implies: withering away until he's almost more ghost than man. He's been given what he thought he wanted, and the result is horrifying. And the head of the executed man that the N.I.C.E. reanimates in order to communicate with the dark spirits is, quite literally, a man without a chest.

The N.I.C.E. has sold itself to a philosophy that rejects the way God created the world. They seek to build a tower to reach the throne of God himself, to take the powers of creation, to make for themselves a "new humanity." And like the first tower of Babel, the people of Belbury end up scattered and undone by the very *real*, very physical and bodily creation they have rejected.

But as Lewis argues in *The Abolition of Man*, the seeds of this insanity are sown early, in the kind of modern education that was taking root in his own day. As we've already seen,

Mark Studdock is the embodiment of this type of education. He is faced by temptations that he has been left utterly unequipped to withstand. But we also get to witness Mark's salvation. The enemy has not *entirely* stripped him of his humanity, for he yet has a chest. It is Mark's chest, that critical third element, that resists both his reason and his raw animal instincts of self-preservation, and causes him to say: "It's all bloody nonsense, and I'm damned if I do any such thing."[6]

At this crucial moment, this moment of Mark being truly *human*, Lewis doesn't use the words "bloody" and "damned" flippantly. This is nonsense that really is bloody —it leads to slaughter and death and destruction. And Mark really will be damned if he goes along with it. At the time, he doesn't understand where his resistance comes from. He doesn't have a logical syllogism that leads him to conclude he must not do this thing, nor does he follow his base animal appetites and desires for survival, or he would have given in long before now. It is the center, the chest, that enables a man to stand firm when everything else in him screams at him to just give in or give up. This is the sort of person that the devil fears, the sort of hero that topples strongholds. In another of Lewis's fictional works, *The Screwtape Letters*, the devil Screwtape warns his nephew Wormwood about this sort of person: "Our cause is never more in danger than when a human, no longer desiring, but still intending, to do [God's] will, looks round upon a universe from which every trace of Him seems to have vanished, and asks why he has been forsaken, and still obeys."[7]

The N.I.C.E.'s men-without-chests philosophy is also internally incoherent. If the universe is raw matter, if it is

---

6 *That Hideous Strength*, 334.

7 C. S. Lewis, *The Screwtape Letters* (New York: Macmillan, 1961), 39.

just atoms bouncing around and reacting with each other, then we have no reason to trust the chemicals in our brains that are *telling* us that the universe is just a bunch of particles of matter and that people are merely bags of protoplasm. As Lewis says elsewhere, "If the universe has no meaning, we should never have found out that it has no meaning".[8] Likewise, if the "greatest good" that Weston argues for is, in fact, the preservation of the species *simply* for the sake of the preservation of the species, then we cannot get any morality or any rules for human behavior from these brute facts. We cannot derive *ought* from *is*. We cannot derive moral laws simply by describing *the way things are*.

Ironically, those who hold to the materialist worldview are often some of the biggest supporters of charitable humanitarian projects. The N.I.C.E. claims to care about humanity, about the environment, about providing jobs for workers, all while working against the way God created the world. But the truth is that, while men can deny the reality of the universe, curse the God of all creation, shake their fists at Him in rebellion, and grasp at the power to "create themselves" or form a new humanity, they cannot escape His world. They are still men, and men cannot actually function as pure matter or pure spirit. Belbury embodies this pendulum swing from materialistic reductionism to a sort of twisted spiritualism, both of which are driven at root by the desire to "be as gods."

Education is primarily concerned with shaping people. It is about creating a certain kind of man or woman. We cannot relay raw facts *without* shaping the worldview of the student, without having an effect on the kind of person that they are and that they will become. Lewis saw this clearly,

---

8 C. S. Lewis, *Mere Christianity* (New York: Macmillan, 1943), 46.

and this is why he objects so strongly to the materialistic, evolutionary education springing up in post-war England. He saw the kind of man it was seeking to create—a man like Mark Studdock, a man without a chest. But he also demonstrates that this sort of education cannot ultimately succeed, because although they try to erase His image, they cannot escape His world.

> And they said, "Come, let us build ourselves a city, and a tower whose top is in the heavens; let us make a name for ourselves, lest we be scattered abroad over the face of the whole earth." But the LORD came down to see the city and the tower which the sons of men had built [...] So the LORD scattered them abroad from there over the face of all the earth, and they ceased building the city (Genesis 11:4-5, 8).

27

AS SPARKS FLY FROM AN ANVIL

Ransom as Jovial Priest-King

> On a sofa before her, with one foot bandaged as if he had a wound, lay what appeared to be a boy, twenty years old. On one of the long window sills a tame jackdaw was walking up and down. The light of the fire with its weak reflection, and the light of the sun with its stronger reflection, contended on the ceiling. But all the light in the room seemed to run towards the gold hair and the gold beard of the wounded man. (Lewis, *That Hideous Strength*)

Ransom has many names: Mr. Fisher-King, the Director, the Pendragon, friend of the *eldila*. Names are important. They are tightly woven with identity. And all of Ransom's names point, in one way or the other, to Jove and to the roles that Jove fulfills. In this chapter, we will look at two of those roles in particular.

In *Planet Narnia*, Ward comments on the lack of attention paid to the "astrological symbolism" in Lewis's work. Jupiter, as we've discussed, is of particular importance in Lewis's writings. Not only is Jupiter the king of the heavens, but the Jovial influence and spirit is one that Lewis sees as "evading us," more so than the other planetary characters. Ward remarks on Jove's influence on the Ransom Trilogy:

> [...] since Jupiter's wisdom is the dominant power in the heavens we should expect to find a considerable focus on Jovial qualities in these inter-planetary adventures. And we do find that. Although Ransom never visits the planet Jupiter, something more important happens: over the course of the trilogy he becomes Jovial himself.[1]

What does it mean that Ransom "becomes Jovial himself"? And how does this Jovial transformation bring both his character and the entire trilogy full circle?

At the end of *Perelandra*, the Oyarsa of Malacandra identifies Ransom in two ways: first *as a man* and then *as an individual*:

> "Look on him, beloved, and love him," said the first. "He is indeed but breathing dust and a careless touch would unmake him. And in his best thoughts there are such things mingled as, if we thought them, our light would perish. But he is in the body of Maleldil and his sins are forgiven."[2]

In this quote, the Oyarsa is introducing Ransom as a member of the human race. What does it mean that Ransom

1 *Planet Narnia*, 47.

2 *Perelandra*, 167.

is a *man*? Ransom, as a man, is fragile. Ransom, as a man, is broken. Ransom, as a man, is in the body of Maleldil. And therefore Ransom, as a man, is *forgiven*. Mortal men, the inhabitants of the Silent Planet, ruled by the Bent One, sequestered under the Moon, cut off from the realm of Deep Heaven, are in the body of Maleldil. For He has dared terrible things. And so Ransom, as a mortal man, is the only one who can fulfill the role that Maleldil has for him.

As an *individual*, we have already discussed how Ransom in particular has been called and prepared for every step of this journey. First, he was kidnapped by Devine and Weston, thereby giving him an opportunity to learn Old Solar. This uniquely prepared him for the next, greater task in which he became a Martial prophet on Perelandra. After passing through Purgatory, he emerged transformed even further. And it is this transformation that enables him to fulfill his final role.

Ward notes that the kingly and sacerdotal roles that Ransom plays in the third book are distinctly *Jovial*. Ransom has become a Priest-King. This is the natural end of a journey that began with a Pilgrim in a dark wood who was taken to Malacandra where he partook of the Martial spirit, which then enabled him to take on the further mission of Prophet on Perelandra. Ransom has been slowly but surely becoming a Christ-figure: subtly in the first book and ever more plainly throughout the trilogy.

Let's consider Ransom as king. When Jane first meets him she is reminded of King Arthur and Solomon, two of the mightiest kings of old. Note the presence of *royalty* in this scene:

> Pain came and went in his face: sudden jabs of sickening and burning pain. But as lightning goes through the darkness and the darkness closes up

> again and shows no trace, so the tranquility of his countenance swallowed up each shock of torture. How could she have thought him young? Or old either? It came over her, with a sensation of quick fear, that this face was of no age at all. She had (or so she had believed) disliked bearded faces except for old men with white hair. But that was because she had long since forgotten the imagined Arthur of her childhood—and the imagined Solomon—for the first time in many years the bright solar blend of king and lover and magician which hangs about that name stole back upon her mind. For the first time in all those years she tasted the word King itself with all linked associations of battle, marriage, priesthood, mercy, and power.[3]

Ransom has seemingly had his youth restored to him, though he still suffers greatly from the wound in his heel. He longs to return to Perelandra, to the "House of Kings," which is the resting place of Melchisedec and Arthur himself, another tie that strengthens Ransom's kingly and Jovial identity. Ward highlights this connection:

> Ransom reminds Merlin that 'Melchisedec is he in whose hall the steep-stoned ring sparkles on the forefinger of the Pendragon.' Ransom is the current Pendragon and Melchisedec is a Hebrew name meaning 'My king is Jupiter.' Melchisedec appears in the Book of Genesis as a priest-king and Lewis knew that, as such, he 'resembles (in his peculiar way he is the only Old Testament character who resembles) Christ Himself,' a resemblance made explicit by the author of the letter to the Hebrews (Heb. 5:5-10). Melchisedec, like Christ,

3 *That Hideous Strength*, 140.

> is associated with bread and wine (Gen. 14:18-20; Luke 22:14-20), and Ransom now survives on that very diet.[4]

Now let's explore Ransom as priest. After his experiences on Perelandra, he becomes a *bridge* between Deep Heaven and the Silent Planet. Priests act as intercessors between God and man. Ransom's role in *That Hideous Strength* drives this home. Remember that the first word of the book is *matrimony*, and that marriage is a central theme in the story. We've already encountered the protagonists, Mark and Jane Studdock, whose marriage is far from ideal. It is Ransom who, just like Christ, our true High Priest, *restores* and *reunites* the Studdocks' relationship. Under Ransom's Jovial influence, Mark and Jane become, respectively, embodiments of Mars and Venus. For this is a crucial part of Ransom's Jovial task: Jove *unites* and Jove also tempers the qualities of the other planets. It is his kingly right to perform marriages, to tie things together, to unite birds and beasts and fairies and men, to bridge worlds and connect heaven and Earth. As Ward says, one of Jupiter's main functions in the third story is to draw "lineages together by his sovereign power" and marry them "by his sacerdotal authority."[5]

This is a "complex web of Jovial-priestly-kingly-Christological imagery,"[6] and to untangle it completely would be to unravel it. The imagery is all linked together—it is what gives us the atmosphere, the *donegality* of the final book. Joining, binding, uniting, breaking down barriers, restoration, salvation, mending what was once broken—these are all things

4 *Planet Narnia*, 50.

5 Ibid., 49.

6 Ibid.

that Ransom does, that Jove does, and that, ultimately, Christ does. Ransom is so tightly joined to Jupiter that he cannot be separated from him. He is a human embodiment of the celestial figure. In the end, he re-unites Mark and Jane in a priestly and kingly act. He bridges Earth and Deep Heaven in an intercessory role. But Ransom is also the wounded healer who returns at last to Perelandra for his own healing:

> "I suppose you *got* to go, Sir?" said Ivy.
>
> "My dear," said he, "what else is there to do? I have not grown a day or an hour older since I came back from Perelandra. There is no natural death to look forward to. The wound will only be healed in the world where it was got."[7]

But before Ransom leaves the Silent Planet, Venus lingers. She is waiting to take him back with her, but she is also at work on Thulcandra. We see Venus's influence as Ransom bestows this kingly and priestly blessing upon Jane: "Go in obedience and you will find love. You will have no more dreams. Have children instead. *Urendi Maleldil.*"[8]

Ransom, in his role as a priest-king, has brought Paradise to the Silent Planet. The boundaries have been broken, and yet the structure has remained. Earth is *still* at the bottom of the Heavens. It has always been that way. And yet mankind is in truth the chief concern of Deep Heaven. Ransom, though a mere man, is yet made in the image of God, as are all of this fallen race. And as a man, he is able to be both priest and king, chasing away darkness as the rising of the Sun chases the horrors of night.

---

7 *That Hideous Strength*, 366.

8 Ibid., 378.

28

HARD, BRIGHT SPLENDOUR

Merlin and Ransom the Elf-Friend

> "In the sphere of Venus I learned war," said Ransom. "In this age Lurga shall descend. I am the Pendragon." (Lewis, *That Hideous Strength*)

One of the conundrums that all readers of the Ransom Trilogy must wrestle with sooner or later is this: what in the world is Merlin doing in *That Hideous Strength*? Part of this confusion comes from putting the book in the wrong category to begin with. If we approach it as a science fiction work in the same vein as either H. G. Wells or Isaac Asimov, two vastly different sci-fi writers, then we will miss out on what Lewis was trying to accomplish. But the Ransom Trilogy is far more complex and doesn't fit neatly into any existing category, unless a category exists for interplanetary adventures that implement a medieval conception of the cosmos. Lewis has far more in common with Dante, Milton, Spenser, and Chaucer than with either Wells or Asimov.

With this in mind, Merlin's presence is far less mystifying. His appearance in a book inspired by medieval cosmology is much less strange and unexpected than Merlin showing up in a science fiction space-travel story. The latter is all UFOs, extraterrestrials, science experiments, and jumping into hyperspace—a world of *Star Trek* and *Star Wars*. The former, in contrast, makes us think of ancient stargazers and mystics, monks hunched over illuminated manuscripts, star charts, and Latin texts, a world in which Merlin would not be out of place at all.

But the question remains: *why*? A straightforward answer, one which Lewis himself would likely approve of, is why not? Merlin is already a perplexing character historically, which is one of the reasons Lewis says he included him: "But the blessing about Merlin (for you and me) is that 'very little is known'—so we have a free hand!"[1] In *That Hideous Strength*, Lewis offers his own addition to the entire mythos surrounding this figure.

But I promise a better answer than that. I believe there is another possible answer that fits with the Medieval Model that Lewis so loved. In order to understand the role that Merlin plays in *That Hideous Strength*, we need to first understand where he fits into the Medieval Model of the cosmos, and in case you were wondering—he *does* fit into the Medieval Model. Recall the *Longaevi*, a term we discussed at length in a previous chapter when talking about the principles of the Triad and Plenitude. As a brief review, the medieval principle of the Triad is an organizational concept that splits things into three. As it is implemented in the model of the

---

1 Lewis to I.O. Evans, Oxford, September 26, 1945 in *Collected Letters*, 2:673.

cosmos, the material realm is divided into three basic components: earth, air, and aether. Additionally, the Principle of Plenitude proposes that every area of the cosmos must be filled—each must be put to "good use." There is no area in which some type of being does *not* exist. The medievals hated waste, and so the *Longaevi* are those creatures that dwell in the space between the earth and aether—"airish beasts," according to Chaucer.[2]

In his chapter on the *Longaevi*, Lewis classifies Merlin as *part-Fairy*. More than this, Merlin is classified as *High Fairy*: "Merlin—only Half human by blood and never shown practising magic *as an art*—almost belongs to [the High Fairy] order."[3] Now, it is true that in *That Hideous Strength*, Merlin explicitly denies that his father was "one of the Airish Men."[4] That said, his character is impossible to separate from all the lore, myth, and legend that hangs about the name *Merlin Ambrosius*.

And not only does this information from *The Discarded Image* tell us something about the character of Merlin, but it also sheds light on Ransom's relationship to him. Merlin, man or part-man, is still one of those "in-between" folk, both in his actual nature and in the time period in which he lived. Dimble attempts to explain this in-between nature of Merlin and creatures like him in this conversation with his wife, Mother Dimble:

> "[...]But about Merlin. What it comes to, as far as I can make out, is this. There were still possibilities for a man of that age which there aren't for a man of ours. The Earth itself was more like an animal

2 Chaucer, *The House of Fame*, line 932.

3 *Discarded Image*, 130.

4 *That Hideous Strength*, 289.

> in those days. And mental processes were much more like physical actions. And there were—well, Neutrals, knocking about."
>
> "Neutrals?"
>
> "I don't mean, of course, that anything can be a *real* neutral. A conscious being is either obeying God or disobeying Him. But there might be things neutral in relation to us."
>
> "You mean eldils—angels?"
>
> "Well, the word *angel* rather begs the question. Even the Oyéresu aren't exactly angels in the same sense as our guardian angels are. Technically they are Intelligences. The point is that while it may be true at the end of the world to describe every eldil either as an angel or a devil, and may even be true now, it was much less true in Merlin's time. There used to be things on this Earth pursuing their own business, so to speak. They weren't ministering spirits sent to help fallen humanity; but neither were they enemies preying upon us. Even in St. Paul one gets glimpses of a population that won't exactly fit into our two columns of angels and devils. And if you go back further...all the gods, elves, dwarfs, water-people, *fate*, *longaevi*. You and I know too much to think they are just illusions."[5]

Here is another reason that Merlin, considered correctly, *must* be in *That Hideous Strength*, and that reason comes down to Ransom and his role in this final book. At the end of *Perelandra*, the Oyarsa of Malacandra introduces Ransom to the Oyarsa of Perelandra, saying: "His very name in his own tongue is Elwin, the friend of the eldila."[6] Lewis's translation of *Elwin* as *friend of the eldila* is intriguing. The name

---

5 *That Hideous Strength*, 281-282.

6 *Perelandra*, 167.

Elwin literally means elf-friend (from Anglo-Saxon *aelf-wine*). As we have already seen, Lewis was as fascinated by language as any philologist, so it is far too simplistic to say that he was merely playing with the phonetic similarity between *elf* and *eldil.* Is there perhaps a *semantic* similarity? I would say there is, and that this connection is embodied in Ransom's character as well as his name. He is both a friend to the residents of Deep Heaven and a friend to the residents of air, the marginal *Longaevi*, with whom Merlin is connected.

How do *eldila*, elves, Merlin, Ransom, and Jove all connect? There are a couple more puzzle pieces to fit into our picture. One such piece has to do with the identity of the *eldila* themselves. Lewis indicates throughout the trilogy that the Oyéresu and the *eldila* exist in separate categories. The Oyéresu are angelic beings: rulers under Maleldil of the planetary realms. But the *eldila* appear to be in a different category altogether, subservient to the Oyéresu. In the opening chapter of *Perelandra*, we saw Lewis the character run into some of these spirits on Thulcandra who are determined to keep him from getting to Ransom's cottage. Remember, it is only "by Jove" that he is able to reach the house at all.[7] The *eldila*, at least the sublunar ones, seem to fall within the category of the *Longaevi*—not immortal, though possessing longer lives than men. Lewis says that the *Longaevi* could be called "fairies," but he was hesitant to use that term

7 Remember that Lewis always uses the exclamation "By Jove" with great significance. Recall the scene at the beginning of *Perelandra*, when Ransom meets Lewis: "By Jove, I'm glad to see you," said Ransom, advancing and shaking hands with me… "I say—you're *all right*, aren't you? You got through the barrage without any damage?" (*Perelandra*, 19). Lewis makes it to Ransom's cottage "by Jove." This connects the end of the first book to the second—for at the end of *Out of the Silent Planet* it is noted that "somebody or something of great importance is connected with Jupiter" (*Out of the Silent Planet*, 158). This role of "connecting" is one of Jove's primary functions as a kingly planet.

because of how tarnished it has been by "pantomime and bad children's books with worse illustrations."[8] He goes on to discuss what our ancestors historically meant by *fairy*. We use the terms *fairies* and *elves* almost synonymously, but they are not identical (though Lewis will often use the term *Faery Elves*, following in Milton's footsteps).

So how does this connect to Ransom? The answer, coming full circle, is Merlin.

Ransom is Elwin—the "friend of the eldila"—but he is also Elwin "Elf-Friend." He is, as we discover later on, the Pendragon, the protector of Logres the true Britain. And his name, Elwin, already points toward this relationship, because the Pendragon has a unique relationship with Merlin, who is himself a "Faery Elf."

And to tie Jupiter into the role of "Elf-Friend" as well, the relationship between Merlin and the Pendragon is, at root, a Jovial one. In *That Hideous Strength*, in the chapter titled "The Descent of the Gods," Glund-Oyarsa, Jupiter himself, descends to Thulcandra. We've already explored the relationship that Jove has with the other Oyéresu as well as with the cosmos, tempering the qualities of the other planetary rulers with his own quality. He is the King of Kings, the *bridge* that connects all of the planetary characters, linking and holding together all of their virtues. In the first chapter of *Perelandra*, Lewis is frightened into thinking that Ransom is being duped into becoming an "unwitting bridge"[9] that allows evil beings into the Earth, but as we explored earlier, while Ransom is indeed becoming a bridge, he is far from unwitting, and the role of bridge is one that allows for the

---

8 *Discarded Image*, 123.

9 *Perelandra*, 12.

salvation of Thulcandra from the forces of darkness rather than its damnation.

In Ransom's relationship to Merlin, we see this role of bridge taken even farther. The relationship is that of a King over a vassal, of the Pendragon over the mage. Ransom has breathed in the air of Mars itself, put it to practice in the sphere of Venus on which he learned the art of war, and has come back to Earth in a desperate hour. His is the lordship of one who has spoken with beings greater and more terrible than Merlin can imagine and has been named by them "friend of the eldila," thus cementing his role as a bridge between worlds, between the world of Deep Heaven, the angelic realm, and the realm of earth and terrestrial inhabitants, including those who dwell in between—the *Longaevi*, the Fairies, the Merlins.

The bridge that Ransom has become is built by the Jovial spirit, a spirit that has been truly leading Ransom all along—through Malacandra and Perelandra and now, at last, to Thulcandra. On the Silent Planet, Ransom not only becomes the image of Jove himself, but, just like every Jovial character, he points to the one even greater than Jove: our Lord Jesus Christ.

29

COMING TO A POINT

St. Anne's and Belbury

"Good is always getting better and bad is always getting worse: the possibilities of even apparent neutrality are always diminishing." (Lewis, *That Hideous Strength*)

Think back to the sweet-smelling islands of Perelandra, where late at night Weston's grotesque visage sits opposite the beauty of the Green Lady, and Ransom is horrified at the juxtaposition. The Un-man is launching all of his arguments, all of his most powerful slings and arrows, seeking to batter down the fortress that is Tinidril's obedience. One of these tactics, as we saw in an earlier chapter, is the attempt to iron out the antithesis between good and evil. The Un-man seeks to eliminate all division and distinction, to blend and smooth until all edges have been removed and black and white have become the mottled gray of an eternal twilight. Of course, the Un-man knows this is impossible, but he doesn't care. He is simply using whatever tool is on hand to accomplish his ends. Satan is the father of lies *because* he knows the truth.

In *That Hideous Strength*, this theme of conflict and antithesis comes to a head. There is, of course, the larger, over-arching conflict between the kingdom of God and the kingdom of darkness, but we see this conflict in microcosm in the two communities of St. Anne's and Belbury. These two communities are constantly being compared, even in the structure of the novel itself. Lewis continually jumps back and forth between Mark's perspective and Jane's. Rather than being distracting, this structure forces constant comparison between Mark and Jane, between Belbury and St. Anne's. They are polar opposites in crucial ways: in their ideologies, in their treatment of their members, in their goals, and in whom they serve.

On one level, we can view the battle between Belbury and St. Anne's as a battle between Gnostics and incarnationalists. A Gnostic prizes knowledge above all else and generally rejects the material realm as the source of evil. Similar to Platonists, Gnostics see physicality as something to be *escaped* rather than embraced. Matter, by its very nature, is not something praiseworthy.

We see Gnosticism very clearly in the minds of the people at Belbury. They are obsessed with sterilization. They don't like *stuff*, especially living stuff. They want a sanitized, static, de-particularized world, a world devoid of anything homey or real, anything with a smell. This is seen most clearly in their destruction of the village of Cure Hardy. Mark rather likes the little town, but his companion only sees it as dirty and noisy and can't wait for the N.I.C.E. to come in and clean it up. They want metal trees and plastic flowers. They want to get rid of fruitfulness or any kind of organic messiness. Cold, frigid, and uninviting, the world that they want to create is a wholesale rejection of the world that God made and pronounced "very good."

Whereas they initially took up this cause in the name of "science" and "progress," the N.I.C.E has now descended into madness, taking orders from a reanimated head powered by dark spirits. The philosophy that began with Weston as materialistic reductionism has now been completely turned on its head. At first, all that existed was matter. The only real things were the physical. But now, escape from that matter and ascendance into a purely "spiritual" realm is all they care about—and it destroys them.

We should not be surprised by this complete switchover from "science" and "progress" to an escape from matter. The Un-Man doesn't care about the truth—only about gaining his desired ends. An ideology that reduces all reality to physical matter often goes hand-in-hand with instrumentalism. If what matters most is being able to accomplish your goals, then you will latch on to whatever serves that purpose best, and what works at one moment may not work the next. In one age it is *rejecting* all spiritual realities and in another it might be embracing *only* spiritual realities. But what is it that links these seemingly opposite views? What does *opposite* even mean, the Un-Man would ask. They are really the same thing. Matter or no matter, spirit or no spirit, these views both reject an essential part of reality. They reject the way God made the world to be.

The incarnationalists, by contrast, hold to the truth while rejecting both of these vain philosophies. By virtue of rejecting both, they attempt to stay in the middle of the road, avoiding the ditch on either side: the one ditch we just discussed (Gnosticism and rejection of materiality) and the other ditch which is materialistic hedonism. Hedonism is the philosophy that considers pleasure and the avoidance of suffering to be the highest good. Materialistic hedonism would say that matter is ultimately all that exists. And if matter is all there is, hedonism takes the enjoyment that we can have of the physical universe and treats it as the *ultimate* good instead of a good to be used to glorify the God who made it. "Eat, drink, and be merry, for tomorrow we die," says the hedonist (Ecclesiastes 8:15, Isaiah 22:13). If matter is the beginning and the end, if all we are is bags of enzymes bouncing around, then we might as well just enjoy ourselves before our enzymes leak out and we return to the primordial goo from which we came.

Being an incarnationalist does not mean treating matter as a god. We must not take any part of creation and treat it as the ultimate thing to be prized. Idolatry is found on both sides of the road: placing either the spiritual or the material realm on a pedestal. Both philosophies misunderstand the nature of creation and end up mistreating both body and spirit. When we idolize any part of creation, we not only fail to worship the true God, we also abuse the good creation that has been given to us. Idolatry doesn't just blaspheme God, but it robs the object of idolatry of the appropriate love and admiration it deserves. Hence, those who worship wealth mistreat wealth itself. By loving a husband or wife or son or daughter beyond all else, we actually despise them. It is only in loving God rightly that we can love our neighbor rightly. It is only by praising and worshiping the Lord of all Creation that we can treat that creation with the stewardship we are commanded.

Incarnationalists recognize that matter can be used in wicked ways, that it can be corrupted and twisted to sinful ends. However, this is no refutation of our calling to use it, enjoy it, and take dominion over it. God created the physical world and called it good. Likewise, we are created to be physical, embodied beings. We are called to enjoy and use God's good creation to His glory. We can no more escape this reality than we can defy the law of gravity. What is even more astounding is that the second Creation does not do away with this characteristic of materiality, but rather *enhances* it. In the coming of Christ, in His death, resurrection, and ascension, we were shown the first fruits of the new world that God is in the process of creating. Far from an ethereal new world full of airy spirits and ghostly harpists, this world is *solid*. A solid that can walk through walls.

The people of Belbury have no category for simple, everyday, physical pleasures. Wither is more a ghost than man, having shed his physicality long ago. In comparison with these walking horrors, when he is deep inside the darkness of Belbury, Mark remembers simple joys almost as if they were a fairy tale:

> Something else—something he vaguely called the "Normal"—apparently existed. He had never thought about it before. But there it was—solid, massive, with a shape of its own, almost like something you could touch, or eat, or fall in love with. It was all mixed up with Jane and fried eggs and soap and sunlight and the rooks cawing at Cure Hardy and the thought that, somewhere outside, daylight was going on at that moment.[1]

We will consider Mark's conversion in more detail later, but here we can see that there is too much of the *incarnational*

1 *That Hideous Strength*, 296-297.

in him for Belbury's efforts to be entirely successful. Mark yet has too much proper love for normal, created things.

In contrast to Belbury and its regimented establishment, the company at St. Anne's is a motley bunch, an unexpected group of men, women, and a bear. They are a humble, lowly fellowship that God uses to do great things and overthrow the enemy. They are joyful, vivacious, and productive, embracing the world in all of its creatureliness. They are homely and familiar. These qualities are the force that drives Jane to the doorstep of St. Anne's. After the horrors of her interrogation and torture under Fairy Hardcastle, waking up in the sunlight to a warm breakfast and a quiet day of reading favorite childhood books seems to Jane like another world—as indeed it is. And in the end, after Belbury has been defeated, it is this world that wins out: a world where physicality is not rejected out of hand, but ordered and kept in its proper place. The conclusion of the book shows a rambunctious celebration of fertility and earthiness and fruitfulness. After Belbury has been overthrown, Venus lingers on Thulcandra. Birds and beasts and men are all paired off. Mark and Jane, having each taken on their rightful roles, are reunited. It is the final victory, a glorification of everything that Belbury was seeking to destroy.

The company at St. Anne's is a group of true human beings. They are not enslaved to any magic or science. They are not earthbound, only believing in pure physicality and rejecting anything spiritual. They are free men and women who are fighting a spiritual battle in order that they may drink tea and read books, plant crops and make babies, teach children and write novels. They have been drawn into this fight because they want to protect the right to live quiet, simple lives that reflect the way God created the world. Matter and spirit both. Earth and heaven. A simple pedestrian on a walking holiday, and mysteries that have angels falling prostrate in adoration and fear.

The primary problem with both Gnosticism and materialism is that they are far too narrow minded, far too small to contain everything that exists. In the end, Christ is the only answer. In Him, everything moves and lives and has its being. The eternal, almighty God took on human flesh and lived at a particular time and in a particular place on this earthly globe of ours. And He conquered principalities and powers by dying a criminal's death and rising again on the third day. This is why a group of old men and women, spinsters and animals, can take down a cruel organization. This is why an estranged, bitter couple can become a picture of a new Adam and Eve. This is why Ransom can change from a frightened, overwhelmed scholar to a shining picture of Jove himself.

> "But God hath chosen the foolish things of the world to confound the wise; and God hath chosen the weak things of the world to confound the things which are mighty" (1 Cor. 1:27, KJV).

30

A WORLD UNMADE

Biblical Imagery

> [...] she had long since forgotten the imagined Arthur of her childhood—and the imagined Solomon too. Solomon—for the first time in many years the bright solar blend of king and lover and magician which hangs about that name stole back upon her mind. For the first time in all those years she tasted the word King itself with all linked associations of battle, marriage, priesthood, mercy, and power. (Lewis, *That Hideous Strength*)

No discussion of *That Hideous Strength* would be complete without talking about the biblical imagery that floods the text. We've already explored the Christological imagery connected with Ransom, but here we will take a look at a few additional important biblical references and allusions.

Allusions are what make great literature like a cave. Even if the only tool we have to explore it is a dollar-store flashlight, even if we can only see a few feet ahead at a time, we can still hear the echoes and know that there is more to see, more to find. An author's use of simple quotation or reference is enough to carve out an entirely new chain of tunnels. And rereading through the years only rewards those explorers who decide to stock up with more head-lamps this time around.

RANSOM & SOLOMON

When Jane meets Ransom, he appears to her as Solomon in all his glory. Solomon is the quintessential example of a Solar king, that is, a king under the influence of Sol (the Sun): wiser than any, magnanimous and generous, glorious in splendor. By describing Ransom in Solomonic terms, Lewis draws on a deep well of allusion, inference, and connections that have been set up for thousands of years. He describes the feeling that Ransom's appearance inspires, but all he really has to do is say *Solomon* and half his work is done. We can taste the word along with Jane. Lewis takes an ancient tapestry and simply rolls it out for us, allowing us to bask in the rich colors and shapes that we have perhaps, like Jane, forgotten about.

Like Solomon, Ransom has been granted wisdom and knowledge beyond that of other mortal men. Through no particular merit of his own, he has been singled out and *chosen*. However, his natural curiosity and thirst for knowledge were key components in how quickly he learned to speak Old Solar. His fascination with the idea of there being an entirely new, non-terrestrial language caught his imagination even while he was still terrified of being in "space." The following experiences on both Malacandra and Perelandra give Ransom a uniquely deep knowledge of both the language of Old Solar as well as the workings of the cosmos. Merlin himself is struck dumb by the knowledge that Ransom possesses:

> "Well answered," said [Merlin]. "In my college it was thought that only two men in the world knew this. But as for my third question, no man knew the answer but myself. Who shall be the Pendragon in the time when Saturn descends from his sphere? In what world did he learn war?"
>
> "In the sphere of Venus I learned war," said Ransom. "In this age Lurga shall descend. I am the Pendragon."
>
> When he had said this, he took a step backwards for the big man had begun to move and there was a new look in his eyes [...] Slowly, ponderously, yet not awkwardly, as though a mountain sank like a wave, he sank on one knee; and still his face was almost on a level with the Director's.[1]

MERLIN & SAMSON

> Then Samson said, "Let me die with the Philistines!" And he pushed with all his might, and the temple fell on the lords and all the people who were in it. So the dead that he killed at his death were more than he had killed in his life (Judges 16:30).

1 *That Hideous Strength*, 271.

Samson is a character that leaps off the page. He is large in both personality and physical stature; he is mighty, rash, and impetuous. He is far from perfect, yet he is God's man in an age where that meant doing mighty and violent deeds. The entirety of his imperfect life and triumphant death are dedicated to delivering Israel from the Philistines.

Similarly, Merlin is a mighty but far from perfect tool in God's hand, a tool to destroy his enemies. Like Samson, he is neither a pure vessel nor completely sinless.[2] Merlin had lived at a time when the lines between light and dark magic were not so clear. In his own time, he had already dabbled with dark powers—powers that were questionable even then, lurking in the shadows that hovered between pagan priest and newly-Christian Briton.

Merlin's role is to destroy the "Philistines" at Belbury, and like Samson, he perishes in the task:

> "It looked as if [Merlin] was on fire…I don't mean burning, you know, but light—all sorts of lights in the most curious colours shooting out of him and running up and down him. That was the last thing I saw: Merlin standing there like a kind of *pillar* and all those dreadful things happening all around him. And you could see in his face that he was a man used up to the last drop, if you know what I mean—that he'd fall to pieces the moment the powers let him go."[3]

Like Samson of old, Merlin is used up to the dregs in the destruction of the enemies of God. We could say Samson is redeemed or purified by his own faithful death, and likewise

---

2 *That Hideous Strength*, 288.

3 Ibid., 359-360, emphasis mine.

Merlin is saved by his. As Ransom informs him: "One of the purposes of your reawakening was that your own soul should be saved."[4]

And in case we were left with any doubt as to Merlin's Samson role, Lewis quotes John Milton's *Samson Agonistes* to refer to Merlin:

> Among them he a spirit of frenzy sent,
> Who hurt their minds,
> And urged them on with mad desire
> To call in haste for their destroyer.[5]

BELBURY & BABEL

Lewis introduces the parallel between Belbury and the tower of Babel in the very title of the book: *That Hideous Strength.* This phrase comes from Sir David Lyndsay's *Ane Dialog* where he describes the Tower of Babel, from which Lewis quotes on the title page:

> The shadow of that hyddeous strength
> sax myle and more it is of length.

With this quote, Lewis clearly establishes the connection between Belbury and the Old Testament story of Babel, a recurring image throughout the book.

At Babel, men attempt to unite in one body (against God's order to multiply and *fill* the Earth) in order to build a tower to the heavens. The people at Belbury attempt a

4 Ibid., 286.

5 Milton, *Samson Agonistes*, lines 1675-1678.

similar disobedience but with a different tactic. They are trying to *remake humanity*, to reject the physical existence that God has given mankind and move into a purely spiritual, bodiless existence, a realm of pure reason and thought. Succumbing to the same sin that has beset mankind since Adam, they are trying to be as God. But at Belbury, Lewis revises the judgment to be more commensurate to the tactic that Belbury employs.

At Babel, God confuses the languages of men, though the languages were still *intelligible* languages. Furthermore, we can assume that each man did not have each his own language, but rather that various individuals were given the same language, which led to the formation of tribes. At Belbury, in contrast, the language is entirely and completely garbled. It ceases to be language at all. It is turned into utter nonsense. These men and women have rejected humanity on God's terms, trying to rebuild it on their own, and so this key part of their humanity (language) is taken from them. Merlin cries out: "*Qui Verbum Dei contempserunt, eis auferetur etiam verbum hominis*" (They that have despised the word of God, from them shall the word of man also be taken away).[6] This judgment is in direct answer to their rebellion. This is another Babel, a reverse Pentecost, in which the languages of men are utterly confused. The name *Belbury* is a play on the words *Babel* and *bury*—a name that is itself a mixing of tongues: Hebrew and Old English.

The Bible is the Great Story and whenever we point back to it in our stories, we not only fill our written creation with ancient truths and wisdom, but we also revive our readers' interest in things that have perhaps become commonplace and ordinary to us. This is the glory of filling

6 *That Hideous Strength*, 348.

our stories with Biblical archetypes. The truth always rings clear and bright, even if it is hidden deep beneath layers of sediment. Echoing through millennia, these stories and allusions resound with the truths of a thousand tales that all point, in the end, to Christ, the One who is the truth, the way, and the life.

31

WOMEN OF THE WEST

True Femininity

> The name *me* was the name of a being whose existence she had never suspected, a being that did not yet fully exist but which was demanded. It was a person (not the person she had thought), yet also a thing, a made thing, made to please Another and in Him to please all others, a thing made at this very moment, without its choice, in a shape it had never dreamed of. And the making went on amidst a kind of splendour or sorrow or both, whereof she could not tell whether it was in the moulding hands or in the kneaded lump. (Lewis, *That Hideous Strength*)

Perhaps one of the most striking characteristics of *That Hideous Strength* in comparison with the other two books is the multitude of female characters. There are no women in *Out of the Silent Planet* (except poor Harry's mother) and there's only the Green Lady in *Perelan-*

dra (though, to be fair, there aren't many characters at all), but we have a long list of female characters in *That Hideous Strength.* Jane Studdock, Mrs. Dimble, Camilla Denniston, Ivy Maggs, Grace Ironwood, Fairy Hardcastle.... Why? Is there any significance to the sudden increase of women?

One simple reason is that true femininity and true masculinity have been major themes throughout the entire trilogy, and these themes come into greater focus in this final installment. In *Out of the Silent Planet,* masculinity formed the background, atmosphere, and theme. Mars, the god of war and quintessentially male, gives the first book its setting and donegality. In *Perelandra,* Venus shapes the story. The goddess of beauty and pleasure is the epitome of all true womanhood, glorious sweetness, and wild fruitfulness. In these two books, we are presented with striking pictures of true masculinity and femininity, deftly woven into the very fabric of the stories. Now, in the last book, we see how Mark and Jane Studdock are meant to be human versions and embodiments of these very characteristics. Belbury is at war with humanity, with everything that makes men *true men* and women *true women.* It is no wonder that Lewis, in bringing this quarrel to Earth, adds a number of women to the cast in order to equal the number of men.

Throughout the book, Jane struggles with accepting a biblical picture of femininity and everything that goes along with it. *Submission* and *obedience* in particular are abhorrent words to her, as they are to many women today. In her struggle, she is confronted with a number of examples of godly womanhood, as well as terrifying examples showing her where her desired "independence" would ultimately lead.

Lewis writes female characters as *real* people, with real strengths and weaknesses, with sins and successes, with glories and vices. But Lewis does not let his characters, male or female, get away with sin. He is a Christian writing in the world God created. And that means exposing sin, in both genders, and exhorting towards repentance. He is adept at picturing what true, free, Christian women should look like, women who believe what the Bible says—about themselves, about the world, and about their place in the world. Mrs. Dimble is one such example of this kind of woman, a woman that Jane learns to imitate. In the beginning of the book, Jane *likes* Mrs. Dimble but considers her with a sort of patronizing superiority. After all, Mrs. Dimble has such "old-fashioned" notions about things (femininity and marriage in particular). And yet there is something comforting and solid and real about Mrs. Dimble that Jane cannot help but be attracted to. Mrs. Dimble is sharp, intuitive, and perceptive, and she guesses at what plagues Jane before Jane herself knows it. As with many of the other women in the story, there is more to Mrs. Dimble than meets the eye.

Jane meets Camilla Denniston when she first comes to St. Anne's. Jane's impression of her is striking:

> Jane now conceived for her that almost passionate admiration which women, more often than is supposed, feel for other women whose beauty is not of their own type. It would be so nice, Jane thought, to be like that—so straight, so forthright, so valiant, so fit to be mounted on a horse, and so divinely tall.[1]

Camilla, who we later find has a loving and strong relationship with her husband, Arthur, is described in almost Martial terminology. She is valiant and forthright, fit to be mounted

1 *That Hideous Strength*, 61.

on a horse, and yet she is very clearly feminine and she has a submissive and obedient attitude towards her husband.

In Grace Ironwood we have an example of a strong woman who has, perhaps, suffered more than we know. She is unmarried and, though there is no reason to suspect that she has romantic feeling towards Ransom, she nevertheless gives him the respect and obedience that she would, in some ways, give to a husband.

An interesting thing to note is the similarity between the names of Grace Ironwood and Fairy Hardcastle. Both first names are feminine and fluid while their surnames contain something firm and unyielding (*iron* and *hard*) followed by an object (*wood* and *castle*). This similarity is no accident. Fairy Hardcastle and Grace Ironwood present two contrasting pictures of womanhood. Just as Belbury and St. Anne's show us two completely different approaches to reality, humanity, and the physical realm, Grace and the Fairy show us how those two worldviews *treat women.*

It can be so easy to think that by emphasizing the differences between the genders, we are somehow ranking them in order of importance. But differentiation does not imply superiority or inferiority. To say that *this* is not *that* is not the same thing as saying that *this* is somehow better than *that.* The lack of this distinction has led to a host of errors.

Fairy Hardcastle is independent, masculine, brittle, and violent. She is coarse, rough, and unfeeling. The irony is that though she thinks she is in control and believes that she has the respect of the men around her, she is in fact just a tool in their hands. She is reprimanded when she acts outside her orders. She is kept on a leash, degraded and disrespected, seen only as a handy person to have around to get things done. She is, in reality, *despised* by her associates. They don't like the way she behaves or approve of her sadistic hobbies.

Mark is at first impressed with her devil-may-care attitude, but it is soon obvious that she is just as much enslaved to the men of Belbury as Mark himself. Fairy Hardcastle's desires may likely have started out very similar to Jane's: to be her own person, to refuse submission to any man or obedience to any rule but her own. The Fairy wants to be her own woman just as the people of Belbury want to be their own humanity. And, as with Belbury itself, the end result is that she has her womanly identity stripped away. None of the men around her see her as a woman at all. Having rejected her womanly calling, the Fairy is only a shell of a woman, used and discarded and uncared for by the men who really pull the strings.

Besides the structure of their last names, Grace Ironwood and Fairy Hardcastle have very little in common. Perhaps the only shared characteristic is a certain stern exterior and a core of steel, though even here the Fairy is inconsistent in her serious demeanor, often treating important matters flippantly. Grace Ironwood, meanwhile, has a calm serenity, a patience and inner strength without brittleness, that Hardcastle lacks entirely. Grace is loyal and devoted to Ransom. She respects him and submits to his wishes in the matters of the Company at St. Anne's. As a result of this, she is respected and given a position of relative importance: running the household and the first one to speak to Jane before she can be admitted to the Director.

The contrast between Grace and the Fairy is not a contrast between hard and soft, strong and weak. Grace is not soft where the Fairy is hard or suppressed where the Fairy is free. No, the contrast is more nuanced than that. Grace is hard, and the Fairy is hard, yet Grace is hard in a *feminine* way, while the Fairy is most decidedly not. Grace knows she is free—*not* to be a man, but free to be a woman. She is free to be what she is. Fairy Hardcastle, on the other hand, thinks she is free to be like a man, yet all she really can be is a sad, broken, confused woman who has lost all of her humanity. In the end, the Fairy despises and rejects *both* true masculinity and true femininity, while Grace, who embraces all of the glorious, biblical differences between masculine and feminine, is set at liberty to be a true human being, not autonomous or androgenous, but in submission to the way God created her to be.

We will now look at Jane: the heroine who has succumbed to the historical failure to properly understand and accept her role as a woman. This failure has created setbacks (and nearly disaster) within the greater cosmic conflict. Jane's personal struggle with the relationship between men and women, particularly between a husband and a wife, is front and center throughout the book.

When Jane meets Ransom for the first time, Lewis pulls out all of the stops on Solar imagery—he even uses the word *solar* itself to describe Ransom, in case we might have missed it. Considering that this is a primarily Jovial book and that Ransom is taking up a distinctly Jovial role, why implement all of the Solar language when Jane first sees Ransom?

The reason becomes clear when we consider that it is from *Jane's* perspective that this language is used and so it is shaped by Jane's character and struggles. This imagery is intimately connected to Jane's identity *as a woman* and her hostility towards men and the very idea of the masculine. Sol is the "worshipp'd male," the "earth's husband,"[2] a purely masculine image which draws a number of allusions to Jane's mind—all images from a time before she became disillusioned. She is overwhelmed by the weight of the word *Obedience*, a word that is part of her organic reaction to the

2 "The Planets", 13.

masculine characteristics she encounters in Ransom. The weight of this idea presses upon her heavily, driven by the influence of Perelandra herself beginning to enter the room, and she nearly (against her better judgment) surrenders completely to Ransom in what would have been an inappropriate fashion. And while she is saved from this error by Ransom ordering the influence to stop and also by Ransom sending Jane from the room, Jane's experience rattles her.

The surrender and submission Jane wants to offer Ransom in this scene is to be directed, instead, to her *own* husband, just as we all must submit to something infinitely more masculine than we can imagine. As Ransom tells Jane: "The male you could have escaped, for it exists only on the biological level. But the masculine none of us can escape. What is above and beyond all things is so masculine that we are all feminine in relation to it."[3] Every Christian, man or woman, is part of the Church, the bride of Christ. And every wife submitting to her own husband in obedience to God is a tiny microcosm of this greater, mysterious relationship.

Our feminist culture accuses Christianity of teaching oppression when it teaches submission, yet it is *Christianity* they have to thank for all the freedoms and privileges that modern women have. Outside of Christ, women are either put on a pedestal or trodden on, and both of these distortions lead to great misery and abuse. It is the Christian church, the bride of Christ, that *opposes* the suppression and mistreatment of women. This does not mean that women are free to be men, but that women are free to be *what we were made to be*. We are not gods and so cannot create ourselves.

Rejection of biblical femininity is ultimately a rejection of the way that God has created the world, and women in

3 *That Hideous Strength*, 313.

particular. This rejection does not lead to freedom, happiness, equality, or respect, but is in fact the way of death and destruction. What most modern feminists call "equality" is in fact just *sameness* which is, simply put, impossible. In trying to make women like men, they succeed only in making women ugly and distorted. Fairy Hardcastle may not be representative of every woman who is trying to do this, but she is a picture of where this way of thinking ultimately leads. Women are not called to be men. Women are called to be true women of God, fearless and valiant. Women who are strong enough to submit without fear, to obey our God without hesitation, and to stand firm on the Word of God and everything it has to say about women and true femininity. Women who are unashamed of what God has created them to be.

32

REBELLION & OBEDIENCE

Mark and Jane's Conversions

> [Mark] was choosing a side: the Normal. "All that," as he called it, was what he chose. If the scientific point of view led away from "all that", then be damned to the scientific point of view! The vehemence of his choice almost took his breath away; he had not had such a sensation before. For the moment he hardly cared if Frost or Wither killed him. (Lewis, *That Hideous Strength*)

Earlier, we saw how Mark and Jane Studdock are the main characters of the last book of the Ransom Trilogy. Mark and Jane, in their own ways, embody the planetary characteristics of the two entities introduced to us in the first two books: Mars and Venus. In this chapter, I want to focus on Mark's and Jane's respective sins, their subsequent redemption, and how this serves to highlight the subject of the self that Lewis frequently addresses in his writings.

Mark and Jane fundamentally struggle with the same issue, but it is one that evidences itself in completely opposite ways. They both struggle with the sin of idolizing the *self*. They have placed the ego on a pedestal in their own hearts and all of their desires, ambitions, and efforts orient themselves to their little god called Themselves. Because they are different people and different genders, this idolatry manifests itself in very different ways. They have different desires and aspirations, but ultimately, they are both self-serving. Their own idea of the self is at the center of all they do.

As we discussed earlier, Mark wants his little idol to have a place at the table with the other elites. He wants *in*. He wants his god to be among the important deities of the world. He wants, most of all, to not stand out. He wants to *belong*. Jane also has a high opinion of the self—and she wants *out*. She is puffed up and vain and wants nothing to do with the petty problems of the men of the College. She just wants to be left alone, to find an intellectual oasis in which she can be the queen of her little academic domain. Belonging is of no interest to her. Jane wants to be set apart, her own self. Both Mark and Jane do not see themselves rightly, do not see or embrace the roles that they are meant to fulfill, roles that are meant to be performed in the context of a *relationship*. They are both too concerned with themselves to see the devastating consequences of neglecting their duties to the other.

As we saw earlier, Jane is meant to exemplify and embody the qualities of Venus. She is meant to be fruitful, submissive, obedient to her husband, glorious, soft, lovely—feminine in the very greatest sense of that word. Her rejection of this role is the source of much that is wrong at the beginning of the book (though Mark is equally culpable for his own sin). Jane struggles to accept the biblical picture of femininity and wifely duties. She is absorbed with her individuality, and the thought of submitting that to anyone, let alone to a man like the one she had married, is abhorrent to her. She wants to be different than "normal" women, even down to the clothes she wears.

> She liked her clothes to be rather severe and in colours that were really good on serious aesthetic grounds—clothes which would make it plain to everyone that she was an intelligent adult and not a woman of the chocolate-box variety—and because of this preference, she did not know that she was interested in clothes at all.[1]

Jane's conversion, therefore, must consist of *obedience*. In order to embrace her role as a true woman and wife, she must accept everything that means. Throughout the book, as Jane spends more time in the presence of Ransom and the company at St. Anne's, as she is increasingly influenced by them, and as she transforms into who she is meant to be, one thing we see is a higher concentration of *poetry* in her own thought. At the beginning of the book, she quotes Donne (the subject of her graduate work), but her ruminations are decidedly dry and didactic, academic in the worst sense of that word. She is thinking of Donne only in order to think of herself. But throughout the rest of the book, the language of Paradise begins to spring up within her, just as it sprang up in Ransom on Perelandra. She is softened, humbled by her experiences. In the end, she is brought to a full realization of how her rejection of her role had hurt her

1 *That Hideous Strength*, 26.

relationship with Mark. She had never attempted obedience to him, never sought to be a true wife to him, despite his own insufficiencies. The final turn, her conversion, comes when she is fully prepared to submit to Mark in every way, to be a true woman, to be an image of Venus. Her idea of herself must be let go. Her idol must be toppled.

> To have surrendered without terms at the mere voice and look of this stranger, to have abandoned (without noticing it) that prim little grasp on her own destiny, that perpetual reservation, which she thought essential to her status as a grown-up, integrated, intelligent person...the thing was utterly degrading, vulgar, uncivilised.[2]

But this is what she must do and this is what she does.

Mark, on the other hand, is meant to be Martial. We have already seen how he lacks many of the essential Martial characteristics. We get glimmers, here and there, of the Martial character peeking through. At one point, we see a reference to Orion (the Great Hunter and a Martial constellation) "[flaming] at him above the tree-tops," but it is revealing that Mark does not "know even that earnest constellation."[3] His modern education has stripped from him even the minimal comfort that he may find in recognizing a familiar constellation in the night sky. In another place we are filled with hope for Mark. He is gradually growing sick of his time at Belbury and longs to return to Jane. He actually makes it off the grounds, but then he comes across the Deputy Director. "And in one moment all that *brittle hardi-*

2 *That Hideous Strength*, 148.

3 Ibid., 70.

hood was gone from Mark's mood."[4] The "brittle hardihood" that gave Mark the push to actually attempt to leave Belbury is a distinctly Martial characteristic.

And in the end, Mark's conversion comes when he finally learns to *rebel.* In contrast to Jane's need to obey, Mark needs to disobey. He releases all of the fears that he had always had of going against the grain, of standing firm even when everything is going to pieces. He finally embraces a certain mindset which both Lewis and Tolkien had a high respect for, a very Norse view of bravery—that defeat is no refutation.[5] This is the height of courage: to fight, not because we think we have any chance of winning, but because we have no other choice, because it is the right thing to do. Maybe the universe *is* a cheat. Maybe the Crooked will always defeat the Straight in the end. Either way, Mark suddenly realizes that this does *not* mean he shouldn't go down with the ship.

> He began to be frightened by the very fact that his fears seemed to have momentarily vanished. They had been a safeguard...they had prevented him, all his life, from making mad decisions like that which he was now making as he turned to Frost and said, "It's all bloody nonsense, and I'm damned if I do any such thing."[6]

Mark's conversion comes at the moment of rebellion. He must stand firm. He must not *belong* anymore. His idol, his desire to protect himself, has been toppled just like Jane's.

4 Ibid., 186, emphasis mine.

5 J. R. R. Tolkien, *The Monsters and the Critics and Other Essays*, ed. Christopher Tolkien (Boston: Houghton Mifflin, 1984), 21.

6 *That Hideous Strength*, 334.

Mark and Jane both must come to know themselves in the context of relationship—with other people, with each other, and with the world as God created it. In the end, they no longer place the ego at the center on a pedestal, but they see themselves as created beings, made to be a certain way by the Creator of the universe. They cannot be a law unto themselves, but they must step into the roles they have been given, in relation to God, the created order, and each other. This means embracing their roles as male and female, as husband and wife, and as Mars and Venus.

33

PULLING DOWN DEEP HEAVEN

Paradise on the Silent Planet

"I am not speaking of the wraiths," said Ransom. "I have stood before Mars himself in the sphere of Mars and before Venus herself in the sphere of Venus. It is their strength, and the strength of some greater than they, which will destroy our enemies."

"But, Lord," said Merlin, "how can this be? Is it not against the Seventh Law?"

"What law is that?" asked Ransom.

"Has not our Fair Lord made it a law for Himself that He will not send down the Powers to mend or mar in this Earth until the end of all things? Or is this the end that is even now coming to pass?" (Lewis, *That Hideous Strength*)

We now come to the end of the trilogy. In *Out of the Silent Planet*, we saw the catalyst that started the whole thing: the lunar boundary had been breached. Weston and Devine constructed their space craft and ventured beyond the sublunar world, past the Moon's frontier, and into Deep Heaven. They broke the Seventh Law themselves, and so spelled their own demise. The people at Belbury, the N.I.C.E. and others, driven by evil powers and their own bent wills, created a Hell on Earth. But having already breached the boundary line, they little thought that they had also enabled Deep Heaven to descend.

Where the conflict was introduced in *Out of the Silent Planet* and continued in *Perelandra*, in *That Hideous Strength* it comes to a crisis. Ransom summarizes this crisis to Merlin:

> "The Hideous Strength holds all this Earth in its fist to squeeze as it wishes. But for their one mistake, there would be no hope left. If of their own evil will they had not broken the frontier and let in the celestial Powers, this would be their moment of victory. Their own strength has betrayed them. They have gone to the gods who would not have come to them, and pulled down Deep Heaven on their heads. Therefore, they will die."[1]

The Oyéresu would not and could not have come to Thulcandra of their own accord. It was forbidden. But with the frontier breached by others, they are now free to descend, meeting the Hell that Belbury has created with the powers of High Heaven. They can do this because not only did Weston and Devine breach the boundary, but they also brought Ransom. This evil act, that of kidnapping an unwilling man to be (as they thought) a sacrifice to Martian inhabitants, worked against them to establish their ultimate defeat, because Ransom, as we've seen, has become a bridge.

---

1 *That Hideous Strength*, 291.

He has become, at last, what he was meant to be from the beginning—the Jovial Priest-King. As he explains to Merlin:

> "Our enemies had taken away from themselves the protection of the Seventh Law. They had broken by natural philosophy the barrier which God of His own power would not break. Even so they sought you as a friend and raised up for themselves a scourge. And that is why Powers of Heaven have come down to this house, and in this chamber where we are now discoursing Malacandra and Perelandra have spoken to me."
>
> Merlin's face became a little pale. The bear nosed at his hand, unnoticed.
>
> "I have become a bridge," said Ransom."[2]

Heaven and Hell meet face to face on the Silent Planet. In a final battle that resounds with biblical imagery (the tower of Babel; Samson's defeat of the Philistines in the temple of Dagon; a sort of inverted Noah's ark[3]), creatures from every realm of the medieval cosmos join together to defeat evil. The Silent Planet is silent no longer—it echoes with roars and chirps and grunts and howls. Merlin, himself now a bridge across which the powers of Deep Heaven can pass, unleashes terror on the people of Belbury. It seems so simple, especially from the viewpoint of those at St. Anne's. They merely wait to hear if Merlin was successful or not. Unlike on Perelandra, this battle does not come to

---

2 Ibid., 288.

3 Belbury, like Noah's ark, attempts to "rescue" mankind. Yet unlike Noah, Belbury seeks to do this by sterilizing creation, by removing the organic and natural, and replacing it with cold science and nature reduced to test tubes in a laboratory. The explosion of animal instinct and energy in this climactic scene directly contradicts the philosophy that undergirds Belbury's project.

physical blows between St. Anne's and Belbury. Between the nature that they sought to destroy and the spiritual realm they sought to control, Belbury is destroyed by the collective power of all three realms of the cosmos—the animals of Earth, Merlin the "fairy" and second bridge, and the strength of Deep Heaven. Paradise has destroyed the schemes of Hell. Unmade, dismantled, un-humaned, the evil that they sought to work on the Earth is thwarted and turned back, sent slinking into the shadows to lick its wounds until the next time it appears with some new scheme.

And then, after the battle is over, Venus remains. The winds and scents of Perelandra, the Lady of Love, weave themselves around St. Anne's and, for a short time, Paradise reigns again on the Earth. Ransom has completed his task. We don't *see* him return to Perelandra, and that's the way he wants it. No drawn-out goodbyes, no tears and sorrow—because he does not take the hope with him, but he leaves it on Thulcandra, with Mark and Jane Studdock, now re-united.

Ransom has worked his last, and perhaps most important, Jovial task: the reunion of Mark and Jane. In this reunion, a great wrong is being righted. Up till now, they have voluntarily remained childless, an evil that Merlin says "of which no less sorrow shall come than came of the stroke that Balinus struck."[4] Their child is one for whose coming "a hundred generations in two lines" have been preparing.[5] Merlin believes the time has passed, that the child can never now be conceived. But the end of this book leaves one to hope. Ransom has fulfilled one last priestly task and, once more moved by proper love, Mark and Jane become husband and wife as they were meant to be.

---

4 *That Hideous Strength*, 275.

5 Ibid., 276.

Indeed, the trilogy ends with an outburst of love between birds and beasts as well as men. Mr. Bultitude finds his Missus; the Dimbles depart together; Ivy is reunited with her husband; all of the beasts are pairing off. This is the work of Venus together with Ransom fulfilling his Priest-Kingly task. But it is also a final tie to Dante. It is an echo of the last words of *The Divine Comedy*, amplified and magnified by being linked to mankind by the Jovial spirit:

> At this point power failed high fantasy
> But, like a wheel in perfect balance turning,
> I felt my will and my desire impelled
> By the Love that moves the sun and other stars.[6]

The Jovial task is complete. Mark and Jane have been restored to their roles. Mars and Venus are reunited, moved back into proper Love, and hope springs from their union, the promise of the coming seed.

6 *Paradiso*, 33.142-145.

Discussion Questions

That Hideous Strength

1. Why do Mark and Jane have an unhappy marriage? What are the different sins and temptations that Mark and Jane each struggle with? How are Mark & Jane "converted" over the course of the book?

2. Compare and contrast the communities of Belbury and St. Anne's. Include discussion of their different philosophies.

3. How does Ransom fulfill his Jovial role in *That Hideous Strength*? How is he a Christ-figure?

4. Discuss Lewis's use of biblical imagery in *That Hideous Strength*. What does this imagery add to the book?

5. How does the modern education system produce "men without chests"? What are some practical ways to combat this sort of education?

CONCLUSION

34

THE INCARNATION & THE EYES OF HEAVEN

Man's Importance in the Cosmos

> Whatever else a modern feels when he looks at the night sky, he certainly feels that he is looking out—like one looking out from the saloon entrance on to the dark Atlantic or from the lighted porch upon dark and lonely moors. (Lewis, *Discarded Image*)

> "Oh, I see it," she said. "I am older now. Your world has no roof. You look right out into the high place and see the great dance with your own eyes. You live always in that terror and that delight, and what we must only believe you can behold." (Lewis, *Perelandra*)

As we, like Ransom himself, near the end of our cosmic travels, there are yet some loose ends to be tied up. We've breathed in the clear air of Malacandra and bathed in the fragrant seas of Perelandra. We've seen the cosmic clash of Heaven and Hell take place on the Silent Planet. Now we return home, back to where we started, after an adventure through the stars. Hopefully, we are wiser.

And so we come back to a familiar stomping ground: the Medieval Model that started it all. In this chapter, I want to consider more fully a theme that we've touched on in numerous places, and that is the *importance* of man within the cosmos. In the Medieval Model, mankind is located as if "at the bottom of a stair whose top is invisible with light."[1] It is this "bottom-dweller" nature that can lead to that marginal feeling when we consider mankind's place in the medieval cosmos. Lewis saw this as one significant defect or flaw of the medieval cosmology. It can cause us to feel insignificant in light of our place beneath the eternal dance of Deep Heaven. But this is at odds with the Biblical account that medieval Christians believed, and so medieval literature often struggled with this apparent dichotomy, because the Bible presents a very different view of humanity's importance in the cosmos. The biblical view of humanity, when considered rightly, gives rise to a very different *emotion*, one seemingly at war with the marginality of man's place in the Medieval Model.

The humble position of mankind in the construction of the medieval cosmos helps to set much of medieval literature and some key events in the right light. Many people assume that medieval Christians put Earth at the center of the cosmos because they saw men as the most important. However, this is entirely false. Think back to Dante—what is at the "center" of the physical universe that he explores? It is Hell itself, found at the center of the Earth. And at the center of Hell, we find Satan himself. Moving closer

1 *Discarded Image*, 74.

and closer to the center is to move further down into the waste bin of the universe, the cosmic septic tank. So, the central location of Earth is actually a *humble* position. Medieval Christians did not struggle with pride in man's place in the cosmos. Rather, they struggled with reconciling man's humble estate with his dignity.

You may be familiar with the often-told story of Galileo and his famous trial. Galileo, after publishing his observations of the heavens in which he supported the Copernican, heliocentric view of the cosmos, was placed on trial by the Catholic church in 1610 and was summarily convicted. Heliocentricity was condemned as heretical by the Inquisition in 1616, and so the Catholic church of the fifteenth century has been branded by most modern historians as backward, superstitious, and anti-science. This conflict is commonly portrayed as a conflict between *religion* and *science*. It is said (inaccurately) that the Christian religion necessitated that Earth be at the center of the cosmos due to the Earth's *importance*. But this was the opposite of the truth. The conflict was not between religion and science—it was between *science* and science. The religious leaders of the time had linked themselves up with the cutting-edge science of the day, the science that was running the show. And Galileo's discoveries would have unhinged all of that. The church's mistake was not dogmatically clinging to "religion," but rather wedding themselves to "science" in the first place.[2]

The harmony, complexity, and order of the Medieval Model is one of the things that Lewis admires most, in addition to the imaginative potential that it possesses. However, there is one aspect of the Model that he sees as distinct-

2 For further reading, see Mitch Stokes's *Galileo* (Nashville: Thomas Nelson, 2011).

ly *unharmonious*, and that is man's symbolized insignificance within the cosmos. He sees this point as a major flaw, for it is at odds with the Bible, which medieval Christians *also* believed and which presents a very different view of humanity's importance, as we discussed before.

"I think that there remained throughout the Middle Ages an *unresolved discord* between those elements in their religion which tended to an anthropocentric view and those in the Model which made man a marginal—almost a suburban—creature," Lewis says.[3] This "unresolved discord" would have grated harshly on Lewis's nerves. He was the sort of man that wouldn't just leave it alone once he had seen it. And it is this discord that he masterfully resolves throughout the Ransom Trilogy.

Lewis's resolution to this tension surrounding man's place in the cosmos involves both a change in trajectory and a particular emphasis on the planetary characters. These two elements come together in the character of Ransom. Ransom embodies the full strength of the Model with this tension resolved, and thus all of the Model's imaginative and emotional power is set free to work in harmony through him.

During the course of the trilogy, Ransom *physically* moves closer to the Earth according to the Medieval Model. In other words, the books have an anthropocentric arc. From the "empyrean ocean of radiance" to Mars, to Venus, the center of each book nears the Earth until the final battle takes place on the Silent Planet itself. Mankind may very well be at the bottom of a stair whose top is bathed in starlight, but in Lewis's view, the eyes of Deep Heaven look *down*. They are intimately concerned with what goes on upon this dull, silent orb at the bottom of the universe.

---

3 *Discarded Image*, 51, emphasis mine.

Why? Because there are rumors spinning through Deep Heaven. As the Oyarsa of Malacandra says in *Out of the Silent Planet*:

> "There was a great war, and we drove [the Bent One] back out of the heavens and bound him in the air of his own world as Maleldil taught us. There doubtless he lies to this hour, and we know no more of that planet: it is silent. We think that Maleldil would not give it up utterly to the Bent One, and there are stories among us that He has taken strange counsel and dared terrible things, wrestling with the Bent One in Thulcandra. But of this we know less than you; it is a thing we desire to look into."[4]

Remember that this last phrase, "it is a thing we desire to look into," echoes 1 Peter 1:12: "To them it was revealed that, not to themselves, but to us they were ministering the things which now have been reported to you through those who have preached the gospel to you by the Holy Spirit sent from heaven—things which angels desire to look into." This thing that angels desire to look into is the Gospel of Jesus Christ—the One who has "dared terrible things."

The Incarnation, just as it is the center of our faith and of the history of the world, is also the center of the universe. *This* is the grand miracle that has given mankind centrality. *This* is what the eyes of Deep Heaven wonder and marvel at. And it happened on Earth. This Silent Planet in whose dust the King of the Universe once walked is now of inestimable *importance*. What our Lord did in the Incarnation shook Deep Heaven. It changed everything, not just for

---

4 *Silent Planet*, 120.

mankind but for the cosmos. Lewis emphasizes the crucial importance of the Incarnation in one of his letters, specifically speaking about Perelandra and what it would come to look like as Tor and Tinidril grow in maturity and set out to fill and subdue the planet:

> The only point I think you are slightly wrong on is that you use the Martian society too boldly as a guide to what Perelandra would become later on. But there is no real parallel. *The Incarnation has come in between*. Malacandra belongs to the old order in which planetary creatures were subjected to the angels: but the angels kneel before Tor [at the end of Perelandra]. There is no limit to the future glories of the world which, needing no redemption itself, yet profits by the Incarnation.[5]

The greater transformation of Ransom into a Christ figure brings the entire focus of this post-Incarnation cosmos back to mankind. Ransom, as both a *man* and a Christ figure, embodies the resolution that has been made between these warring emotional effects. In Ransom, we see the glory and wonder of the translunary world. He becomes the bridge to Deep Heaven where the eternal dance of light and love carries on, untouched by sin and death and decay. But we also see *ourselves*, the center of cosmic attention, created in the image of God, existing, like Ransom, "in the body of Maleldil," our sins forgiven, and all worlds holding their breath as they stare down and wonder, *what next*?

Deep Heaven stoops, desiring to look into the mysterious doings of Earth and mankind because *Christ* descended

5 Lewis to Victor M. Hamm, Oxford, August 11, 1945 in *Collected Letters*, 2:667, emphasis mine.

to Earth. In taking on man's flesh and nature, He bound them to Himself and they have died and risen to the heavenly places in Him. Ransom is a bridge; but he is a bridge modeled after an even greater Bridge that not only unites Heaven and Earth, but unites His people to Himself and to His Father through the Spirit.

Both Ransom's physical and spiritual journeys bring the focus down to Earth in a particular way. Mankind is both fallen and sinful, but also reborn and redeemed in Christ. Lewis seamlessly holds these two things together, no longer clashing, but working together in harmony. In having the music of the spheres descend to Earth, Lewis makes the medieval cosmos sing in harmony with a no longer Silent Planet. And its song is a hymn of praise.

35

RECOVERING THE DISCARDED IMAGE

Looking to the Stars

"She comes more near the Earth than she was wont to—to make Earth sane. Perelandra is all about us and Man is no longer isolated. We are now as we ought to be—between the angels who are our elder brothers and the beasts who are our jesters, servants, and playfellows." (Lewis, *That Hideous Strength*)

Chart the stars. Draw a diagram of the entire cosmos, if you can, if you have time enough and world enough. Put the sun at the center. Or the Earth. Do you feel any different? By now, we have hopefully caught a glimpse of what a man felt centuries ago when he looked up into the night sky. We have felt the maternal warmth of Venus, the hardy courage of Mars, Sol's golden touch, the Moon's cold wandering beam, Saturn's leaden weight, Mercury's playful dance, and the kingly mirth of Jove. But why does it *matter*? After all, isn't it all just make-believe? At the end of all our exploration, we come back to where we started and ask ourselves once more: what is so important about the Medieval Model of the cosmos? Why was it so important to C. S. Lewis? Why did he care about recovering an image of the world that is, factually speaking, false?

BREATHING SILVER

Remember what Lewis called myths before he was converted: "Lies breathed through silver." There was something attractive, beautiful, and deeply moving about myth, about these stories that shaped the fabric of Lewis's imagination. He loved them deeply, and yet his rational side constantly warred with his romantic side—for the stories simply were not true. However, in discussions with Tolkien and other friends, Lewis came to recognize the *truer* truth that was contained in all the old stories. A tale does not have to be *factually* true in order to communicate deep truths—truths which may not always fit into the pages of a technically pristine textbook.

Some truths are too large to be communicated by anything *but* myth, and the reason for this echoes back to a theme that has continually popped up again and again in our discussion of the Ransom Trilogy: the world is not made up of physical material alone. The world is physical and spiritual just as a man is body, soul, and spirit. To dissect and try to isolate just one part and pretend that it is the whole is to fall into a deep pit of error. Just as Weston reduced the world to the material in *Out of the Silent Planet*, or as Belbury attempted to escape the material world into a sterilized existence in *That Hideous Strength*, a worldview that has no place for myth is missing an integral part of what it means to be human. It is like looking at the world through the wrong end of the telescope, presenting a distorted picture of reality.

We are story-telling creatures because we are created in the image of a story-telling God. He is the great Author, weaving together a complex history full of heroes and villains, side plots and side characters. He uses motifs and archetypes. He has favorite themes and tropes. He keeps track of every thread. No sparrow escapes His notice. He writes epics between rival anthills, comedies involving frogs, tragedies about field mice, dramas in the deepest oceans. Our Lord is a master Weaver. He spins galaxies and whirlwinds, stitches garments for the forests, unrolls the mountains and hills like a Persian rug, embroiders the stories of men's lives into an enormous tapestry, and encompasses the entirety of human history—from the first shiver of Adam's chest as he drew his first breath, to the final trumpet call when all shall be remade.

To be human, to be created in His image, is to tell stories.

And so we *need* myth, stories, and legends. We need the tales of other times. We need to know the way other men throughout the history of the world have seen this world and how they have explained it. We need to be, as Lewis says, "myriad-minded."[1] And we need to encourage the type of education that promotes this sort of thinking, an education unlike the one Mark Studdock received. We want men who can rule both mind and appetite, who understand the role that myth plays in the lives of mankind. We want men with chests.

---

1 "The Planets", 14.

THE HEAVENS DECLARE

The Medieval Model of the cosmos presents to us an old way of seeing the universe. It introduces ideas to us that have become so out of date as to be completely foreign. We like to see ourselves as "enlightened," and we use the term *medieval* to indicate backwards, old-fashioned, unenlightened, or dark. But in this study guide, we have looked back into the "dark ages" and found something surprising. Rather than gloom and midnight darkness, we have stumbled into a grand hall blazing with light and life and dance—a world of golden edges and scarlet banners, a world full to the brim with music and living creatures, a world where monks and scribes cannot write anything down without decorating the margins with birds and beasts and flowers and swirls of gold. There is no space uninhabited, no spot where there is not some creature that has been made to sing the praises of its Creator.

This picture of the cosmos is much closer to the one presented in the Bible. We have grown accustomed to letting science, a science influenced by materialistic reductionism and evolution, teach us about the world. How does the *Bible* speak of the heavens? Of angels and archangels and seraphim? Of principalities and powers? Of dragons and unicorns and Leviathan and armies of flame? It can't all be metaphorical.

And then we have a Baby in a manger. The God of all creation, born of a woman under heaven and placed in a manger. How do the wise men come to the place? A star leads the way. Every modern astronomer will tell you that this is impossible. How could a star in the heavens actually lead the wise men to a specific part of the country, let alone a specific house in a specific city? It seems impossible, yet it happened. Stars are more than atoms bouncing around in the dead expanse of space. Stars are personal. They have names (Psalm 147:4). They sing (Luke 2:13-14). When we object that stars are "just" huge balls of flaming gas, Lewis has an answer for us: "Even in your world, my son, that is not what a star is but only what it is made of."[2]

We are often far too quick to let modern science inform our metaphysics. We reject what the Bible clearly teaches in favor of a materialistic, reductionistic science. Scientific accuracy will be cold comfort in a world devoid of all awe, wonder, mystery, life, and soul. A thing is much more than what it is *made* of.

GO OUTSIDE

It is a cool spring evening in North Idaho. I can hear frogs and crickets perform clashing symphonies in the creek below the hill. The wood of the porch steps is damp under my bare feet from an earlier rainstorm, but now the clouds have cleared. The sky is the color of a peacock's tail and the mountains to the east are purpling slowly, darkening from dusty grape to a deeper mysterious wine.

I watch the stars emerge. Jupiter, their captain, leads the way first. Low and bright and burning, he rides above the treetops, lord of the heavens. The blue at the edge of the world becomes black before I realize it and now the sky is spattered with stars like droplets of shimmering paint. So chaotic at first—a random, star-speckled sky. But then my eye starts to connect the dots. I see Orion, the Great Hunter, charging across the sky in full pursuit of some unknown

---

2 *The Voyage of the* Dawn Treader, 209.

quarry. Perhaps the Great Bear and her cub? Lyra sings and the twins dance to her melody. The Pleiades are a comfort in their familiar shape.

I don't feel lost anymore. The sky is full of eyes that look down on the Earth in breathless wonder. For He has dared terrible things. What is man that You are mindful of him? We feel small beneath the vast cathedral of light and life that arches overhead—tiny, insignificant, forgotten maybe. And yet…and *yet.*

Go outside on a clear night. Wherever you are and whatever constellations dance over your head in your sky, take the time to learn their names. They are creatures, like us. They have the same God. They sing with voices and move in praise and love for their Creator and ours. See them with eyes that have learned the right stories, that have believed the true myths. Will we walk differently? Will it change us? What will it be in us when we remember it when we lie down to die?

Because here is the truth: the Gospel does not leave *anything* alone. It doesn't leave stones unturned or grass unruffled. It is a breeze blowing or water rushing. It transforms. And when it transforms, the transformation touches everything. What does Christ have to do with Jupiter? *Everything.* What does Jupiter have to do with our growth in maturity? *Everything.* Why? Because of Christ, all things are made new.

So, is the Medieval Model of the cosmos true? Well, what does Lewis say?

> I have made no serious effort to hide the fact that the old Model delights me as I believe it delighted our ancestors. Few constructions of the imagination seem to me to have combined splendour, sobriety, and coherence in the same degree. It is possible that

> some readers have long been itching to remind me that it had a serious defect; it was not true.
>
> I agree. It was not true. [...] But the meaning of the words 'know' and 'truth' in this context has begun to undergo a certain change.[3]

Certainly, Lewis agrees that the actual *physical* arrangement of the Medieval Model is not true—as in, it is not technically accurate. We have known this from the beginning. Lewis never argues that we should *return* to a Ptolemaic system or reject the knowledge that our technological advancements have enabled us to gain. No, Lewis's project is at the same time simpler and more complex than that. He wants to recover this discarded image, not to *supplant* the current factual framework, but to restore truths which erroneous ideologies have stripped from that framework. In the Ransom Trilogy, he undertakes an imaginative reconstruction project to restore wonder and awe. He desires to reawaken a sense of *place*, of that bottom-heavy security that our medieval fathers felt when they looked up at the heavens, knowing their place in the cosmos, knowing they were not forgotten, but that the eyes of Deep Heaven and deeper were fixed back at them in wonder.

And so we will end with this last question: what do *you* see when you look up? See God's creation. See the heavens, resounding with praise and glory. See deep heaven, swirling with light and life. Then see even deeper—see Christ and look out with joy.

We are redeemed. We need not fear the dark.

---

3 *Discarded Image*, 216.

APPENDIX A

Timeline

The Life and Writings of C. S. Lewis

APPENDIX A

1898 Clive Staples Lewis (called "Jack" by his friends and family) is born on November 29th in Belfast, Northern Ireland. His parents are Albert J. Lewis (1863-1929) and Florence Augusta Hamilton Lewis (1862-1908). His brother Warren was born on June 16, 1895.

1908 Lewis's mother (Florence) dies of cancer on August 23rd. Lewis is enrolled at Wynyard School in Watford, Hertfordshire in September.

1911 Lewis is enrolled as a student at Cherbourg House which was a prep school near Malvern College where Warnie was enrolled. Lewis is there until June 1913.

1914 In April, Lewis meets Arthur Greeves (1895-1966), who was (besides his brother) Lewis's most intimate friend. On September 19, Lewis starts private study with W. T. Kirkpatrick, "The Great Knock," in Great Bookham Surrey. He studied with Kirkpatrick until April 1917.

1916 Lewis makes his first trip to Oxford to take a scholarship examination.

1917 From April to September, Lewis is a student at University College, Oxford. He enlists in the British army (three years after the outbreak of WWI) and starts officer's training in Keble College, Oxford. Lewis is commissioned as an officer in the 3rd Battalion, Somerset Light Infantry, on September 25. He comes to the front line in the Somme Valley, France on his 19th birthday.

1918 April 15: Lewis is wounded on Mount Berenchon during the Battle of Arras. He returns to duty in October, assigned to Ludgerhall, Andover, England.

1919 February: "Death in Battle" (poem) is Lewis' first publication in something besides school magazines. January 1919 to June 1924: Lewis resumes his studies at University College, Oxford.
Published: *Spirits in Bondage: A Cycle of Lyrics*, Lewis's first published book, poetry, published under the name "Clive Hamilton."

1920 During the summer, Mrs. Janie King Moore (1873-1951), the mother of Paddy Moore (a fellow soldier and friend of Lewis's who died in the war) and her daughter, Maureen, move to Oxford and rent a house in Headington Quarry. Lewis lives with the Moores from June 1921 onward.

1921 May: Lewis' essay "Optimism" wins the Chancellor's English Essay Prize. There is no extant copy of "Optimism" to date.

1924 October 1924 to May 1925: Lewis is a stand-in philosophy tutor at University College.

1925 May 20: Lewis is elected a Fellow of Magdalen College, Oxford, where he is a tutor in English Language and Literature for twenty-nine years until leaving for Magdalene College, Cambridge, in 1954.

1929 Lewis becomes a theist: "In the Trinity Term of 1929 I gave in, and admitted that God was God, and knelt and prayed...."
September 24: Albert Lewis (Lewis's father) dies.

1931 Lewis becomes a Christian. See Lewis's *Surprised by Joy*: "When we [Warnie and Jack] set out [by motorcycle to the Whipsnade Zoo] I did not believe that Jesus Christ was the Son of God, and when we reached the zoo I did."

1933 Regular meetings of the Inklings, a group of Lewis's literary friends, begin. They meet regularly, several times a week, for the next 16 years, either in Lewis's rooms at the College, at The Eagle and Child (a local pub known to regulars as The Bird and Baby), or other pubs. Members of the Inklings included J. R. R. Tolkien, Warnie (Lewis's brother), Hugo Dyson, Charles Williams, Dr. Robert Havard, Owen Barfield, Weville Coghill, and others.
Published: *The Pilgrim's Regress*

1935 Lewis agrees to write a volume on 16th century English literature for the Oxford History of English Literature series.

1936 Published: *The Allegory of Love*

1937 Lewis receives the Gollancz Memorial Prize for Literature for *The Allegory of Love.*

1938 Published: *Out of the Silent Planet*

1939 September: Charles Williams moves from London to Oxford with the Oxford University Press at the outbreak of WWII. He joins the Inklings and became a regular member.
Published: *The Personal Heresy* (essay collection) and *Rehabilitation and Other Essays* (essay collection).

1940 Published: *The Problem of Pain*

1941 Published: May 2 to November 28, The Guardian publishes 31 "Screwtape Letters" in weekly installments.
In August, Lewis gives four live radio talks over the BBC on Wednesday evenings from 7:45 to 8:00. Another 15-minute session, answering questions received in the mail, was broadcast on September 6. These talks were known as "Right and Wrong."

1942 January and February: Lewis gives five radio talks on Sunday evenings from 4:45 to 5:00, on the subject "What Christians Believe."
September 20 to November 8: Sundays at 2:50 to 3:05 p.m., Lewis gives a series of radio talks known as "Christian Behavior."
Published: *Screwtape Letters*, *Preface to Paradise Lost*

1943 February: Lewis gives a series of lectures at the University of Durham that are published later in the year as *The Abolition of Man.*
Published: *Perelandra, The Abolition of Man*

1944 February 22 to April 4: Lewis gives the pre-recorded talks known as "Beyond Personality." Together, all of Lewis's BBC radio talks were eventually published under the title *Mere Christianity.*
Published: *The Great Divorce* (as weekly installments in *The Guardian*)

1945 Charles Williams dies on May 15.
Published: *That Hideous Strength*, *The Great Divorce*

1946 Lewis is awarded honorary Doctor of Divinity by the University of St. Andrews.

1947 Published: *Miracles*

1948 Lewis is elected a Fellow of the Royal Society of Literature.
Published: *Arthurian Torso* (critical study of Charles Williams' poetry)

1950 Published: *The Lion, the Witch, and the Wardrobe*

1951 January 12: Mrs. Moore dies.
Lewis loses the election for the position of Professor of Poetry at Oxford to C. Day Lewis. In December, he declines election to the Order of the British Empire.
Published: *Prince Caspian*

1952 Lewis is awarded the honorary degree of Doctor of Letters by Laval University in Quebec.
September: He meets Joy Davidman Gresham, fifteen years younger than him (b. April 18, 1915–d. July 13, 1960).
Published: *Mere Christianity*, *The Voyage of the* Dawn Treader

1953 Published: *The Silver Chair*

1954 June: Lewis accepts the Chair of Medieval and Renaissance Literature at Magdalene College, Cambridge.
Published: Review of Tolkien's *The Fellowship of the Ring*, *The Horse and His Boy*

1955 January: Lewis begins his duties at Cambridge. While at Cambridge, he lives at Magdalene College during the week in term and at The Kilns in Oxford on weekends and vacations. Lewis is elected an Honorary Fellow of Magdalen College, Oxford, and a Fellow of the British Academy.
Published: *The Magician's Nephew*, *Surprised by Joy*

1956 Lewis receives the Carnegie Medal in recognition of *The Last Battle.*
April 23: Lewis enters into a civil marriage with Joy Davidman at the Oxford Registry Office for the purpose of giving her British citizenship in order to prevent her deportation by British authorities.
December: A bedside marriage is performed in accordance with the rites of the Church of England in Wingfield Hospital.
Published: *The Last Battle*, *Till We Have Faces*

1958 July: Lewis and Joy go to Ireland for a holiday.
August 19 and 20: Lewis makes tapes of ten talks on the four loves in London.
Lewis is elected an Honorary Fellow of University College, Oxford.
Published: *Reflections on the Psalms*

1959 Lewis receives the honorary degree of Doctor of Literature from the University of Manchester.

1960 April 3 to April 14: Learning of the return of Joy's cancer, Lewis and Joy, with Roger Lancelyn Green and his wife, go to Greece.
July 13: Joy dies at the age of 45, not long after returning from Greece.
Published: *The Four Loves*, *Studies in Words*, *The World's Last Night and Other Essays* (essay collection)

1961 Published: *A Grief Observed*, *An Experiment in Criticism*

1963 Friday, November 22: Lewis dies at 5:30 p.m. at The Kilns, one week before his 65th birthday. This is the same day on which President Kennedy is assassinated and Aldous Huxley dies. He had resigned his position at Cambridge during the summer and was elected an Honorary Fellow of Magdalene College, Cambridge.

Works published posthumously:

Letters to Malcolm: Chiefly on Prayer (1964)
The Discarded Image (1964)
Of Other Worlds (essay collection, 1966)

Studies in Medieval and Renaissance Literature (1966)
Letters to an American Lady (1967)
Spenser's Images of Life (1967)
Weight of Glory (1970)
God in the Dock (1970)
Dark Tower and Other Stories (1977)
Selected Literary Essays (1980)
All My Road Before Me (Lewis's diary, 1991)
Collected Poems (1994)
Collected Letters, Vol. I and II (2004)
Collected Letters, Vol. III (2007)

APPENDIX B

Glossary

Characters, Places, and Old Solar

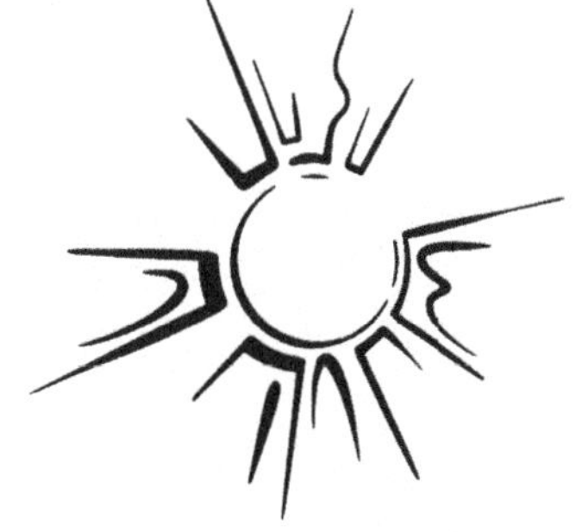

APPENDIX B

A

ALCASAN, Francois: a French-Arab radiologist who was executed. The N.I.C.E uses his head for their experiments.

ARBOL: the sun (see entry *Sol*).

ARBOL HRU (Old Solar): gold; literal translation "the Sun's blood".

AUGRAY: the *sorn* that meets Ransom in *Out of the Silent Planet* and helps him get to Meldilorn.

B

BELBURY: the headquarters of the N.I.C.E., located near the village of Edgestow.

BENT ONE, the: the devil, Satan, the Dark Oyarsa of Thulcandra.

BRACTON COLLEGE: a college in the University of Edgestow; Mark Studdock is a Senior Fellow of sociology there.

BRAGDON WOOD: an ancient woodland which is part of Bracton College and considered to be the resting place of Merlin.

BRIZEACRE, Dr.: a psychiatrist at Bracton College.

MR. BULTITUDE: the last of the seven bears of Logres.

BUSBY, James: Bursar of Bracton College; former clergyman.

C

CRAH (Old Solar): the last part of a poem.

COSSER: a member of the N.I.C.E. sociology department; he manipulates Mark Studdock into writing propaganda about what is going on in Cure Hardy.

CURE HARDY: a village close to Edgestow and Belbury; next on the N.I.C.E.'s list of places to demolish.

CURRY: Sub-warden of Bracton College; leader of the Progressive Element.

D

DAISY: a member of the Women's Auxiliary Institutional Police (see entry *Waips*).

DENNISTON, Arthur: a former friend of Mark Studdock's; member of the company at St. Anne's and husband of Camilla; some readers think Denniston will be the next Pendragon after Ransom leaves (likely because of the name "Arthur"). More evidence points to Mark Studdock as the next Pendragon, at least until his and Jane's promised child is ready to take up the mantle.

DENNISTON, Camilla: tall and valiant; a member of the company at St. Anne's and wife of Arthur; we find out from Ransom that Camilla is pregnant ("You carry its [Logres'] future in your body"). Some use this as an argument that Camilla's child will be the next Pendragon. There is no reason to infer this, necessarily, as Ransom could simply be referring to the presence of a second generation of the True Britain or Logres and not its leader.

DEVINE, Dick (also LORD FEVERSTONE): Devine is an old school fellow of Ransom's from Wedenshaw (not someone Ransom was very fond of) and is a close associate of Weston's. His primary aim in going to Malacandra is to gather wealth. He reappears in *That Hideous Strength* as Lord Feverstone and is deeply ingrained in the workings of Belbury. Devine dies in a great landslide/earthquake at Edgestow.

DIMBLE, Cecil (Dr. Dimble): Fellow of Northumberland; was Jane Studdock's tutor in her last year as a student; expert on Arthurian legend and a member of the company at St. Anne's; Dimble is the only other human character besides Ransom to fluently speak Old Solar.

DIMBLE, Margaret (Mrs. Dimble or Mother Dimble): the wife of Dr. Dimble and member of the company at St. Anne's; the Dimbles have no children but she is an "unofficial aunt" to her husband's students.

E

EDGESTOW: village near Belbury; Edgestow is destroyed by a great earthquake at the end of the book.

ELDIL (pl. *eldila*, sometimes *eldils*): angelic beings who inhabit space; they do not eat, breed, breathe, or die and possess different sort of bodies; there are both good and bad *eldila* (Tellurian or earthly *eldila* which exist beneath the lunar boundary).

F

FEVERSTONE, Lord: (see entry *Devine, Dick*)

FIELD OF ARBOL: the Solar System.

FILOSTRATO, Professor: a physiologist who works for the N.I.C.E. and believes that he has been the one to keep the head of Alcasan alive; he is a large Italian eunuch whose goal is to free humanity from the constraints of materiality; he is decapitated in the laboratory by Straik and Wither.

FIRIKITEKILA: a *pfifltrigg* on Malacandra.

FROST, Augustus: a psychiatrist for the N.I.C.E.; a hard materialist, Frost views emotions as mere chemical reactions; he (along with Wither) knows the true nature of the head; in the end, under the influence of the dark *eldila*, Frost burns to death by locking himself in the Objective Room.

G

GLOSSOP: close friend of Hingest.

GLUNDANDRA (see entry *Jupiter*)

GOULD: a member of the N.I.C.E.

GREEN LADY, the (Tinidril, Embla, Baru'ah, Yatsurah): the first "woman" on Perelandra; the Queen of Perelandra; wife of Tor; Ransom is sent to Perelandra to help prevent the fall of that world which the Un-man attempts to accomplish by the temptation of the Green Lady; she is named Tinidril-Oyarsa-Perelendri on the Holy Mountain at the end of *Perelandra*.

H

HANDRA (Old Solar): earth (the element).

HANDRAMIT (Old Solar): the low, watered country; gorge or canyon.

HARANDRA (Old Solar): the high country.

HARDCASTLE, Fairy: the head of the N.I.C.E.'s Institutional Police, as well as its female auxiliary unit, the Women's Auxiliary Institutional Police (Waips); she is killed by a tiger in the banquet hall at Belbury.

HARRY: village boy who works for Devine and Weston and was intended by them to be taken to Malacandra; Harry's mother asks Ransom to fetch him home and Ransom is kidnapped in Harry's place.

HINGEST, William (Bill the Blizzard): Bracton fellow and physical chemist; Hingest leaves Belbury after seeing what it is all about but is murdered shortly after.

HLAB-ERIBOL-EF-CORDI (Old Solar): the language of Old Solar itself.

HLERI: a she-*hross*.

HLUNTHELINE (Old Solar; future): to long for or yearn; irrational striving for the recreation of an experience.

HMĀN (Old Solar; pl. *hmāna*): man.

HNAKRA (Old Solar; pl. *hnéraki*): an aquatic beast on Malacandra; it has snapping jaws and is born in the northern mountains; the *hrossa* love to hunt it.

HNAKRAPUNT (Old Solar; pl. *hnakrapunti*): slayer of the *hnakra.*

HNAU (Old Solar): rational, sentient creatures with a soul/spirit.

HNOHRA: a *hross.*

HNOO: a *hross.*

HONODRASKRUD (Old Solar): Malacandrian weed; pinkish-white, edible but the *hrossa* do not eat it "for choice."

HRESSA-HLAB (Old Solar): a shortened name for the language of Old Solar, specifically as used by the *hrossa* on Malacandra.

HRIKKI: young she-*hross.*

HRINHA: a *hross* in Meldilorn who ferries Ransom to the island.

HROSS (Old Solar; pl. masculine *hrossa*, pl. feminine *hressni*): one of the three *hnau* species on Malacandra; they have a thick black coat and short legs with webbed feet; six to seven feet high; a whiskered head and short tail; crested *hrossa* in the west are around ten feet high; they live around one hundred and sixty earth years and marry at the age of forty; they are poets and water-workers.

HRU (Old Solar): blood.

HUMPHREY: a doctor that Lewis calls on to be ready for Ransom when he returns from Perelandra.

HYOI: a *hross*; the first *hnau* Malacandrian that Ransom meets; teaches Ransom Old Solar and much about the

Fields of Arbol; tells Ransom that he must go to Oyarsa; takes Ransom on a hunt for the *hnakra* and, with Ransom, becomes *hnakrapunt* before he is shot by Weston and Devine.

I

IRONWOOD, Grace: a doctor and psychologist; member of the company at St. Anne's and close friend to Ransom.

J

JEWEL: Canon Jewel is an elderly priest in Bracton College. He is against the proposed sale of college land but is outvoted.

JULES, Horace: a novelist and reporter; he is the appointed Director of the N.I.C.E., but Wither and Frost really pull the strings and he is not aware of the true nature of their work; he is strongly anti-religious and opposes the presence of clerics at Belbury; he is shot by Fairy Hardcastle at the banquet.

JUPITER (Jove, Glundandra): *Fortuna Major*; the greatest of the seven planets; Jove is lord and king; festal and joyous, a king at his leisure; he binds all the planets together; also known as the Wounded Planet (due to the dark, blood-like mark on his surface).

K

KANAKABERAKA: the first *pfifltrigg* that Ransom meets on Malacandra; he works on a carving of Ransom.

KITTY: a member of the Women's Auxiliary Institutional Police (see entry *Waips*).

L

LEN: a member of the N.I.C.E. who captures Mr. Bultitude.

LEWIS (character): friend of Ransom; helps Ransom in his preparations for his journey to Perelandra and assists him when he returns.

LUNA (the Moon, also Sulva): Luna marks the boundary between the sublunar and translunar realms; below the moon all is silent and Earth is sealed off from the rest of the Field of Arbol according to the Seventh Law.

LUR: a "green sea" on Perelandra where Tor is taken to be instructed and guided.

LURGA (see entry *Saturn*)

M

MACPHEE, Andrew: a close friend of Ransom's; an Ulster Scot who is a scientist, a rationalist, and skeptic; he is a member of the company at St. Anne's albeit with certain conditions (he is not allowed to go search for Merlin because he is not a Christian); based on Lewis's tutor Kirkpatrick.

MAGGS, Ivy: a former part-time maid for Jane Studdock; she is kicked out of town by the N.I.C.E. and joins the company at St. Anne's; her husband, Tom, is in prison for petty theft.

MALACANDRA (planet, Mars): *Infortuna Minor*; god of war and battle; he produces iron in the earth and courage and sturdy hardiness in men.

MALACANDRA (Oyarsa): the ruling angelic being of Mars.

MALELDIL: the Triune, Christian God.

MALELDIL the YOUNG: Jesus Christ; the Son of God and second Person of the Trinity.

MARS: see entry *Malacandra (planet)*

MELDILORN: the island on Malacandra where Ransom goes to meet the Oyarsa.

MERCURY (planet, Viritrilbia): lord of language and meaning; his metal is quicksilver.

MERLIN, Ambrosius: buried and asleep for 1500 years in Bragdon Wood and awakened in *That Hideous Strength*; he is sought for by both the members of the N.I.C.E. and the company of St. Anne's; Merlin becomes a vessel by which the powers of Deep Heaven can come down to Thulcandra and defeat the people of Belbury; this is also the means by which his soul can be saved; Merlin is "used up" by this act and is buried in the collapse of Belbury.

MYRTLE: Mark Studdock's twin sister.

N

N.I.C.E: the National Institute of Co-ordinated Experiments.

O

O'HARA, Captain: second-in-command to Fairy Hardcastle; works with Mark on the newspaper articles about Alcasan.

OLD ONE, the: God the Father; the first Person of the Trinity.

OYARSA (pl. Oyerésu): angelic beings; a higher order of *eldila* who rule over each of the planets.

P

PERELANDRA (planet, Venus): *Fortuna Minor*; the goddess of love and fertility; the maternal planet; she produces copper in the earth and amorousness in men.

PERELANDRA (Oyarsa): the ruling angelic being of Venus.

PFIFLTRIGG (pl. *pfifltriggi*): one of the three *hnau* species on Malacandra; in appearance they are described as reptilian, like grasshoppers, and frog-like; small and hairless; having many fingers and making a rasping sound when they move and having a piping laugh; they are matriarchal and short-lived; they live in the forests and mines on Malacandra's old ocean beds; they are the craftsmen and artisans, the makers.

R

RANSOM, Dr. Elwin (Mr. Fisher-King, the Director, the Pendragon, the Pedestrian): a philologist and fellow of Cambridge College; around forty to fifty years old at the beginning of the trilogy.

S

SATURN (planet, Lurga): *Infortuna Major*; he produces lead in the earth and melancholy in men; the god of time.

SID: a member of the N.I.C.E. who captures Mr. Bultitude.

SOL (the Sun): produces gold in the earth and generosity and wisdom in men; he produces fortunate events.

SORN (pl. *séroni*): one of the three *hnau* species on Malacandra; about eighteen feet tall; white, thin, and elongated bodies; they have narrow, conical heads and solemn faces; they have thin hands like a bird and are covered in transparent feathers; they are the philosophers and intelligentsia.

ST. ANNE'S: a town near to Edgestow where there is a manor in which Ransom has set up his company.

STEELE: head director of sociology at the N.I.C.E; he does not approve of Mark Studdock; he is killed by an elephant at the banquet.

ST. ELIZABETH'S: Jane Studdock's old college.

STONE: a Belbury employee who appears to be out of favor with the N.I.C.E.; Mark meets him in Wither's office; he searches for Merlin.

STRAIK, Reverend: Welsh; the "mad parson" of the N.I.C.E.; he believes in power over all else and that science is the instrument that God is using to build His kingdom on Earth; Straik has undergone excessive brainwashing; he is killed by Wither who stabs him to death in the laboratory after they decapitate Filostrato.

STUDDOCK, Jane (Tudor): twenty-three years old; wife of Mark Studdock; she is working on her doctorate on Donne's "vindication of the body"; she has delayed having children and is accused by Merlin of thus having prevented the birth of the next Pendragon; she has visions that enable St. Anne's to gather vital information which helps them in their conflict with Belbury.

STUDDOCK, Mark: sociologist and fellow of Bracton College; husband of Jane Studdock; he is ambitious but more obsessed with being a part of the "inner ring" than anything else.

SULVA: see entry *Luna (the Moon)*

SURNIBUR (Old Solar): the speech of the *sorns*.

T

TAI HARENDRIMAR (Old Solar): the Hill of Life; a place in Perelandra where Ransom meets Tor and Tinidril after his fight with the Un-man.

THIRD ONE, the: the Holy Spirit; the third Person of the Trinity.

THULC (Old Solar): silent.

THULCANDRA: Earth, the Silent Planet, the Wounded World; the terrestrial, sublunar realm which is blocked off from the rest of the Field of Arbol by the Seventh Law (which is broken by Weston and Devine).

TINIDRIL: (see entry *Green Lady, the*)

TOR (Ask, Baru, Yatsur): the King of Perelandra; husband of Tinidril (see entry *Green Lady, the*); he is taken to Lur (a "green sea") where he learns many things; he is named Tor-Oyarsa-Perelendri on the Holy Mountain at the end of *Perelandra.*

U

UN-MAN, the: Ransom's name for Weston after he has been possessed by the devil on Perelandra.

V

VENUS: see entry *Perelandra (planet)*

VIRITRILBIA: see entry *Mercury (planet)*

W

WAIPS: the Women's Auxiliary Institutional Police run by the N.I.C.E.

WESTON, Edward Rolles: a great physicist who discovered "Weston rays"; he is driven by a desire to see the human race survive and builds a space-ship to send mankind out onto other planets; he is possessed by a devil (perhaps Satan) and comes to Perelandra; while possessed, he is killed by Ransom who smashes his head in with a rock under the mountain on Perelandra; his body falls into a fiery chasm.

WHIN: a *hross*; Hyoi's friend.

WINTER: a member of the N.I.C.E.

WITHER, John: the Deputy Director of the N.I.C.E.; he is the true leader (rather than Jules); he is a dedicated servant of the "Macrobes" (dark *eldila*) and because of his interactions with them, his humanity is "withering" and his ghost appears frequently around Belbury; he is finally killed in the laboratory by Mr. Bultitude (the last of the seven bears of Logres) after Wither has killed both Filostrato and Straik.

WONDELONE (Old Solar): to long for or yearn for something from the past while remaining satisfied that that thing is gone and may not return.

APPENDIX C

INDEX

Allusions, Quotations, and Translations

APPENDIX C

As you've seen throughout the course of this book, C. S. Lewis was a master of quotation and allusion. His works echo with the sheer enormity of the knowledge he had of classical literature, poetry, and mythology. Sometimes Lewis will give us the source of these quotations, but more often they are slipped in where we hardly notice them. They don't shout for attention, yet they give a richness and maturity to his writing. In addition to direct quotations, Lewis will also use allusion (a reference to some other work or author). He also uses phrases in other languages without proffering a translation.

In this appendix, you will find an index of most of the allusions and direct quotations that appear throughout the Ransom Trilogy, as well as translations of phrases in other languages. This is very likely not a comprehensive index, as more comes to the surface with every rereading.

Note: All page numbers are taken from the Scribner paperback editions.

Out of the Silent Planet

Note

"Mr. H.G. Wells's fantasies"

H. G. Wells (1866–1946) was a pioneer in science fiction as a genre, for whom Lewis had a great respect and admiration, despite having a very different philosophy and cosmology.

Chapter 1

"Lo, the poor Indian" (p. 16)

From Alexander Pope's *Essay on Man.*

Chapter 5

"a second Danaë" (p. 33)

Danae is a figure from Greek mythology. Zeus came to her in the form of golden rain and by her begat Perseus.

"sweet influence" (p. 33)

From John Milton's Paradise Lost, 7.373–375:

> [...] the grey
> Dawn, and the Pleiades, before him danced,
> Shedding sweet influence.

See also see Job 38:31.

> "Can you bind the cluster of the Pleiades,
> Or loose the belt of Orion?"

"happy climes that ly
Where day never shuts his eye
Up in the broad fields of the sky." (p. 34)

John Milton, *Comus* (1634), epilogue

Chapter 8

"Wellsian fantasies" (p. 48)

Reference to the creatures found in the science fiction of H. G. Wells and those others influenced by him who wrote within the same genre.

Chapter 9

"basso profundissimo" (p. 53)

Italian: "deepest bass"

Chapter 11

"faute de mieux" (p. 67)

French: "in necessity; for want of a better alternative."

"He remembered how H.G. Wells's Cavor had met his end on the Moon" (p. 71)

Cavor is a character from Wells's book *The First Men in the Moon*. Cavor tells those who dwell on the Moon about the human wars. He is presumably then killed by them, likely in order to prevent any more humans coming to the Moon to spread their bloodthirsty ways.

Chapter 15

"albs, devas *and the like*" (p. 95)

Alb (from Latin *albus* meaning "white or bright") is used rather obscurely by Lewis here to refer to mythical angelic beings. *Deva* is a word used in many Eastern religions to refer to angelic beings.

Chapter 17

"rather like one of Arthur Rackham's dwarfs" (p. 112)

Arthur Rackham (1867–1939) was an English illustrator. Rackham was considered to be a forerunner of Britain's Golden Age of Illustration and he illustrated a large number of mythologies of various cultures, fantasies, and children's stories.

Chapter 18

"a thing we desire to look into" (p. 121)

"To them it was revealed that, not to themselves, but to us they were ministering the things which now have been reported to you through those who have preached the gospel to you by the Holy Spirit sent from heaven—things which angels desire to look into" (1 Peter 1:12).

Chapter 19

"the undoubted work of Mr. Woolworth" (p. 127)

Woolworth's was a large American company with branches in Great Britain known for its cheapness and poor quality.

"The stars in their courses were fighting against Weston." (p. 127)

"They fought from the heavens;
The stars from their courses fought against Sisera."
(Judges 5:20)

Chapter 22

"Bernardus Silvestris" (p. 151)

Silvestris was a twelfth-century Platonist philosopher and poet; his *Cosmographia* (or *De mundi universitate*) speaks of the creation of the universe and talks about things like the music of the spheres and *oyarses* (planetary figures).

"I asked C.J. about it" (p. 151)

Likely referring to Oxford philosopher and historian, Clement C. J. Webb of Magdalen College.

"Aristotle" (p. 152)

Famous Greek philosopher (c. 384–322 B.C.).

"Kipling" (p. 152)

Rudyard Kipling (1865–1936), English journalist, poet, and novelist. Kipling was known for using the phrase "but that is another story" in many of his short stories. The phrase pops up in seven of his short stories that appear in the collection titled *Plain Tales from the Hill.*

Postscript

"deeper than Chaliapin" (p. 153-154)

Feodor Chaliapin (1873–1938) was a Russian opera singer.

"you remember Chaucer's "airish beasts'?" (p. 155)

Geoffrey Chaucer (c. 1340–1400) was a famous middle English poet. The reference to "airish beasts" or "beasts of air" is found in *The House of Fame*, preceded by a mention of Plato:

> For in this regioun, certein,
> Dwelleth many a citezein,
> Of which that speketh dan Plato.
> These ben the *eyrish bestes*, lo!
> (emphasis mine)

"Ypres Salient" (p. 156)

Ypres Salient is an area around Ypres in Belgium which was the site of some of the largest battles of World War I. There are currently over 100 military cemeteries in the Ypres Salient area.

"The author whom I mentioned to you [...] 'For it was well said of the great Africanus that he was never less alone than when alone, so, in our philosophy, no parts of this universal frame are less to be called solitarie, since the withdrawing of men and beasts signifieth but the greater frequency of more excellent creatures.'" (p. 158)

Cicero (c. 106–42 B.C.) was a Roman statesman and author. This is a quote from *De officiis*, 3.2. "Africanus" refers to Roman general Scipio Africanus.

"If there is to be any more space-travelling, it will have to be time-travelling as well...!" (p. 158)

Perhaps a reference to Lewis's agreement with Tolkien that he would write a space-travel story and Tolkien would write a time-travel story. This could be Lewis's subtle "passing of the torch" to J. R. R. Tolkien. Lewis ended up writing his own time travel story that is linked to the Ransom Trilogy called *The Dark Tower* which was published posthumously by Walter Hooper.

Perelandra

Dedication

"To Some Ladies at Wantage"

The "ladies at Wantage" were nuns of the Community of St. Mary the Virgin which was founded in 1848. They lived in a convent at Wantage, south of Oxford. Sister Penelope, one of the nuns, wrote more than forty letters to Lewis between 1939 and 1957. In her first letter, written in August 1939, she thanks Lewis for writing *Out of the Silent Planet.* In 1944, Lewis wrote an introduction for Sister Penelope's translation of Athanasius' *On the Incarnation.*

Chapter 1

"Mr. Wells's Martians" (p. 11)

H. G. Wells (1866–1946).

"or his Selenites" (p. 11)

From H. G. Wells's *The First Men in the Moon* (1901); this is one name for the inhabitants of the Moon originating from the Greek goddess Selene whose name in Greek (Σελήνη) literally means "moon."

"I was seeing the archon of Mars" (p. 17)

Greek *archôn* (ἀρχων) meaning "leader" or "ruler"; was once used to refer to any one of the nine high magistrates in ancient Athens. This word was used by the Gnostics in first-century Christian and Jewish circles to refer to the seven rulers of the seven celestial spheres, each of which was linked up with one of the planets, much like Lewis's Oyarses.

"Natvilcius" (footnote on p. 17)

Natvilcius is a name made up by Lewis. It is a Latinized form of *Nat Whilk*, which is an Anglo-Saxon phrase meaning "I know not whom," the equivalent of saying "author unknown" or "anonymous." Lewis sometimes used *Nat Whilk* or *N. W.* as a pseudonym, especially with his earlier published poems. *A Grief Observed* (1961), Lewis's meditations on the death of his wife, was initially published under the name N. W. Clerk.

"Leave your familiar alone…" (p. 18)

Familiar is a term used to refer to an attendant spirit to a magician, sometimes taking the form of an animal.

Chapter 2

"in his own photosome or whatever we should call it" (p. 21)

"Photosome," Greek: "light-body."

"principalities and powers" (p. 21)

"For we do not wrestle against flesh and blood, but against principalities, against powers, against the rulers of the darkness of this age, against spiritual hosts of wickedness in the heavenly places" (Ephesians 6:12).

"There's a man called Schiaparelli" (p. 23)

Giovanni Schiaparelli (1835–1910) was an Italian astronomer.

"hopes deferred" (p. 26)

"Hope deferred makes the heart sick" (Proverbs 13:12).

"all the earth became full of darkness and cruel habitations" (p. 26)

> "[...] the dark places of the earth are full of the haunts of cruelty" (Psalm 74:20).

Chapter 3

"a sceptical friend of ours called McPhee" (p. 29)

We meet this character (McPhee) again in *That Hideous Strength*, though Lewis apparently decided to change the spelling to "MacPhee."

"The reason why the thing can't be expressed is that it's too definite *for language"* (p. 30)

"I suspect that all these difficulties may be put down to a single cause: the cause Mendelssohn had in mind when he wrote: 'The thoughts that are expressed to me by music that I love are not too indefinite to be put into words, but on the contrary too definite'" (C. S. Lewis, *Spenser's Images of Life*, 115).

Chapter 4

"garden of the Hesperides" (p. 40)

The garden of the Hesperides was a garden in Greek mythology which was located at the foot of the Atlas Mountains in northwest Africa. The Hesperides (Greek: "daughters of evening") were said to be the three (or sometimes more) daughters of Atlas and Hesperis (or Erebus and Night...as is usual with Greek mythology, identifying parentage can be difficult). These goddesses guard a tree with golden apples in the center of this garden, aided by the dragon Ladon.

"Cyclops" (p. 40)

Greek mythology; the cyclops were one-eyed giants, at least one of which was a son of Poseidon.

"the verse in Pope, 'die of a rose in aromatic pain'" (p. 42)

Alexander Pope (1688–1744), *An Essay on Man* I, 200.

"'Sober certainty of waking bliss'" (p. 44)

John Milton (1608–1674), Comus, 263.

"Circe or Alcina" (p. 48)

Circe is a sorceress in Greek mythology who lives on the island of Aeaea, where she is known to turn visitors into animals. Alcina is a wicked sorceress appearing in *Orlando Furioso* by Ludovico Ariosto (1474–1533); she has the same unbreakable habit as Circe of turning people into beasts.

"a Titian satyr" (p. 49)

A satyr is a half-human creature in Greek mythology with the ears and tail of a horse. This creature was often depicted by the Italian painter Tiziano Vecelli, who was known more commonly as Titian (c. 1490–1576).

Chapter 5

"walking before him as if on the other side of a brook, was the Lady herself" (p. 51)

See Dante, *Purgatorio* 18.34-42. When Dante first sees Matilda, she is walking on the other side of a brook. Lewis, in a letter to Charles A. Brady, pointed out the parallel between his Green Lady and Dante's Matilda. (C. S. Lewis to Charles A. Brady, Oxford, October 29, 1944, *Letters*, 2:630).

"Artemis" (p. 56)

Artemis was the Greek goddess of hunting and also the moon. Later she becomes associated with nature in general as well as childbirth (and also chastity). She is given the name Diana in Roman mythology.

"Mænad" (p. 56)

In ancient Greece, a female who participated in festivities performed to honor the god Bacchus or Dionysius, who is the god of wine and fertility.

"Maleldil Himself wept when He saw it" (p. 58)

"Therefore, when Jesus saw her weeping, and the Jews who came with her weeping, He groaned in the spirit and was troubled. And He said, 'Where have you laid him?' They said to Him, 'Lord, come and see.' Jesus wept. Then the Jews said, 'See how He loved him!' And some of them said, 'Could not this Man, who opened the eyes of the blind, also have kept this man from dying?' Then Jesus, again groaning in Himself, came to the tomb. It was a cave, and a stone lay against it" (John 11:33–38).

Chapter 6

"Giant's Causeway" (p. 63)

A natural wonder with basalt columns on the coast of Antrim, Northern Ireland.

"Something like a shooting star seemed to have streaked across the sky" (p. 65)

"I saw Satan fall like lightning from heaven" (Luke 10:18). See also Revelation 8:10-11: "Then the third angel sounded: And a great star fell from heaven, burning like a torch [...] The name of the star is Wormwood. A third of the waters became wormwood, and many men died from the water, because it was made bitter."

"the first of worlds to wake after the great change" (p. 71)

The "great change" refers to the Incarnation.

Chapter 7

"inter-sidereal" (p. 77)

Latin, *inter* (between) and *sidus*, *sideris* (star); literally "between the stars" or "between constellations." In the context of Weston's comments, he could be using it to mean "between galaxies."

"God is a spirit" (p. 79)

"God is Spirit, and those who worship Him must worship in spirit and truth" (John 4:24).

"your hell a picture of the urge or nisus" (p. 80)

Nisus, Latin: "exertion," "striving," "forward urge".

"qui dort dîne" (p. 84)

French: literally "he who sleeps dines." Colloquially, this could be translated "he who sleeps forgets his hunger."

Chapter 8

"when the morning stars sang together" (p. 92)

> "Where were you when I laid the foundations of the earth [...]
> When the morning stars sang together,
> And all the sons of God shouted for joy?"
> (Job 38:4, 7)

Chapter 9

"a man who had been on the Somme" (p. 94)

Ransom had fought as a soldier in World War I. The Somme is a river in northern France where there were horrific battles in the summer of 1916. Thousands of soldiers were killed. This is also one of many Martial references that we see crop up throughout Ransom's growth on Perelandra.

"it is for this that I came here, that you may have Death in abundance" (p. 98)

"I have come that they may have life, and that they may have it more abundantly" (John 10:10). Also alluded to by G. K. Chesterton: "Schopenhauer hovering over the future; but it was also Manichaeus rising from the dead; that men might have death and that they might have it more abundantly" (G. K. Chesterton, *The Everlasting Man* in *The Collected Works of G. K. Chesterton*, Vol. 2, 386).

"Are you certain that He really wishes to be always obeyed?" (p. 99)

Echoing Adam's words from *Paradise Lost* after he has sinned and is shown by the archangel Michael the future of his offspring and the coming Messiah:

> Henceforth I learn that to obey is best
> And love with fear the only God, to walk
> As in His present, ever to observe
> His providence, and on his sole depend.
> (12.561–564)

"Felix peccatum Adae" (p. 104)

Latin: literally "Happy/blessed sin of Adam." See also chapter seventeen: "the sin whereby it came is called Fortunate."

Chapter 10

"the Prince of Darkness is a gentleman" (p. 110)

Shakespeare, *King Lear*, 3.4.

"Mephistopheles" (p. 110)

Mephistopheles is a demon, first appearing in the late medieval German legend of Faustus.

"Paradise Lost" (p. 110)

John Milton (1608–1674), English poet. Lewis discusses Satan's character at length in *A Preface to Paradise Lost* (1942).

"Agrippina" (p. 113)

Iulia Agrippina (A.D. 15–59) was the second wife of the Roman emperor Claudius. She had two husbands before Claudius and she is thought to have poisoned him. She was also the mother of Nero, who had her executed after he became emperor. She was a cruel and merciless woman.

"Lady Macbeth" (p. 113)

The wife of the title character in Shakespeare's *Macbeth*. She is the one to prod him into murdering his King and seizing the throne for himself. In the end, her guilt drives her to madness and eventually suicide.

Chapter 11

"'Tis not in mortals to command success" (p. 120)

Joseph Addison (1672–1719), English poet, *Cato*, 1.2.

"Men were at war, and white-faced subalterns and freckled corporals who had but lately begun to shave, stood in horrible gaps or crawled forward in deadly darkness" (p. 121)

World War II. Another Martial reference.

"Horatius stood on the bridge" (p. 121)

Publius Horatius Cocles (literally, "the one-eyed") was a Roman hero in the late sixth century B.C. He and only two companions defended a bridge (the Pons Sublicius) over the Tiber against the approaching Etruscan army so that the Romans could demolish the bridge. He then leapt into the river, completely armored, and swam across it, not having lost any of his weaponry. It is said he lost one eye in the conflict, hence his cognomen.

"Constantine" (p. 121)

Constantine the Great (c. 280–337), Roman emperor. He became a great defender of Christianity. After he fell gravely ill, he requested to be baptized in the Jordan River. He died shortly after.

"fallings from him, vanishings" (p. 123)

Line from *Ode. Intimations of Immortality from Recollections of Early Childhood* (line 148) by William Wordsworth (1770–1850), an English poet ("fallings from us, vanishings").

"lose his nerve as St. Peter had done, and be, like St. Peter, forgiven" (p. 125)

See Peter's betrayal of Jesus, Matthew 26:69–75.

"sat before Him like Pilate" (p. 126)

See Matthew 27.

"the slaying before the foundation of the world" (p. 126)

"All who dwell on the earth will worship him, whose names have not been written in the Book of Life of the Lamb slain from the foundation of the world" (Revelation 13:8).

Chapter 12

"When I wake up after Thy image, I shall be satisfied" (p. 128)

> "I shall be satisfied when I awake in Your likeness."
> (Psalm 17:15)

"Eloi, Eloi, lama sabachthani" (p. 130)

"My God, My God, why have You forsaken me?" (Matthew 27:46).

"The Battle of Maldon" (p. 132)

Old English poem dating from the tenth century about the battle of Maldon which took place c. 991 between the Anglo-Saxons and the Viking invaders.

"My hounds are bred out of the Spartan kind, so flew'd so sanded..." (p. 134)

Shakespeare, *A Midsummer Night's Dream*, 4.1.

"All the good things are now–a thin little rind of what we call life, put on for show, and then–the real universe for ever and ever." (p. 143)

Here, Lewis has Weston express Friedrich Nietzsche's view of the world, the idea that all of the good things in life (beauty, art, etc.) are simply an Apollonian veil (or thin rind) that we draw over the vast abyss of reality in order to cope and not dissolve into hopelessness.

Chapter 14

"Æneid" (p. 148)

The epic poem of Vergil (70–19 B.C.), a Roman poet.

"Chanson de Roland" (p. 148)

The Song of Roland, an Old French epic poem about Charlemagne, his valiant soldiers, and their fight against the Saracens in Spain.

"Kalevala" (p. 148)

Finnish work of national epic poetry, compiled by Elias Lönnrot in the nineteenth century.

"The Hunting of the Snark" (p. 148)

A nonsense poem (1876) by Lewis Carroll (born Charles Dodgson, 1832–1898), who is best known for his children's book *Alice in Wonderland.*

"a rhyme about Germanic sound-laws" (p. 148)

Lewis himself wrote a rhyme like this when he was a tutor in Oxford. Part of the text of this poem (see below) can be found in Walter Hooper's Preface to Lewis's *Selected Literary Essays.* The entire poem appears to only exist in one of Lewis's personal notebooks which Walter Hooper has in his possession.

From *W. GMNC* to *Primitive O.E.*
Vowel Changes.

AU, AI, Ă, Ā, EU, IU.

When Hors and Hengist turned the prow
From home, they brought Germanic AU
And AI from Baltic woods afar
And short Ă and the longer Ā
And EU and its companion IU;
Through all whose fates I mean to see you.

A > Æ̂

The short Ă soon began to wag,
WĂGAN turned WÆGN, DĂGS turned DÆ̂G;
Or, by a following nasal bitten,
More often as an "O" was written;
Ã nasalized (in some cold lough),

Followed by an X, became an ŌH;
Said Hengist "BRĀXTA, DÃHTA ought-ter
Be rather sounded BROHTE, þOHTE."
To whom thus Hors replied with scorn…

"He had picked up a big, jagged stone from beside the stream" (p. 155)

"And he [David] chose for himself five smooth stones from the brook" (1 Samuel 17:40).

"the face smashed out of all recognition." (p. 155)

"And I will put enmity
Between you and the woman,
And between your seed and her Seed;
He shall bruise your head,
And you shall bruise His heel."
(Genesis. 3:15)

Chapter 15

"a wound in his heel" (p. 160)

Genesis 3:15 (see previous entry).

"But on the third day he was well" (p. 162)

"[...] He was buried, and […] He rose again the third day according to the Scriptures" (1 Corinthians 15:4).

"He looked to see an angel with a flaming sword" (p. 165)

"So He drove out the man; and He placed cherubim at the east of the garden of Eden, and a flaming sword which turned every way, to guard the way to the tree of life" (Genesis 3:24).

Chapter 16

"I rounded this ball when it first arose from Arbol." (p. 168)

Here, Lewis echoes Tolkien's idea of sub-creation in which created beings are given the power to create parts of the world/worlds (on different levels) by God. In Tolkien's *Ainulindalë* (the first part of *The Silmarillion*), we see him implementing this idea of sub-creation when he has Ilúvatar (God) grant the power of creation to his angels (the Ainur) who sing the world into existence. Here is appears that the Oyarsa was given a certain amount of creative power in the fields of heaven.

"one of Maleldil's sayers" (p. 168)

Referring to the Apostle Paul, Galatians 4:1–7.

"concentric wheels" (p. 170)

"The appearance of their workings was, as it were, a wheel in the middle of a wheel" (Ezekiel 1:16). In one of his letters, Lewis writes that he owes a "heavy debt to Ezekiel" for the way he described the *eldila* (Letter to Mary Willis Shelburne, Oxford, March 4, 1953, *Letters*, 3:302).

"A faint breath, as Virgil says, reaches even the late generations" (p. 172)

Vergil, *Aeneid* 7.646.

Chapter 17

"Tor and Tinidril, Baru and Baru'ah, Ask and Embla, Yatsur and Yatsurah" (p. 177)

Tolkien says that the names *Tor* and *Tinidril* "are clearly Tor and his elf-wife Idril blended with Tinuviel (the second name of Luthien)". See Tolkien's letter of July 17, 1971, to Roger Lancelyn Green, quoted in Green & Hooper, *C. S. Lewis: A Biography* (San Diego: Harcourt, 1974), 177.

A *baru* was a master of divination or soothsayer in ancient Assyro-Babylonian religion, responsible for offering purification sacrifices. *Baru'ah* appears to be an invented female form of this name.

Ask and *Embla* are the first two human beings according to old Norse creation myth. They are mentioned in both the *Prose Edda* (written by Snorri Sturluson in the thirteenth century) and *Poetic Edda* (compiled in the thirteenth century but drawing on older sources).

Yatsur is Hebrew. It is a masculine noun meaning "form" or "member." It is also the passive participle of the verb *yatsar* which means "to frame, fashion, form, or create." *Yatsurah* is likely an invented female form.

"The Great Dance does not wait to be perfect..." (p. 183)

Chalcidius (a fourth-century writer) is likely the inspiration for Lewis's idea of the Great Dance. Alanus was a French twelfth-century writer who further developed this concept. For more on this, see Lewis's *The Discarded Image*, pages 55 and 58.

"This is the Morning Star which He promised to those who conquer" (p. 185)

"[...] and I will give him the morning star" (Revelation 2:28).

"Glund...Lurga...Neruval!" (p. 185)

The planets Jupiter, Saturn, and Uranus.

"Let me wash your foot in this pool'...the King kneeled before him in the shallow water" (p. 189)

"[...] He poured water into a basin and began to wash the disciples' feet" (John 13:5).

That Hideous Strength

Dedication

"J. McNeill"

Jane Agnes McNeill (1889–1959) was a friend of both C. S. Lewis and his brother W. H. ("Warnie") Lewis who lived in Belfast. She appears in *Surprised by Joy* under the name "Janie M."

Motto

"Sir David Lyndsay"

David Lyndsay was a Scottish herald to King James V of Scotland and the last major poet of the old Scots tradition (1486–1555). His poem *Ane Dialog* is a dialogue regarding the current state of the church and nation in light of the history of the world. Its full title is *Ane Dialog betuix Experience and ane Courteour* (1555). Lyndsay was writing at the time of the Reformation in Scotland and was one of the early readers of Tyndale's translation of the Bible, advocating to get it into the hands of the common man. He frequently satirized the abuses of church authority in his writings, and the tower of Babel in *Ane Dialog* is meant to represent all of this abuse. This David Lyndsay is not to be confused with the modern science fiction author David Lindsay, whose book

Voyage to Arcturus (1920) was another one of Lewis's literary inspirations.

"that hyddeous Strength"

Refers to the tower of Babel. See Genesis 11:4-9. Lyndsay used the word "Strength" here in the older sense of "stronghold" or "bulwark".

Preface

"The Abolition of Man" (p. 7)

A series of lectures given by C. S. Lewis for the University of Durham in 1943 and published later that year by Oxford University Press.

"Olaf Stapledon" (p. 8)

An English writer and philosopher (1886–1950), author of the science fiction novel *Last and First Men* (1930). This is one of the books that drove Lewis himself to dive into the "scientifiction" genre. Lewis disliked the philosophy that was being put forward by the authors in this genre, but also recognized that it could support the weight of a worldview.

"Numinor and the True West, Tolkien" (p. 8)

J. R. R. Tolkien (1892–1973), author, professor, and friend of Lewis's. His *The Lord of the Rings* was published in 1954–1955 after nearly twenty years of writing and rewriting. He had great encouragement to finish this work from Lewis and other colleagues in weekly meetings of the literary club called the Inklings. *That Hideous Strength* was written in 1943 and so references or allusions to Tolkien's writings are a result of Lewis's readings of the early manuscripts or pieces that Tolkien read aloud to his friends. This would explain Lewis's use of *Numinor* for Tolkien's *Númenor*. The history of Númenor and the True West can primarily be found in *The Silmarillion* which was published after Tolkien's death in 1977, although it was written before *The Lord of the Rings*.

Chapter 1: Sale of College Property

"John Donne" (p. 12)

One of the English metaphysical poets (1572–1631). See Lewis's 1938 essay "Donne and Love Poetry in the Seventeenth Century" in *Selected Literary Essays*, edited by Walter Hooper (Cambridge: University Press, 1969), 106–125.

"Love's Alchymie" (p. 14)

From John Donne's *Songs and Sonnets* (1631).

"Henry de Bracton" (p. 15)

A medieval English lawyer (c. 1210–1268) who wrote an important work on common law. He argues that the King, far from being above the law, is actually subject to it: "The King is under the Law for it is the Law that maketh him a King" (quoted and translated by C. S. Lewis in *English Literature in the Sixteenth Century*, 48). Lewis also quotes this line directly in *The Horse and His Boy*: "No. The King's under the law, for it's the law that makes him a king. Hast no more power to start away from thy crown than any sentry from his post" (*The Horse and His Boy*, 167).

"it was still sweet in the mouth" (p. 15)

"[...] evil is sweet in his mouth" (Job 20:12).

"Watson" (p. 16)

Character created by Sir Arthur Conan Doyle (1859–1930); Watson is a friend and assistant to the character Sherlock Holmes and is the one writing down the stories of Sherlock's adventures.

"Distributivism" (p. 17)

Also called *distributism*; an economic theory which had some traction in the early twentieth century, particularly among Roman Catholics. Some of its most well-known supporters were G. K. Chesterton and Hilaire Belloc.

"Inigo Jones" (p. 18)

English architect and designer (1573–1652).

"Bunyan" (p. 18)

John Bunyan (1628–1688), English Puritan preacher and writer. Best known as the author of *Pilgrim's Progress.*

"Walton's Lives*"* (p. 18)

Izaak Walton (1593–1683) was an English ironmonger and linen draper who wrote two well-known books, one of which, the *Lives*, is a collection of short biographies of several prominent poets and writers of the time, including John Donne, George Herbert, and Richard Hooker.

"Strabo's Balacthon*"* (p. 19)

"Strabo" most likely refers to Walafrid Strabo (808–849), a Benedictine monk, theologian, and poet. When he was young, Strabo set to verse a piece written by his tutor, including many images of hell, purgatory, and paradise which is often considered a precursor to Dante's *Divine Comedy*. And yet, no poem titled "Balacthon" by Strabo can be found. Lewis apparently pulled different strands together to create this fictitious history of Bragdon and he himself wrote these poetic lines in Middle English.

"Cromwell" (p. 20)

Oliver Cromwell (1599–1658) was an English Puritan general and statesman. He was the leader of the parliamentary army during the English Civil War. Cromwell ruled over the British Isles as Lord Protector of the Commonwealth for the last five years of his life (1653–1658) after Charles I was executed in 1649.

"Merlin who was the Devil's son" (p. 20)

The Welsh monk Nennius (c. A.D. 800) is commonly credited with compiling the *Historia Brittonum* (History of the Britons). In this work, there is found a story taking place around A.D. 430 about a boy named Ambrosius who had been gifted with prophetic powers and who had no human father. In Welsh legend, Merlinus (Myrddin Wyllt) was actually the name of a bard and seer who lived in the late sixth century (much later than the Ambrosius mentioned above). Still later, around 1140, Geoffrey of Monmouth wrote the *Historia Regum Britanniae* (History of the Kings of Britain) in which we find the story of a young prophet, also lacking a human father (6.17–19). The boy is called Merlin and he appears as a magician in other parts of the book. Geoffrey of Monmouth was the one who Latinized the Welsh name Myrddin Wyllt into Merlinus and associated this figure with the Ambrosius of earlier legend. Geoffrey's History can be credited with setting off the tradition of medieval Arthurian literature. This tradition took off particularly well in France (see Chrétien de Troyes, 1130–1191, and Malory's *Le Morte d'Arthur*). By the thirteenth century, it was commonly thought that Merlin's lack of a human father meant that he was the son of the Devil himself.

"Sir Kenelm Digby" (p. 20)

English diplomat and philosopher (1603–1665), known for his eccentric pursuit of astrology, alchemy, science, and poetry.

"Collins the poet" (p. 20)

William Collins (1721–1759), a pre-Romantic poet.

"George the Third" (p. 20)

King George III (1738–1920), the "mad king."

"Nathaniel Fox" (p. 20)

Fictional WWI poet invented by Lewis.

"a late version like Malory's" (p. 29)

Sir Thomas Malory (c. 1405–1471) wrote *Le Morte d'Arthur* (The Death of Arthur, published in 1485) which is a large collection of Arthurian stories. The book has gone through many editions and it is the primary source for most of the many English versions of the King Arthur story that followed. The first manuscript version of the book was discovered in 1934.

"he knows all about the Grail" (p. 29)

The Holy Grail is described as a chalice, bowl, or sometimes a stone. Its first appearance is in an unfinished romance by Chrétien de Troyes, *Perceval* (or *Le Conte del Graal*), written around 1190. There are many versions of the tale, with the Grail having different functions, but eventually the most common version of the legend says that it is the cup that Christ drank from during the Last Supper which Joseph of Arimathea then also used to collect the blood of Christ after His crucifixion. The Grail is a magical object with miraculous healing power, granting eternal youth. The "Grail Keeper" (called the Fisher King, the Wounded King, or the Maimed King) is a mysterious figure who is the last in a long line of guardians of the Grail.

"Layamon goes out of his way to tell you" (p. 29)

An English poet of the late twelfth or early thirteenth century, Layamon is best known for his long poem written in early Middle English, *Brut* (c. 1190), which chronicles the history of Britain from the Fall of Troy up through the seventh century. It is named after the mythical founder of Britain, Brutus of Troy who is said to be a descendant of Aeneas, the hero of Vergil's *Aeneid.* It is the first extant text written in English to mention Arthur by name.

"listen to an essay on Swift" (p. 31)

Jonathan Swift (1667–1745), English satirist and essayist.

Chapter 2: Dinner with the Sub-Warden

"Non-Olet" (p. 32)

Latin for "[it] doesn't stink." The full phrase is *Pecunia non olet* ("Money doesn't stink") and is usually attributed to the Roman Emperor Vespasian when speaking of the tax money collected from the public urinals.

"Clausewitz" (p. 33)

Karl von Clausewitz (1780–1831), Prussian general in World War I, military theorist, and author of various works on warfare.

"Othello's occupation would be gone" (p. 33)

Shakespeare, *Othello* 3.3, line 357.

Chapter 3: Belbury and St Anne's-on-the-Hill

"Hingest" (p. 54)

This name appears to be a derivation of "Hengist." Hengist and Horsa were two brothers who, in the fifth century A.D., led the first group of Anglo-Saxons to Britain. Hengist becomes the first of the Kings of Kent. In Nennius's *Historia Brittonum*, Hengist's daughter is given to Vortigern in marriage. This is also where Hengist's death is recorded, in the same section as one of the earliest appearances of Arthur.

"de Broglie" (p. 55)

Louis-Victor, Duc de Broglie (1892–1987) was a French physicist and won the Nobel Prize in 1929. In June 1921, de Broglie was at a ceremony in Oxford where C. S. Lewis, as an undergraduate, made an appearance for winning an award for an essay contest. Lewis wrote in a letter to his brother: "From a great deal of snobbish reference, which sounded less vulgar in Latin, I gather he [de Broglie] is of a great house" (*Letters*, 1:557).

"Almanac de Gotha" (p. 55)

A directory of European royalty and higher nobility, it was first published in 1763 by C. W. Ettinger in Gotha in Thuringia, Germany.

"Peter Rabbit" (p. 60)

Beatrix Potter, *The Tale of Peter Rabbit* (1902).

"Romance of the Rose" (p. 60)

A thirteenth-century French allegorical poem, *Roman de la Rose*. It is comprised of two sections, written by Guillaume de Lorris and Jean de Meung. For more on *Roman de la Rose*, see chapter three in Lewis's book *The Allegory of Love*.

"Klingsor's garden" (p. 60)

A setting in Richard Wagner's opera *Parsifal* (1882), which was based on a thirteenth-century epic poem, Wolfram von Eschenbach's *Parzifal*. Klingsor is a wicked sorcerer who has stolen the Holy Lance and Parsifal is an Arthurian knight who attempts to retrieve it. He comes into Klingsor's garden where he encounters enchantments that he must resist.

"the one book that lay on the table in the middle of the room [...] 'The beauty of the female is the root of joy to the female as well as to the male'" (p. 61)

This book that Jane finds is a made-up book, as Lewis points out in two letters (*Letters*, 3:699 and 3:1360):

To Ruth Pitter, Oxford, January 31, 1956, "The passage is, so far as I know, my own invention, influenced, I think, by Coventry Patmore. I am not now sure that it is very relevant in its place."

To Rosamund Cruikshank, Cambridge, July 31, 1962, "The bit Jane reads at St Anne's is my own."

"divinely tall" (p. 61)

Alfred Tennyson (1809–1892), English poet; "A Dream of Fair Women" (stanza 22):

> At length I saw a lady within call,
> Stiller than chisell'd marble, standing there;
> A daughter of the gods, divinely tall
> And most divinely fair.

"my name is Camilla" (p. 61)

Very possibly named after the warrior-princess and huntress Camilla from Vergil's *Aeneid*, 7.803–817, and 11.498–835. This would be in keeping with the other Martial language that Lewis uses to describe Camilla.

Chapter 4: The Liquidation of Anachronisms

"to behave like the Sword of Siegfried" (p. 74)

In Richard Wagner's opera *Götterdämmerung* (Twilight of the Gods: 2.4), Siegfried places his sword Notung between himself and Brünnhilde, whom he is wooing for his brother Gunther. She accuses Siegfried of having "extorted lust and love" from her, but he points to this act of placing his sword between them to deny the charge. So, to "behave like the sword of Siegfried" is to prevent sexual intercourse.

"I might have got like that frightful woman in Ibsen" (p.75)

Henrik Ibsen (1828–1906) was a Norwegian poet and playwright.

"They will gnaw their tongues and not repent" (p. 76)

"Then the fifth angel poured out his bowl on the throne of the beast, and his kingdom became full of darkness; and they gnawed their tongues because of the pain. They blasphemed the God of heaven because of their pains and their sores, and did not repent of their deeds" (Revelation 16:10–11).

"Cyrus" (p. 78)

Cyrus the Great, King of Persia (c. 600–530 B.C.).

"There is no turning back once you have set your hand to the plough" (p. 78)

"[...] Jesus said to him, 'No one, having put his hand to the plow, and looking back, is fit for the kingdom of God'" (Luke 9:62).

"Know you not that we shall judge angels?" (p. 78)

"Do you not know that we shall judge angels? How much more, things that pertain to this life?" (1 Corinthians 6:3)

"The obituary (in Raleigh's fine phrase) was an instrument which the Deputy Director's talents well fitted him to play." (p. 79)

Sir Walter Alexander Raleigh (1861–1922) was the first holder of the Chair of English Literature at Oxford and a Fellow of Merton College, Oxford (the same college at which J. R. R. Tolkien was also a Fellow and Professor of English Language and Literature). He is not to be confused with Sir Walter Raleigh the Renaissance poet and explorer of the late sixteenth century. Raleigh died a few months before Lewis began studying English at Oxford. This "fine phrase" is pulled from a letter written on January 25, 1912, to Edmund Gosse. "I do find the obituary a difficult instrument to play."

"Saeva sonare verbera, tum stridor ferri tractaeque catenae" (p. 88)

Vergil, *Aeneid*, 6.557–558 (Latin line numbers): "the cruel sounding of whips with the grating of dragging iron chains" (translation mine).

Chapter 5: Elasticity

"in the famous words, 'nasty, poor, brutish, and short'!" (p. 110)

Thomas Hobbes (1588–1679) was an English philosopher. This is a quote from his most famous book *Leviathan*, written in 1651: "the life of man, solitary, poor, nasty, brutish, and short" (*Leviathan*, 1.13).

"run by a Mr. Fisher-King" (p. 111)

The Fisher King is a figure in high medieval Arthurian legend. He is first introduced by Chrétien de Troyes in *Le Conte del Graal* (see note on the Holy Grail on page 340 of this book). The Fisher King often appears as either an old fisherman or else a king afflicted with an incurable wound. In de Troyes, Perceval meets the Fisher King in the guise of a fisherman who helps him. But later on, he meets the same man as a wounded king lying abed. While there, Percival sees a strange procession of servants pass by the bed, carrying the Grail and other strange artifacts. However, he keeps silent, not knowing that by asking about the Grail, he could have secured the Fisher King's healing.

"the Sura" (p. 112)

A *sura* is the name for a chapter of the Koran. Here, Lewis uses the word as a name for the primarily fictitious figure of a "great native Christian mystic."

Chapter 6: Fog

"a cloud no bigger than a man's hand" (p. 120)

"Then it came to pass the seventh time, that he said, 'There is a cloud, as small as a man's hand, rising out of the sea!'" (1 Kings 18:44)

"hasn't read her Ovid. Ad metam properate simul" (p. 125)

Ovid (c. 43 B.C.–A.D. 18) was a Roman poet during the time of Augustus Caesar; this quote is from his *Ars Amatoria* (The Art of Love) 2.727: "hasten to the goal together" (translation mine).

"Dunne" (p. 127)

John William Dunne (1875–1949) was a British soldier who fought in the Boer War. Later in his life, he turned to philosophy and specifically achieved some recognition and influence with his theory on the nature of time and consciousness as it relates to precognitive dreams/visions, called "serialism."

"witches prophesying on a blasted heath" (p. 127)

See the opening scene of *Macbeth.*

"the Stagyrite" (p. 128)

Aristotle (384–322), the famed Greek philosopher, who was born in Stagira, Macedonia.

"Gestapo" (p. 131)

The secret police of Nazi Germany.

"Ogpu" (p. 131)

The secret police of the Soviet Union from 1922–1934.

Chapter 7: The Pendragon

"I live like the King in Curdie" (p. 146)

George MacDonald (1824–1905) was a Scottish novelist and a great inspiration to Lewis. MacDonald wrote *The Princess and Curdie* (1883). The king in this book lived on bread and wine.

"Brobdingnag" (p. 147)

Gulliver's Travels (1726) by Jonathan Swift (1667–1745); Brobdingnag is the land of the giants visited by the title character.

Chapter 8: Moonlight at Belbury

"Trespassed beyond your proper sphere, Miss Hardcastle" (p. 158)

Tongue in cheek reference from Lewis to medieval cosmology. This whole conflict began when Weston and

Devine trespassed "beyond their proper sphere" (the sub-lunar realm).

"Be glad thou sleeper and thy sorrow offcast. I am the gate to all good adventure" (p. 160)

Geoffrey Chaucer, *The Parliament of Fowls*, lines 131–132.

> This is the wey to al good aventure.
> Be glad, thow redere, and thy sorwe of-caste.

"the Curdie books" (p. 160)

George MacDonald, *The Princess and the Goblin* (1872) and *The Princess and Curdie* (1883).

"Mansfield Park" (p. 160)

Jane Austen (1775–1817). *Mansfield Park* was her fourth novel, written in 1814.

"experimentum crucis" (p. 163)

Latin: "Critical experiment."

"A king cometh [...] who shall rule the universe with righteousness and the heavens with judgment" (p. 175)

> "Behold a king will reign in righteousness
> And princes will rule with justice."
> (Isaiah 32:1)

Chapter 9: The Saracen's Head

"The Saracen's Head" (chapter title)

During the Crusades, *Saracens* was the name for Muslims or Arabs. The turbaned head of a Muslim was often used as a symbol in heraldry. Such a head would also appear as decoration on the signs of inns and taverns. But, in a play on words, Lewis uses this term to refer to Alcasan.

"and then, as one of the poets says, he "discovered in his mind an inflammation swollen and deformed, his memory." (p. 181)

Christopher Hassall (1912–1963) was an English actor, lyricist, and poet. This quotation is from his three-part poem "S.O.S. … Ludlow," 3.14–15.

"All lies in a passion of patience…Taliessin through Logres" (p. 191)

Charles Williams (1886–1945) was a British novelist, poet, playwright, and theologian. He was a member of the Inklings and a good friend of Lewis's. This line is from his poem "Mount Badon" in *Taliessin through Logres* (1938) which is a cycle of Arthurian poems.

"Mr. MacPhee probably approves of no poets except Burns" (p. 191)

Robert Burns (1759–1796) was a famous Scottish poet.

"the Pendragon of Logres" (p. 192)

The term *Pendragon* originally was simply an ancient title for a Welsh or British chief or leader, likely meaning "head dragon." Geoffrey of Monmouth writes that Merlin was the one to give this title to King Arthur's father Uther, who was then known as Uther Pendragon. The idea of this title being passed on after Uther appears to be an original idea of Lewis's, as it has no historical precedent. *Logres* is a Latinized version of *Lloegyr* which was the ancient Welsh name for that part of what we now know as England (from Angle-land) that was connected with Arthur.

"Jane washed up under the attentive eye of Baron Corvo, the jackdaw" (p. 192)

"Baron Corvo" is the pseudonym of the English writer Fredrick Rolfe (1860–1913). Lewis described his style as "one of the most preposterous I have ever read, and I doubt if I ever saw so much pedantry combined with so much ignorance" (letter to Arthur Greeves, The Kilns, October 1, 1934, *Letters,* 2:143). *Corvus* is Latin meaning "raven."

"Faustus" (p. 198)

A fictional character based on the historical Johann Georg Faust (c. 1480–1540), a German magician and astrologer from the early sixteenth century. He became a character of folk legend after his death and is the main character of several famous plays, including those written by Marlowe and Goethe, and musical compositions, including those by Wagner and Berlioz.

"Prospero" (p. 198)

Shakespeare, *The Tempest*; Prospero is a magician living in exile with his daughter Miranda on a small island.

"Archimago" (p. 198)

Edmund Spenser (1552–1599), *The Faerie Queene*; Archimago is a deceitful sorcerer.

"after the fall of Numinor" (p. 198)

In Tolkien's *The Silmarillion*, the fall of Númenor marks the end of the Second Era. This story is similar in many ways to the story of the Tower of Babel.

"Paracelsus" (p. 198)

Paracelsus (1493–1541), whose real name was Theophrastus von Hohenheim, was a Swiss alchemist, astrologer, and physician during the German Renaissance.

"Agrippa" (p. 198)

Heinrich Cornelius Agrippa von Nettesheim (1486–1535) was a German alchemist, philosopher, and physician.

"Bacon" (p. 198)

Francis Bacon (1561–1626) was a famous English statesman, author, and philosopher. His many writings include the unfinished *The New Atlantis* (1626).

"the last vestiges of Atlantean magic" (p. 198)

Tolkien's story of Númenor is an adaptation of the Atlantis myth. In the *Timaeus*, Plato describes Atlantis as an island in the Western ocean which had disappeared and had supposedly been submerged beneath the sea for nine thousand years before Solon lived. He heard the tale from an Egyptian priest, and then told it to the son of a friend, who passed it on to his grandson, who then told it to Socrates.

"élan vital" (p. 200)

French: "life-force".

"Panpsychism" (p. 200)

The idea that everything material, including plants and inanimate objects, have some element of individual consciousness as well as humans and animals.

"Anima Mundi" (p. 200)

Latin: "spirit or soul of the world/earth."

Chapter 10: The Conquered City

"ultra vires" (p. 204)

Latin: "unauthorized or acting beyond one's legal power".

"the sadness that came over him had novelty in it ... Brother Lawrence" (p. 221)

Brother Lawrence was born Nicolas Herman (1614–1691) in the province of Lorraine in eastern France. In 1640, after fighting in the Thirty Years' War, he entered a Carmelite monastery in Paris and at that time he took the name Lawrence of the Resurrection. On Brother Lawrence's death, his abbot compiled two books from his notes and letters. The books together came to be known as *La pratique de la présence de Dieu* (The Practice of the Presence of God).

Chapter 11: Battle Begun

"They had tried to do that to Merlin" (p. 230)

The story goes that Merlin was sent for by King Vortigern after the king had made three attempts to build a fortress which collapsed each time he tried. The King's seers advised him to find a fatherless child, kill it, and sprinkle its blood over the building project. The King finds the boy (Merlin) but Merlin bests Vortigern's seers by revealing the true reason that Vortigern's fortress would not stand: beneath the building site is a great lake containing two dragons. By this action, Merlin cements his role as a "prophet."

"John Buchan" (p. 243)

John Buchan was a Scottish writer and politician (1875–1940). He was the fifteenth Governor General of Canada, serving from 1935 until his death in 1940. However, despite his many political honors and appointments, he is primarily remembered for writing the adventure stories of Richard Hannay (*The Thirty-Nine Steps*, *Greenmantle*, *Mr. Standfast*, and others).

Chapter 12: Wet and Windy Night

"It is one of Barfield's "ancient unities" (p. 258)

Owen Barfield (1898–1997) was a British author, poet, and philosopher and one of Lewis's closest friends.

For more background on the "ancient unities" mentioned here, see chapter ten of *Miracles* by Lewis.

"the Great Disaster" (p. 262)

The end of Atlantis/fall of Númenor.

Chapter 13: They Have Pulled Down Deep Heaven on Their Heads

"in the cup-shaped land of Abhalljin, beyond the seas of Lur in Perelandra" (p. 271)

Abhalljin, a name which Lewis invented, is a form of the word *Avalon*. Avalon is the island where it is said that King Arthur was taken after he was mortally wounded in battle, in order that he might be healed. It is said that he will then one day return to Britain. In British lore, it is thought that Glastonbury Tor is the island of Avalon. The area surrounding the Tor is below sea level, and without man-made dikes and drainage, the entire area would be watery and marshy, making the Tor an island surrounded by the Vale of Avalon. Lur is the "green sea" where Tor was taken for a time and received instruction (see *Perelandra*, 180).

"the stroke that Balinus struck" (p. 275)

Sir Balin was a knight of King Arthur's court, also known as the Knight with Two Swords. In an impetuous act (sometimes out of rage and in other versions in self-defense), he injures the Grail King Pellam with the Holy Lance (the spear that was used to pierce Christ). Because of this sacrilege, the land becomes a barren wasteland for years. The story appears in Malory's *Le Morte d'Arthur.*

"Apuleius" (p. 276)

Lucius Apuleius Madaurensis (c. A.D. 124–170) was a Latin prose author and rhetorician. He is most famously known for his *Metamorphoses* or *The Golden Ass* which contains the first written version of the story of Cupid and Psyche.

"Martianus Capella" (p. 276)

Latin author from Carthage (c. A.D. 360–428).

"Hisperica Famina" (p. 276)

An early medieval text dating from around the sixth century in Ireland or Wales.

"the poem about Heaven and Hell eating into merry Middle Earth" (p. 281)

Possible reference to William Blake's poem *The Marriage of Heaven and Hell*, though the actual line "eating into merry

Middle Earth" is difficult to track down. It may be a reference to an obscure medieval text, or potentially even a line from an unpublished poem circulated amongst the Inklings.

"the bit in the Bible about the winnowing fan" (p. 281)

> Likewise the oxen and the young donkeys that work the ground
> Will eat cured fodder,
> Which has been winnowed with the shovel and fan.
> (Isaiah 30:24)

"Or like Browning's line: "Life's business being just the terrible choice." (p. 281)

Robert Browning (1812–1889) was a well-known English poet and playwright. This quotation is from *The Ring and the Book*, 10.1235–1237:

> White shall not neutralise the black, nor good
> Compensate bad in man, absolve him so:
> Life's business being just the terrible choice.

"fate, longaevi" (p. 282)

Fate is the plural form of the Italian *fata*, meaning "fairy." *Longaevi* is a Latin word used by Martianus Capella meaning "long-livers" or "those who live long lives." For more on the *Longaevi*, see chapter six in *The Discarded Image* and chapter fourteen of this book.

"magia *of Merlin… the new* goeteia" (p. 283)

These are two Greek words for "magic": *magia* (from μαγεία meaning "magic" generically and *goeteia* (from γόητες meaning "sorcerers"). Typically, *magia* was used to refer to "white" or "good" magic, while *goeteia* was connected with "dark" or "black" magic associated with demons.

"the last of the seven bears of Logres" (p. 284)

Lewis wrote, "The VII bears and the Atlantean Circle (in *That Hideous Strength*) are pure inventions of my own, filling the same purpose in the narrative that 'noises off' wd in a stage play" (Lewis to Charles Moorman, Oxford, February 10, 1952, in *Letters*, 3:232). The Atlantean Circle is mentioned in *That Hideous Strength*, page 225.

"the days when Nimrod built a tower to reach heaven" (p. 285)

Genesis 10:8ff.

"I am not the son of one of the Airish Men. That was a lying story." (p. 289)

In medieval cosmology, there were other beings (spirits of the air) who were thought to have possibly fathered Merlin (see chapter six in *The Discarded Image*). These *Longaevi*, including fairies, were not necessarily evil. See also chapter twenty-eight in this book.

"the time when Logres was only myself and one man and two boys" (p. 289)

Merlin may be speaking of an episode in Malory's *Le Morte d'Arthur* about Merlin, Sir Ector, young Arthur, and Kay (Kay being the "churl" spoken of).

Chapter 14: "Real Life is Meeting"

"Waddington has given the best answer. Existence is its own justification. The tendency to developmental change [...]" (p. 292 and 293)

C. H. Waddington (1905–1975) was an English developmental biologist, embryologist, geneticist, and philosopher. The quote here is paraphrased from his *Science and Ethics* (1942). Lewis attacked Waddington and his philosophies in *The Abolition of Man*, summarizing Waddington's position with the phrase "existence is its own justification."

"Huxley himself [...] Romanes lecture" (p. 293)

Thomas Henry Huxley (1825–1895) was an English biologist and popular scientific writer. He was popularly known as "Darwin's Bulldog" for his determined advocacy for Darwinism. The "Romanes lectures," free public lectures given at the Sheldonian Theatre in Oxford, were founded in 1891 by Huxley's friend George Romanes (1848–1894), also a biologist.

"Mark had read somewhere of "things of that extreme evil which seem innocent to the uninitiate" (p. 296)

From G. K. Chesterton's (1874–1936) *The Everlasting Man* (1925).

"Some such dress Jane had seen worn by a Minoan priestess on a vase from old Cnossus" (p. 301)

Also spelled Knossos (Greek Κνωσός) Cnossus was the chief city on the island of Crete during the Minoan period.

"Titian" (p. 311)

Tiziano Vecellio (c. 1490–1577) was an Italian painter. In *Surprised by Joy*, Lewis includes Titian among a list of people that he calls "the resonant, dogmatic, flaming, unanswerable people."

"You had better agree with your adversary quickly" (p. 313)

"Agree with your adversary quickly, while you are on the way with him, lest your adversary deliver you to the judge, the judge hand you over to the officer, and you be thrown into prison" (Matthew 5:25).

"Yes, by the splendour of Christ, we will send them one! 'Upon them He a spirit of frenzy sent To call in haste for their destroyer.'" (p. 314)

From John Milton's lesser-known *Samson Agonistes*, a drama about the Philistines gathering in the temple of Dagon where Samson was brought to perform for them (Judges 16:21–31). Ransom uses this line to refer to Merlin, which further cements Merlin's role as a Samson type:

> Among them he a spirit of frenzy sent,
> Who hurt their minds,
> And urged them on with mad desire
> To call in haste for their destroyer.
> (lines 1675–1678)

Chapter 15: The Descent of the Gods

"See thou do it not!" he had said. "Have you forgotten that they are our fellow servants?" (p. 318)

"And I fell at his feet to worship him. But he said to me, 'See that you do not do that! I am your fellow servant, and of your brethren who have the testimony of Jesus. Worship God! For the testimony of Jesus is the spirit of prophecy'" (Revelation 19:10).

"Then he said to me, 'See that you do not do that. For I am your fellow servant, and of your brethren the prophets, and of those who keep the words of this book. Worship God'" (Revelation 22:9).

"the slayer of Argus" (p. 319)

In Greek mythology, Argus Panoptes ("all-seeing") was a many-eyed giant who was a servant to Hera, wife of Zeus. Hera tasked Argus with guarding Io (a priestess and Zeus's lover who had been turned into a cow by Hera in her jealousy) in order to keep Zeus from finding her. Mercury was asked by Zeus to find a way to kill Argus and Mercury succeeded by putting Argus to sleep with his magic pipe. It is said that Hera placed the hundred eyes of Argus into the tail of the peacock in honor of her slain servant.

"Mercury and Thoth" (p. 319)

Mercury is the Roman name for Hermes and Thoth is the Egyptian god of the moon, writing, and arithmetic, with whom the Greeks also associated Hermes.

"all Arabia breathing from a box" (p. 319)

Alexander Pope, *The Rape of the Lock* (1714), 1.133-134.

> This casket India's glowing gems unlocks,
> And all Arabia breathes from yonder box

Shakespeare, *Macbeth* 5.1: "All the perfumes of Arabia will not sweeten this little hand."

"the inconsolable wound with which man is born" (p. 320)

See Lewis's essay "The Weight of Glory." There he talks of "the inconsolable secret in each one of you–the secret which hurts so much." This idea can also be found in *Surprised by Joy* (the "inconsolable longing"), in *The Pilgrim's Regress* (Mr. Wisdom mentions "the sorrow that is born with us"), and in *Reflections on the Psalms* (Lewis talks about our hope being to escape from time "and so cure that always aching wound").

"King William said, Be not dismayed…" (p. 321)

A line from an anonymous song called "The Boyne Water" which celebrates the battle of the Boyne, which was fought in 1690 between the Protestant army led by the newly crowned William of Orange and the Catholic army led by the deposed James II.

"Merlin saw in memory the wintry grass of Badon Hill" (p. 321)

The Battle of Badon was fought in the late fifth or early sixth century between the Britons and the Anglo-Saxons. King Arthur was the leader of the victorious Briton force.

"Mars, Mavors, Tyr" (p. 322)

Mavors is an old form of the name Mars. Tyr is a Germanic deity who was also identified with Mars.

"The Golden Bough" (p. 337)

The Golden Bough: A Study in Comparative Religion is a book by Scottish anthropologist Sir James George Frazer (1854–1941), published between the years 1880–1915.

Chapter 16: Banquet at Belbury

"made him all the cheer that a beast can make a man" (p. 348)

Malory, *Le Morte d'Arthur* XIV.6.

"So full of sleep are they at the time when they leave the right way" (p. 350)

Dante, *Inferno* 1.11–12:

> I had become so sleepy at the moment
> When I first strayed, leaving the path of truth.

Chapter 17: Venus at St Anne's

"Looked like steel in colour…like a Valkyrie" (p. 360)

Valkyrie literally means "chooser of the slain." In Norse myth, the Valkyrie were Odin's handmaidens who conducted slain warriors from battle into Valhalla. Also used to refer to women warriors. This echoes back to Camilla's name which is likely pointing to Camilla the warrior-princess from Vergil's *Aeneid.*

"Like starlight, in the spoils of provinces" (p. 361)

From Ben Jonson's play *Volpone, or The Foxe* (1606).

"Barbarossa" (p. 366)

Frederick I Barbarossa (c. 1123–1190) was King of Germany and Holy Roman Emperor from 1155 to his death in 1190. He is the subject of many legends and, like King Arthur, it is thought that he was cast into an enchanted sleep from which he will one day awake, perhaps at the end of the world.

"Enoch or Elijah" (p. 366)

Genesis 5:24 and 2 Kings 2:11.

"the Third Heaven" (p. 367)

Venus, the third sphere according to medieval cosmology.

"Aphallin" (p. 367)

Another form of the name Avalon invented by Lewis.

"there was a moment in the Sixth Century" (p. 367)

The highest point in King Arthur's reign was the battle of Mount Badon or Badon Hill which took place around A.D. 500.

"Mordred" (p. 367)

Mordred was either a nephew or natural son of King Arthur. Mordred tried to dethrone Arthur and was killed in this attempt. Arthur was mortally wounded and so taken to Avalon.

"Sidney" (p. 367)

Sir Philip Sidney (1554–86) was an English poet, scholar, and soldier. Lewis called him "dazzling": "he is that rare thing, the aristocrat in whom the aristocratic ideal is really embodied" (from *English Literature in the Sixteenth Century*, 324).

"Cecil Rhodes" (p. 367)

Rhodes was an English businessman (1853–1902) and politician. He served as prime minister of the Cape Colony from 1890 to 1896. He was a chief representative of British imperialism in southern Africa. Between 1964–1978, present-day Zimbabwe was named Rhodesia in his honor.

"the successor of Arthur and Uther and Cassibelaun" (p. 367)

Uther Pendragon was Arthur's father. Cassivellaunus was a British tribal chief and one of Julius Caesar's fiercest opponents in Julius's second expedition to Britain in 54 B.C. He led an alliance of combined British forces against the Roman troops. In Geoffrey of Monmouth's *Historia Regum Britanniae*, he calls him Cassibelaunus and records how he became King of Britain after his older brother's death, thus making him a predecessor to Uther Pendragon.

"As one of the modern authors has told us, the altar must often be built in one place that the fire from Heaven may descend somewhere else" (p. 368)

Charles Williams, *He Came Down from Heaven* (1938).

"If we've got an ass's head, it is by walking in a fairy wood" (p. 368)

Shakespeare, *A Midsummer Night's Dream.*

"How right Sam Weller was when he called Mr. Pickwick an angel in gaiters!" (p. 368)

Charles Dickens (1812–1870), *The Pickwick Papers.*

"Trahison des clercs" (p. 370)

French: "the treason of clerks;" also the title of the main work by French writer Julien Benda (1867–1956).

"Cine Cerere et Baccho" (p. 374)

Part of a Latin saying: *sine Cerere et Libero friget Venus* ("without Ceres and Bacchus, Venus will freeze"), that is, "without food and wine, love will cool."

"'She comes more near the Earth than she was wont," quoted Dimble, "to make men mad.'" (p. 374)

From Shakespeare's *Othello*, 5.2, 113–114, in which "she" refers to the Moon, not Venus: "It is the very error of the moon. She comes more nearer earth than she was wont. And makes men mad."

"So geht es im Schnützelpützhaüsel!/Da singen und tanzen die Maüsel!" (p. 376)

Anonymous eighteenth-century German song.

Rough translation:

> So it goes in the Schnützelputzhäusel
> (a sort of house)
> The singing and dancing of the mice!

"Beauty too rich for use, for earth too dear" (p. 378)

William Shakespeare, *Romeo and Juliet* 1.5.

BIBLIOGRAPHY

Alighieri, Dante. *The Divine Comedy*. Ed. and trans. Mark Musa. New York: Penguin Books, 1995.

Barfield, Owen. *Owen Barfield on C. S. Lewis*. Middletown: Wesleyan University Press. 1989.

Calvin, John. *Institutes of the Christian Religion*. Ed. John T. McNeill. Louisville: Westminster John Knox Press, 2006.

Carpenter, Humphrey. *J. R. R. Tolkien: A Biography*. Boston: Houghton Mifflin Harcourt, 2014.

Chapman, Allan. *Gods in the Sky: Astronomy from the Ancients to the Renaissance*. London: Channel 4 Books, 2002.

Chaucer, Geoffrey. *The House of Fame*.

Coleridge, Samuel Taylor and Henry Nelson Coleridge. *Specimens of the Table Talk of the Late Samuel Taylor Coleridge*. London: John Murray, 1851.

Daigle-Williamson, Marsha. *Reflecting the Eternal: Dante's Divine Comedy in the Novels of C. S. Lewis*. Massachusetts: Hendrickson Publishers, 2015.

Downing, David C. *Planets in Peril.* Massachusetts: University of Massachusetts Press, 1992.

Dunbar, H. Flanders. *Symbolism in Medieval Thought and Its Consummation in* The Divine Comedy. New Haven, CT: Yale University Press, 1929.

Gilbert, Douglas and Clyde Kilby. *C. S. Lewis: Images of his World.* Grand Rapids, MI: Eerdmans, 1973.

Green, Roger Lancelyn and Walter Hooper. *C. S. Lewis: A Biography*, revised & expanded edition. London: HarperCollins, 2002.

Jacobs, Alan. *The Narnian: The Life and Imagination of C. S. Lewis*. London: SPCK, 2005.

Leithart, Peter J. *Ascent to Love: A Guide to Dante's* Divine Comedy. Moscow, ID: Canon Press, 2001.

Lewis, C. S. *The Abolition of Man.* New York: Macmillan Publishing Company, 1955.

———. *The Allegory of Love: A Study in Medieval Tradition.* London: Oxford University Press, 1936.

———. *All My Road Before Me: The Diary of C. S. Lewis, 1922-1927*, ed. Walter Hooper. London: HarperCollins, 1991.

———. *Christian Reflections*. Grand Rapids: Eerdmans, 1995.

———. *The Collected Letters, Volume I*, ed. Walter Hooper. London: HarperCollins, 2000.

———. *The Collected Letters, Volume II*, ed. Walter Hooper. London: HarperCollins, 2004.

———. *The Collected Letters, Volume III*, ed. Walter Hooper. London: HarperCollins, 2006.

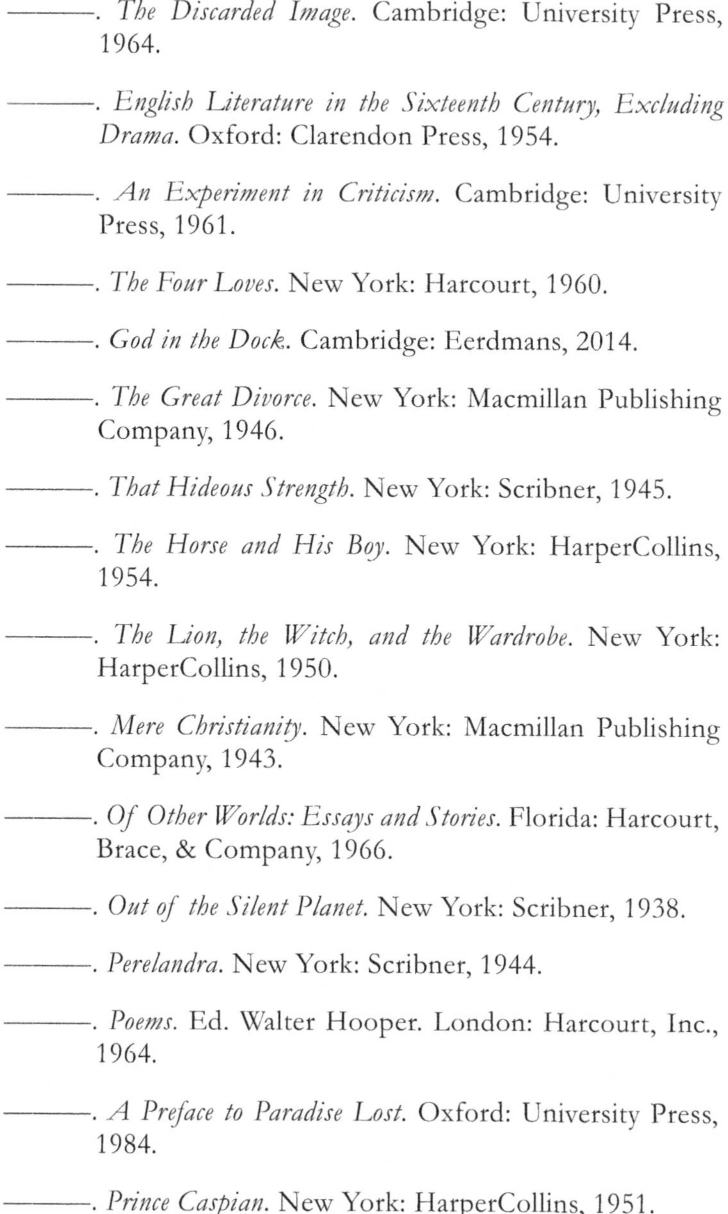

———. *The Discarded Image*. Cambridge: University Press, 1964.

———. *English Literature in the Sixteenth Century, Excluding Drama*. Oxford: Clarendon Press, 1954.

———. *An Experiment in Criticism*. Cambridge: University Press, 1961.

———. *The Four Loves*. New York: Harcourt, 1960.

———. *God in the Dock*. Cambridge: Eerdmans, 2014.

———. *The Great Divorce*. New York: Macmillan Publishing Company, 1946.

———. *That Hideous Strength*. New York: Scribner, 1945.

———. *The Horse and His Boy*. New York: HarperCollins, 1954.

———. *The Lion, the Witch, and the Wardrobe*. New York: HarperCollins, 1950.

———. *Mere Christianity*. New York: Macmillan Publishing Company, 1943.

———. *Of Other Worlds: Essays and Stories*. Florida: Harcourt, Brace, & Company, 1966.

———. *Out of the Silent Planet*. New York: Scribner, 1938.

———. *Perelandra*. New York: Scribner, 1944.

———. *Poems*. Ed. Walter Hooper. London: Harcourt, Inc., 1964.

———. *A Preface to Paradise Lost*. Oxford: University Press, 1984.

———. *Prince Caspian*. New York: HarperCollins, 1951.

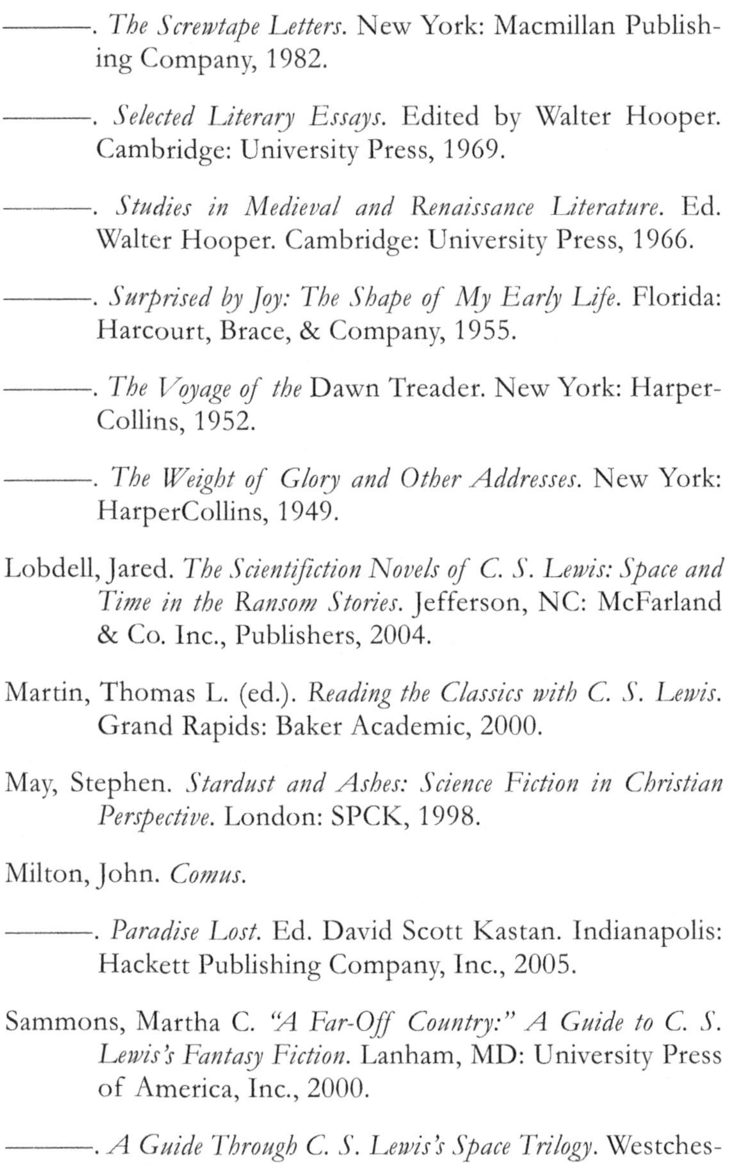

———. *The Screwtape Letters*. New York: Macmillan Publishing Company, 1982.

———. *Selected Literary Essays*. Edited by Walter Hooper. Cambridge: University Press, 1969.

———. *Studies in Medieval and Renaissance Literature*. Ed. Walter Hooper. Cambridge: University Press, 1966.

———. *Surprised by Joy: The Shape of My Early Life*. Florida: Harcourt, Brace, & Company, 1955.

———. *The Voyage of the* Dawn Treader. New York: HarperCollins, 1952.

———. *The Weight of Glory and Other Addresses*. New York: HarperCollins, 1949.

Lobdell, Jared. *The Scientifiction Novels of C. S. Lewis: Space and Time in the Ransom Stories*. Jefferson, NC: McFarland & Co. Inc., Publishers, 2004.

Martin, Thomas L. (ed.). *Reading the Classics with C. S. Lewis*. Grand Rapids: Baker Academic, 2000.

May, Stephen. *Stardust and Ashes: Science Fiction in Christian Perspective*. London: SPCK, 1998.

Milton, John. *Comus*.

———. *Paradise Lost*. Ed. David Scott Kastan. Indianapolis: Hackett Publishing Company, Inc., 2005.

Sammons, Martha C. *"A Far-Off Country:" A Guide to C. S. Lewis's Fantasy Fiction*. Lanham, MD: University Press of America, Inc., 2000.

———. *A Guide Through C. S. Lewis's Space Trilogy*. Westchester, IL: Cornerstone Books, 1980.

Schakel, Peter J. *Imagination and the Arts in C. S. Lewis: Journeying to Narnia and Other Worlds*. Columbia, MO: University of Missouri Press, 2002.

Schwartz, Sanford. *C. S. Lewis on the Final Frontier: Science and the Supernatural in the Space Trilogy*. New York: Oxford University Press, 2009.

Sidney, Sir Philip. *The Defence of Poesie*, ed. Albert Feuillerat. Cambridge: University Press, 1923.

Stokes, Mitch. *Galileo*. Knoxville: Thomas Nelson, 2011.

Tolkien, J. R. R. *The Tolkien Reader*. New York: Ballantine Books, 1966.

———. *The Fellowship of the Ring*. New York: Houghton Mifflin, 1994.

———. *The Letters of J. R. R. Tolkien*. Ed. Humphrey Carpenter. Boston: Houghton Mifflin, 1981.

———. *The Monsters and the Critics and Other Essays*. London: HarperCollins, 1997.

———. *Tree and Leaf*. New York: HarperCollins, 2012.

Ward, Michael. *Planet Narnia: The Seven Heavens in the Imagination of C. S. Lewis*. New York: Oxford University Press, 2008.

ROMAN ROADS PRESS

INHERIT THE HUMANITIES

Roman Roads Press is a publisher of classical Christian curriculum for the home and classroom.

Visit DeeperHeaven.com for resources on using *Deeper Heaven* as a curriculum or for group study, including an answer key for the discussion questions found in this book.

Visit RomanRoadsPress.com to learn about our curriculum, resources, and books. Our mission is to provide tools for you and your family to "inherit the humanities."

The Old Western Culture curriculum guides high school students and adults through the great books of Western civilization. The name comes from a phrase coined by C. S. Lewis in his lecture *De Descriptione Temporum*, and represents the ideas and stories that were held in common by all educated men and women until recent times. Learn more at www.oldwesternculture.com

Old Western Culture

Inherit the Humanities

THE GREEKS

VOLUME 1 *The Epics*

VOLUME 2 *Drama & Lyric*

VOLUME 3 *The Histories*

VOLUME 4 *The Philosophers*

THE ROMANS

VOLUME 5 *The Aeneid*

VOLUME 6 *The Historians*

VOLUME 7 *Early Christianity*

VOLUME 8 *Nicene Christianity*

CHRISTENDOM

VOLUME 9 *Early Medievals*

VOLUME 10 *Defense of the Faith*

VOLUME 11 *The Medieval Mind*

VOLUME 12 *The Reformation*

EARLY MODERNS

VOLUME 13 *Rise of England*

VOLUME 14 *Poetry and Politics*

VOLUME 15 *The Enlightenment*

VOLUME 16 *The Novels*